Level 2 • Part 2
Integrated Chinese
中文听说读写

TEACHER'S HANDBOOK

Corresponds to Third Edition

Compiled by Zheng-sheng Zhang
Yuehua Liu, Tao-chung Yao, Nyan-Ping Bi,
Liangyan Ge, Yaohua Shi

Cheng & Tsui Company

Boston

This book is for use only by classroom teachers whose schools have obtained it directly from Cheng & Tsui Company. It may not be resold to anyone nor distributed outside the schools without the express written consent of Cheng & Tsui.

Copyright © 2014 Cheng & Tsui Company, Inc.

All rights reserved. No part of this publication may be reproduced or transmitted in any form or by any means, electronic or mechanical, including photocopying, recording, scanning, or any information storage or retrieval system, without written permission from the publisher.

All trademarks mentioned in this book are the property of their respective owners.

16 15 14 13   1 2 3 4 5 6 7 8 9 10

Published by
Cheng & Tsui Company, Inc.
25 West Street
Boston, MA 02111-1213 USA
Fax (617) 426-3669
www.cheng-tsui.com
"Bringing Asia to the World"™

ISBN 978-0-88727-696-5

Cover Design: studioradia.com

Cover Photographs: Man with map © Getty Images; Shanghai skyline © David Pedre/iStockphoto; Building with masks © Wu Jie; Night market © Andrew Buko. Used by permission.

The *Integrated Chinese* series includes books, workbooks, character workbooks, audio products, multimedia products, teacher's resources, and more. Visit www.integratedchinese.com for more information on the other components of *Integrated Chinese*.

Printed in the United States of America.

The Integrated Chinese Series

Textbooks Learn Chinese language and culture through ten engaging lessons per volume. The third edition features full-color design, more communicative activities, up-to-date vocabulary, expanded cultural notes, and exciting new storylines.

Workbooks Improve all four language skills through a wide range of integrated activities that accompany the lessons in the textbook.

Character Workbooks Practice writing Chinese characters and learn the correct stroke order.

Audio CDs Build listening comprehension with audio recordings of the textbook narratives, dialogues, and vocabulary, plus the pronunciation and listening exercises from the workbooks.

Teacher's Handbooks Create a successful language program with this bilingual manual of strategies for teaching specific characters, vocabulary, and grammar—along with the pedagogical rationale underlying these strategies.

Textbook DVDs Watch the *Integrated Chinese* story unfold with live-action videos of the textbook dialogues and cultural segments for each lesson.

Integrated Chinese Digital Bookbag

Find everything you need to support your course in one convenient place: FREE teacher resources, image gallery, sentence drills, and more. The *Integrated Chinese* Digital Bookbag is a great new way to provide your students with access to Cheng & Tsui's suite of outstanding digital products:

- **Online Textbook** Enjoy 24/7 on-demand access to the online version of the *Integrated Chinese* textbook.

- **Online Workbook** Access automatic grading, voice recording and playback, and Classroom Management to export capabilities to BlackBoard, in addition to all of the print features of this workbook.

- **MP3 Audio Downloads** Deepen students' listening skills with recordings of all audio from the textbook and workbook. Bonus tracks with alternate, slower versions of the dialogues are included.

- **Online Character Workbook** Receive on-demand access to the exact content found in the printed Character Workbook. Download a page anytime, anywhere for immediate practice.

- **Companion Website** Supplement your lesson plans with FREE teacher resources like classroom slideshows and related images, as well as PDF downloads of the tests, quizzes, sample syllabi, and daily class schedules from the teacher handbook.

Please see the next page for suggested additional publications to supplement your *Integrated Chinese* course.
To order call 1-800-554-1963 or visit **www.cheng-tsui.com**

Downloads

Users of this book have free access to additional downloadable teacher's resources. To obtain printable versions of the sample syllabi, quizzes and tests in Simplified and Traditional characters, audio downloads, and more, you simply need to register your product key on Cheng & Tsui's website.

Instructions:

1. Visit **www.cheng-tsui.com/downloads**.
2. Follow the instructions to register your product key.
3. Download the files.

For technical support, please contact support@cheng-tsui.com or call 1-800-554-1963.

If you have purchased a used copy of this book, or one without a valid product key, you may purchase a new key on our website (**www.cheng-tsui.com**) or by contacting our customer service department at 1-800-554-1963.

Your Product Key: ANUQ-E5AD

Titles of Related Interest

Teaching Chinese as a Foreign Language
Theories and Applications
Second Edition
Edited by Michael E. Everson, Yun Xiao

Practical essays on how to teach Chinese as a second language.

Tales and Traditions
Readings in Chinese Literature Series
Compiled by Yun Xiao, et al.

Level-appropriate adaptations of Chinese legends and folktales.

Chinese in Motion
An Advanced Immersion Course
By Yi Lin

A fieldwork-based curriculum that teaches professional-level Chinese language. Especially suited for students who are studying abroad.

Visit **www.cheng-tsui.com** to view samples, place orders, and browse other language-learning materials.

Contents 目录

Preface 序 vii

I. General Information   I. 概论

How to Use This Handbook   本手册使用须知 ix

Layout of Individual Chapters   章节安排 xi

Sample Syllabus   教学提纲范例 xx

Sample Daily Schedule I   逐日教学进度表范例一 (以每周四节课为例) . . . xxii
based on four sessions a week

Sample Daily Schedule II   逐日教学进度表范例二 (以每周五节课为例) . . xxvii
based on five sessions a week

General Principles and Useful Resources   总体教学原则及资源 xxxii

II. Teaching Suggestions   II. 教学参考意见

Lesson 11: Chinese Festivals   第十一课：中国的节日 1

Lesson 12: Changes in China   第十二课：中国的变化 17

Lesson 13: Travel   第十三课：旅游 29

Lesson 14: Life and Wellness   第十四课：生活与健康 43

Lesson 15: Gender Equality   第十五课：男女平等 57

Lesson 16: Environmental Protection and Energy Conservation   第十六课：环境保护与节约能源 71

Lesson 17: Money Management and Investing   第十七课：理财与投资 85

Lesson 18: Chinese History   第十八课：中国历史 99

Lesson 19: Interviewing for a Job   第十九课：面试 109

Lesson 20: Foreigners in China   第二十课：外国人在中国 121

III. Workbook Answer Key   III. 《学生练习本》答案 133

IV. Sample Quizzes and Tests   IV. 考试测验范例 173

Publisher's Note

When *Integrated Chinese* was first published in 1997, it set a new standard with its focus on the development and integration of the four language skills (listening, speaking, reading, and writing). Today, to further enrich the learning experience of the many users of *Integrated Chinese* worldwide, Cheng & Tsui is pleased to offer this Teacher's Handbook for the revised and updated third edition of *Integrated Chinese*. We would like to thank the many teachers and students who, by offering their valuable insights and suggestions, have helped *Integrated Chinese* evolve and keep pace with the many positive changes in the field of Chinese language instruction. *Integrated Chinese* continues to offer comprehensive language instruction, with many new features and useful shared resources available on our website at **www.cheng-tsui.com**.

The Cheng & Tsui Chinese Language Series is designed to publish and widely distribute quality language learning materials created by leading instructors from around the world. We welcome readers' comments and suggestions concerning the publications in this series. Please contact the following members of our Editorial Board, in care of our Editorial Department (e-mail: **editor@cheng-tsui.com**).

Professor Shou-hsin Teng *Chief Editor*
Graduate Institute of Teaching Chinese as a Second Language
National Taiwan Normal University

Professor Dana Scott Bourgerie
Department of Asian and Near Eastern Languages
Brigham Young University

Professor Samuel Cheung
Department of Chinese
Chinese University of Hong Kong

Professor Hong Gang Jin
Department of East Asian Languages and Literatures
Hamilton College

Professor Ying-che Li
Department of East Asian Languages and Literatures
University of Hawaii

Former members of our Editorial Board

Professor Timothy Light *(emeritus)*
Western Michigan University

Professor Stanley R. Munro *(emeritus)*
University of Alberta

Professor Ronald Walton *(in memoriam)*
University of Maryland

Preface

It has been more than fifteen years since *Integrated Chinese* (IC) came into existence in 1997. During these years, amid the historical changes that have taken place in China and the rest of the world, the demand for Chinese language teaching and learning materials has grown dramatically. We are greatly encouraged by the fact that *IC* has not only been a widely used textbook at the college level in the United States and beyond, but also has become increasingly popular with high school classes. One major factor for the success of *IC* has been the steadfast support from the teachers of Chinese, whose feedback greatly facilitated the repeated revisions of the series throughout the years.

In a sense, this new Teacher's Handbook accompanying the third edition of *IC* is our way of repaying the teachers who have adopted *IC* as the textbook for their classes. The aims of the handbook are to make *IC* easier to use and Chinese language teaching more effective. With those guiding principles for its compilation, this handbook is an expansion of the series that is aimed solely at Chinese language teachers. In this handbook, we have provided discussions of the general principles on teaching Chinese, information on useful resources for teaching, sample syllabi and schedules, answer keys, as well as specific suggestions on teaching the language points in each lesson. Instead of being prescriptive, the content here is intended to alleviate the burden on teachers, who are welcome to utilize its features selectively and adaptively based on their actual needs.

Some of the pedagogical practices recommended in this handbook may not be as prevalent in all corners of the Chinese-teaching field. As the user will notice, in this handbook we have tried to achieve a new balance between grammar on one side and vocabulary and characters on the other, attaching greater importance to the analysis of specific words and characters. In particular, we have regularly highlighted the phonetic and semantic components in Chinese characters and used them to relate different words and characters by pointing out their shared components. While we firmly believe in the pedagogical value of these practices, we encourage teachers to prioritize their teaching activities based on their students' proficiency levels in different language skills.

In general, materials in this handbook are arranged in order to optimize their effectiveness in the classroom. For instance, the placement of mechanical drills before more communicative activities is prompted by the need for scaffolding. For the same reason, the arrangement of different activities on a given language point usually progresses from easy to difficult and from controlled to more open-ended. Elsewhere, however, the rationale may not be as obvious. For example, at certain places one may find tips on vocabulary and characters mixed together with those on grammar. In these cases, we felt it more effective to group together grammar explanations and vocabulary tips linked by a common theme.

The current volume is the result of a long course of preparation. The *IC* authors have provided a large number of grammar notes, tips on teaching aids and class activities, detailed lesson plans, drill exercises, sample syllabi and course schedules, but it took the sustained efforts of Professor Zheng-sheng Zhang, compiler of this handbook, to edit and reorganize these materials. He is also responsible for many of the added materials in the volume, especially the general instructional principles and most of the tips on teaching vocabulary and characters.

As we prepared this handbook, we have accumulated more academic and intellectual debts than we can possibly acknowledge here. As we said above, the Chinese teachers at both college and high school levels have always been a primary source of support and inspiration for us. To them we feel eternally indebted. Specifically, we would like to thank those teachers who contributed to the tests and quizzes for this publication: Mei Xu (quizzes 15 and 20, midterm exam, and final exam), Qiaona Yu (quizzes 11–14 and unit tests 11–14), and Chuan Lin (quizzes 16–19 and unit tests 16–19). We also wish to take the opportunity to express our gratitude to those who have helped us in different ways. Among many others, our particular thanks go to our editors at Cheng & Tsui.

How to Use This Handbook
本手册使用须知

This handbook contains a collection of teacher resources which are not generally found in the textbook itself. They include the following:

   a. General guidelines for instruction
   b. Useful resources
   c. Tips and suggestions for teaching language points including characters, vocabulary, pronunciation, and grammar
   d. Notes on frequently encountered student errors
   e. Answer key to the student workbook
   f. Sample quizzes and tests

It is important to bear in mind that this manual provides flexible guidelines which teachers can use to develop their own detailed lesson plans. In other words, it should not be regarded as a book of "recipes" to follow. The reasons for this are as follows:

- Although some sample syllabi and daily schedules are suggested at the beginning of the handbook, we have left the time restrictions open, so that teachers can decide, based on student response, how much time should be spent on each item. While some attempt is made to sequence the language points, ultimately it is up to the teacher to decide the best order.

- While lesson plans need to address the reviewing and recycling of lesson content, this manual does not generally dictate the manner in which this should be done. This should not be interpreted as an indication that going over the materials once is enough. Review and repetition are essential, but the extent and frequency of the review should depend on the individual teacher's needs.

本手册为教师提供一般而言并不见之于课本本身的诸多资源，包括：

   a. 教学实践的一般原则
   b. 实用性资源
   c. 汉字、词汇、发音和语法等语言点的教学提示
   d. 关于学生常见错误的提示
   e. 《学生练习本》中的练习答案
   f. 考试测验范例

请记住本手册并不提供详尽的教程计划。换言之，本手册不同于一本可以按部就班地效仿的"食谱"。原因在于：

- 虽然本手册开篇处提供若干教学提纲范例及逐日教学进度表范例，但是教师必须根据学生的接受情况、反应来调整各项活动所需的时间。尽管我们在手册中对语言点的教学顺序做出一些建议，但是最佳安排最终仍然应由教师自己决定。

- 教案必须顾及对教材内容的复习和再循环，本手册与之不同，一般没有刻意规定对教材内容的复习和再循环的方式。这不应被理解为教材内容只需学习一遍即可。复习和回顾是绝对必要的，但是复习的幅度和频率应该由教师本人来决定。

- Neither is this handbook systematic and exhaustive in covering all vocabulary and grammar points. Each grammar point is not given the same weight, and so the discussion length can vary. Additionally, because some of the grammatical points are simpler than others, there might not be need for further explanation for all grammar items.

- Not all of the suggested activities need to be completed. In this sense, the handbook is more like a menu rather than a "recipe book."

- 另外，本手册对词汇和语法点的讨论并不是系统性的或详尽无遗的。各语法点所占份量轻重不一，讨论的篇幅疏密互见，而且有的语法点因为比较简单，所以无需再进行提示。

- 对本手册建议的活动，教师不必逐一、全部完成。在这个意义上，本手册更像一个菜单，而不是一本"烹调菜谱"。

Layout of Individual Chapters
章节安排

This Teacher's Handbook is the second of a two-volume set for Level 2. While it is similar to the two Level 1 volumes in many ways, a number of differences are clearly noticeable.

One major difference between Level 2 and Level 1 is the greater need to prioritize. When students first start learning the language, the number of target items is relatively small and fundamental to the language. Because of this, students are expected to master them completely; that is, to both understand and use them in speech, and to be able to read and write them. Starting in Level 2 the number of words taught increases exponentially and the grammar is more complex. It is no longer realistic to expect students to master everything presented to them. This is especially true of the increasing number of written and formal expressions, many of which may not occur in spoken language in the first place. We therefore try to provide explicit suggestions on prioritizing—for example, which items are not crucial to the lesson and therefore need not be dwelt upon at length.

Since most basic grammar has been covered in Level 1 of this textbook, some of the grammatical content in Level 2 functions as in-depth practice for grammatical items that have already been taught, while the rest ties together related items that were presented separately in the past. Although we do introduce some new grammar points, including some points used more often in written Chinese, as well as some modal particles, it can be safely said that at this level, grammar is no longer the focus of the language practice that *Integrated Chinese* provides. Instead, building students' vocabulary has become the main focus. We therefore recommend spending more time on vocabulary practice, including key vocabulary items, verbs, adjectives, and abstract nouns presented in the Level 2 textbooks' new vocabulary sections.

本教师手册为二年级系列的两卷之第二卷。虽然与一年级的两卷有明显的渊源关系，但也有几个明显的区别。

一个主要的区别是二年级与一年级相比更有必要进行适当的取舍。当学生刚开始学习一种外语时，接触的生词、语法项目都很少，也比较基本，老师可以要求学生对所学的要"听说读写"全面掌握。但是到了二年级，随着学的词汇急速增加、语法复杂程度不断加大，学生就很难全面掌握所有学的内容。特别是有越来越多出现于书面语体或很正式的口语的词语，就不能要求学生全面掌握其用法。为此我们特别做一些提示，指出本课的哪些词汇或语法项目只要求理解，而不要求能说和写。

本教材在 Level 1 中将汉语基本语法都涵盖了。Level 2 有的语法部分是对已学过的语法项目进一步加深学习，有的是过去分散学的内容做一个小结。我们也教了一些新的语言点（或叫作语法点），其中有一些书面语虚词、有些表示语气用法的。可以说，语法已经不是 Level 2 语言学习的重点，重点转向词语。也就是说，扩大词汇量已成为学习的重点。因此我们建议多做一些词语练习（包括重点词语和生词中的动词、形容词、抽象名词等）。

The layout of individual chapters, while remaining fairly similar to that of Level 1, has also changed somewhat to reflect this need to sharpen the focus. What follows is a list of the headings found in each individual chapter.

Chapter Structure

The chapter structure is given at the beginning of each chapter. The contents of each chapter are given below in order of appearance.

Lesson Focus

Each chapter begins with a list of the lesson's main points.

Instead of restating all of the focal elements from the textbook, we have selected some of the main themes for more detailed treatment.

Priorities

To sharpen the focus further, we have added a new category called "Priorities" (取舍), which is used to underscore our belief that the most important thing is not to cover all the material presented in a lesson but to make judicious choices to best accomplish the main objectives of the lesson. To that end, we offer some tentative suggestions on what need not be covered when circumstances do not allow.

Focal Themes Teaching Suggestions

We have added a new category called "Focal Themes Teaching Suggestions" (重点主题教学建议) to highlight the focal themes. In this section, suggestions are given on teaching aids/props and how to approach new materials, as well as detailed advice on how to develop and deepen the course material. As emphasized elsewhere, this volume is not to be treated as a recipe book, but rather as a resource that can be used selectively. These teaching suggestions are offered in this same spirit.

章节的格式虽无大变，但为了突出重点也作了相应的改动。以下是每一章所包括的内容。

章节结构

章节结构出现在每一章的开头。以下按其出现的顺序，依次介绍每一部份的内容。

本课重点

每章开头列出本课的焦点语言点。

我们不是简单地重复主课本中每课开头所列出的重点项，而是选一些主题，作重点处理。

取舍

为了更好地凸显焦点，我们增添了一个称为"Priorities"(取舍)的新条目。这是用来强调最重要的并不是教完每一课的内容，而是为完成这一课的主要目标而做出合理的选择。为此，我们提出一些初步的建议，即情况不允许时什么内容可以略去不教。

焦点主题教学建议

为了进一步凸显焦点成分，我们还增添了一个叫"Focal Themes Teaching Suggestions"(重点主题教学建议)的新条目。在这部分，我们提供一些关于教学辅助材料、新内容的切入、详细教学步骤方面的建议。但我们说过，本书不应当作菜谱来用，而是应当视为选择性采用的资源库。这些教学建议也是本着这个精神而提出的。

Sequencing and Suggestions for Key Grammar and Vocabulary

Renamed from "Teaching Suggestions and Sequencing of Important Language Points" (重要语言点的教学建议与顺序), this section still takes up the greater part of each chapter. Most of the space is devoted to vocabulary instruction, reflecting our belief in the importance and challenge of vocabulary acquisition in Chinese. This part also complements the main textbook, where information on the teaching of individual vocabulary items is limited to the vocabulary list and notes on selected items.

The principles used for sequencing the vocabulary items in a lesson remain the same as in Level 1. They are given below.

Unlike the vocabulary lists in the main textbook, in this handbook the words and structures are not presented in their order of appearance in the text as this may not be the best way to present and practice them. Instead, the items are grouped according to how closely they are associated either semantically or syntactically, such as verbs with their objects, or nouns with their modifiers, and so on.

A typical entry for a language point may include the following:

Characters

Here teachers are alerted to whatever clues that exist, be they for meaning and/or sound, which can be used to make the characters appear more logical to students. In addition, we also include tips on how to draw connections between characters that share common components.

Especially important are the phonetic clues that have been somewhat neglected in the teaching of Chinese. For example, when introducing the character 妈, we suggest pointing out that it shares the same sound component as 吗. In this way, we can concentrate on the tonal differences in the characters, as it is no longer necessary to go over the "ma" pronunciation again. Relating the new character to the old also helps students get a handle on the new character, as well as being a helpful way to review.

主要语法和词汇的排序和教学建议

本部分即是一年级的"Teaching Suggestions and Sequencing of Important Language Points"(重要语言点的教学建议与顺序),仍占每一章最大的篇幅。词汇教学也仍然是中心内容,反映了我们关于汉语"词汇重要、词汇难"的信念。本部分也是对于主课本的补充。那里的词汇部分只限于词汇表和对一些词条的选择性的注释。

每一课的语言点的排序原则仍然与前三册相同,特陈述如下。

生词和语法点不像主课本那样按课文中出现的先后顺序排序。那种排序不一定利于教和练。本手册尽量将相关的内容放到一起,譬如在语义上有联系的词语或句法结构中相关的成分(如动词与其宾语,名词与其修饰语等)。

手册中对一个语言点的处理通常会包括如下几点内容:

汉字

此处就汉字中可能包含的语音符号和语意符号对教师提出提示,这些符号可以帮助学生认识到汉字的结构规律,同时也可帮助他们联想到包含相同成分的其它汉字。

汉字中的声符尤为重要,而这些声符在中文教学中往往没得到足够的重视。例如,在学到"妈"这个字时,不妨指出其中的语音符号与"吗"的声符相同,这样做使我们除了声调以外不必再过于强调"妈"的发音。把新出现的字和已学过的字联系起来既帮助新字的掌握,又能起到复习作用。

There will be fewer notes on characters in Level 2 as most of the areas of difficulty have already been dealt with in Level 1. However, this does not imply that no more attention should be paid to character composition. Indeed, you will still find notes on character composition for some vocabulary items.

Pronunciation

There will also be fewer notes on pronunciation, as most of the areas of difficulty have been dealt with in Level 1. However, this does not imply that no more attention should be paid to pronunciation.

Meaning

Under this heading a number of meaning-related tips are given, for example the difference between the literal meanings of the component morphemes and the actual meaning of the word.

Word Structure

For some items with multiple syllables, a note on word composition is provided. When words contain multiple syllables, the issue of internal grouping of syllables becomes relevant. For example, the correct grouping of 服务员 should be 服务 + 员 rather than 服 + 务员. This is especially important when the correct structure is not apparent. For example, in 汽车站, both 汽车 and 车站 are words in their own right. Yet the correct structure is really 汽车 + 站, rather than 汽 + 车站. Knowing the breakdown of a word should be helpful for the comprehension and retention of a vocabulary item.

Chinese Gloss

As part of the effort to encourage the use of Chinese, a new vocabulary item is explained in Chinese whenever possible. This has the dual benefit of recycling old vocabulary and conveying the meaning better when simple English glosses do not work, as for kinship terms.

Usage

Usage notes are used to address the subtle differences in the use of lexical items. For example, even though 父母 means the same as 爸妈, the former cannot be used to address parents face to face.

跟前三册相比，汉字的注释减少了，因为很多难点在一年级已经教过了。但这并不意味着汉字的结构不再需要注意。有些词汇还是会有汉字注释。

发音

跟前三册相比，发音的注释也减少了，因为很多难点在一年级已经教过了。但这并不意味着发音不再需要注意。

词义

在此会提供一些跟词义有关的提示，如实际词义和构词语素字面意思之间的差别。

单词结构

有些多音节词有构词注释。当一个词含有不止一个音节时，单词内部的组合结构就有讲究了。例如，"服务员"一词中正确的组合结构是"服务＋员"而不是"服＋务员"。在答案并非显而易见时，这种提示就尤为重要。例如，在"汽车站"中，"汽车"和"车站"都各自是一个词。但是这儿正确的组合结构应该是"汽车＋站"而不是"汽＋车站"。正确了解单词内部结构有助于对单词的理解和记忆。

中文解释

为了尽量多用中文，我们尽可能为生词提供中文解释。这样做有两个好处，一方面可以复习学过的词语，另一方面可以在英文解释不够准确的情况下更好地表达词义，例如亲属称谓等。

用法

用法说明是用来提示相关词语之间词义上的细微差别。例如，虽然"父母"与"爸妈"同义，但是前者不用于当面称呼父母。

Regional Variation

The linguistic scene is China is extremely diverse. To prepare students for extensive regional variations, we provide some regional variants of standard usages. For example, the preferred term for 水平 in Taiwan is 水准 and 和 is often pronounced hàn. Even though 行 can no longer be used as the verb to mean "walk" in Mandarin, it is still used this way in Cantonese, as was true of classical Chinese as well.

In addition to exposing students to the linguistic reality of the Chinese-speaking world, giving regional variants also has added benefits for heritage students, who may be able to use this kind of information to relate to their own dialects.

Culture

Cultural notes are given for some vocabulary items as needed. For example, for the character 瘦, the significance of the sickness radical will be pointed out. Traditionally, to be thin is to be sick; an out of date compliment is 你胖了. Cultural notes like these not only serve to highlight the distinctness of Chinese culture, they will also help in the retention of characters and words. These cultural notes do not overlap with those given in the textbook, which are more general in nature, related to the topic of the lesson rather than individual vocabulary items.

Explanation

Here additional explanations of the more difficult grammatical structures are given, along with suggestions for teaching.

Suggested Modes for Practice

Some items (such as those that occur only in rhetorical questions) are not suited for practice in the usual way (for example, with Q&A exercises). For such items, an explicit suggestion for a mode of practice is given.

区域变异

中国的语言极其多样化。为了让学生更好地应对极其普遍的区域变异，我们告诉他们一些标准用法的地区性变体。例如，"水平"在台湾通常说"水准"，"和"在台湾可能发成 hàn。虽然"行"在普通话中通常不再用作表示"行走"的动词，但是在粤语和文言文中仍用于这一意义。

除了帮助学生正视中国各地区间的语言差异外，这一条目对有华裔背景的学生尤为有益，有助于他们跟自己的方言联系起来。

文化

有必要时，有些生词有文化注释。例如，在讨论"瘦"字时，我们会指出其"病"字头。中国人传统上认为"瘦"与"病"有关，而"你胖了"曾经是一句恭维语，尽管现在已经不合时宜了。这样的文化解释不仅有助于彰显中西文化的不同，而且有助于学生对词和字的记忆。这些文化解释与主课本中的文化点并不重复，因为主课本中的文化点涉及的是更宽泛的内容，相关的是课文的主题而不是个别单词的词义。

解释

此处会对难度较高的语法结构作出解释，并提供一些教学提示。

建议练习方式

有些语言点（如只出现在反问句中的词语）不适于用一般的方式练习（如问答练习）。为此我们就合适的练习方式提出一些具体的建议。

Q&A Practice

This is typically the first exercise to be used when a word has been introduced. The Q&A format has the following pedagogical advantages:

With a Q&A sequence, students can listen to and use the word right away. Given the similarity in word order between questions and answers in Chinese, the question provides built-in structural scaffolding for the answer. Teachers should try to take advantage of this fact and encourage students to pay attention to the structure of each question and echo it in their answer.

Jeopardy

This format is named after the popular TV game show, and it has a number of uses:

If the answer is too involved or too open-ended, asking the question reduces the difficulty level and allows students to focus on the targeted item more.

This can be used if the target item is unlikely to appear in a question. Even though students will not be using the target item in their questions, they will at least see the target item in the answer, which their questions must be based on.

The format can also be used if the questions from the teacher sound unnatural for lack of sufficient context or appear intrusive. By asking students to provide questions to match the answers, we turn the question-answer sequence into practice of form, which need not always be natural.

Finally, the use of the format can get students to ask questions, instead of only answering them. Students should not always be at the receiving end of questions. There will be times when students don't know the answer and hence want to ask questions! With better facility in asking questions, students will feel more comfortable initiating conversations and controlling the direction a conversation takes.

问答练习

这通常是介绍一个生词后最先进行的练习。从教学法上来说,问答练习有如下优点:

在问答程序中学生可以听到并马上用到刚学的单词。由于中文中问句和答句的词序相同,问句本身即为答句提供结构上的铺垫。教师应利用这一点,鼓励学生充分注意问句的结构并在答句中对其进行模仿。

绝处逢生

与流行的电视游戏节目同名,这个练习有几个用处:

如果答案太复杂或者太过宽泛,可以通过提问来降低难度,并把注意力集中在要练习的词语上。

这种练习也可以用于那些不太出现于问句的语言点。虽然学生不会在问句中用到这个语言点,他们得根据回答提出相应的问题,而从这些回答中就可接触到这个语言点。

如果教师的问题因语境不明而听起来不够自然或者显得突兀,不妨采用这个模式。通过让学生提出与答句对应的问句,我们可以将问答程序变为语法练习,而语法练习不必总是非常自然的。

最后,这个练习方式可以鼓励学生提问,而不仅仅限于回答问题。在问答活动中学生不应该永远是被问者。有时候学生会因为不知问题的答案而要发问!在发问的能力得到提高之后,学生才会更加得心应手地跟他人展开交谈或者在交谈中改变话题。

Fill in the Blanks

This format is used to focus on target items, which is not easy to do with other kinds of exercises. The typical items to go into blanks are grammatical words like prepositions, aspect markers, particles, and so on. Another use of the format is to contrast two items by requiring students to fill in blanks with either of the two items.

Sentence Completion

This format can be used when the use of questions is not appropriate or possible, for example, when practicing connectives. The use of this format allows a fine balance between creativity and control/scaffolding.

Transformation

This is used to highlight the difference in form between two related structures, for example, that between the two ways of expressing time duration, e.g., either before an object or after an object (我学了两年的中文了 vs. 我学中文学了两年了).

Translation

This exercise is used mostly to highlight the differences between Chinese and English.

Collocation

This is used to illustrate the use of the target items in typical contexts.

Other combinations

In the textbook, component characters are sometimes listed alongside the vocabulary items. Extending this practice, we single out word components when appropriate. We try, whenever appropriate, to provide new contexts for the word component, in order to help students strengthen their retention. For example, in addition to the word 中文, we also give information on 文. We also try, whenever appropriate, to provide new contexts for the word component, in order to help students strengthen their retention. For example, when 茶 (tea) is introduced, related combinations such as 红茶 (black tea), 绿茶 (green tea), 中国茶 (Chinese tea), and 英国茶 (English tea) are also given. Instead of being an extra burden for students, the extra information may be helpful in the following ways:

填空

这种练习可用于凸显那些不易用其他方式练习的词语。用来填空的通常为介词、体态词、语气词等语法成分。另一用法是让学生通过对相关两个词语的对比而选定其中之一填空。

完成句子

这个方式可在用问句练习不合适或不可能时采用，如练习关联词语时。用这种练习方式既能保持控制/提供支持也允许学生发挥一定的创造力。

转换

这种练习用于突显两种相关句型之间的联系和差异，例如有关动作延续时间的两种表达法之间的差异（我学了两年的中文了 vs.我学中文学了两年了）。

翻译

这类练习主要用于彰显中英文的差异。

搭配

这是用来显示所介绍的词语的典型搭配语境。

其他组合

课本的生词表在某些单词之下选择性地分列组成该词的字。仿照这种做法，本手册在适当的时候也讨论组成特定单词的字。例如，我们不仅介绍"中文"这个单词，我们也讨论这个词中的"文"。如果我们认为适当，我们还会介绍有关特定组词成分的语境，以帮助学生强化记忆。例如，在介绍"茶"的时候，我们会列举诸如"红茶"、"绿茶"、"中国茶"和"英国茶"一类的组合。它们不会给学生造成额外负担；相反，它们会在下列诸方面有帮助：

- As Chinese is unrelated to most students' mother tongues, very little can be done to relate Chinese to their native languages, making vocabulary acquisition in Chinese particularly challenging. Therefore, in order to help students retain new material, we need to do everything possible to connect it to other elements within Chinese.

- Situating the word components in a broader context helps to clarify the meaning of these components. For example, presenting 汽车、马车 and 火车 together shows that the meaning of 车 is "vehicle" rather than "car."

- Presenting new combinations serves as review of older materials.

The information about word components and supplementary combinations is typically given at the very end, after the main target word is practiced. We recommend that teachers adhere to this sequence as well. This may help prevent erroneous analogies by students.

Not all of the supplementary words supplied here need to be given to students. They certainly should not be expected to use all of the supplementary words. They are given more for their mnemonic values than anything else.

Exercises for the Main Text

In this section, we have suggested a number of exercises to help students become familiar with the text.

How to make most of reading aloud: In order to encourage students to associate sound with shape, we suggest projecting the text on screen and highlighting the parts being read. To engage more students and ensure comprehension, we suggest assigning the roles of speakers and interpreters for conversational text.

A list of questions related to the text is also given to check comprehension and help students practice listening and speaking.

- 对于大多数学生来说，中文与他们的母语没有亲族关系，很难使中文与他的母语发生联系。这一点使得他们对中文词汇的学习尤为困难。因此，为了帮助学生掌握新的内容，我们必须尽量将这一新内容与中文中的其它成分联系起来。

- 将所学的组词成分置于更大的语言环境中使该组词成分的意义更加清晰。例如，将"汽车"、"马车"、"火车"放到一起可以更清楚显示"车"的意思是 vehicle 而不是 car。

- 介绍新组合也是复习的过程。

有关组词成分和补充复合词的信息通常放在最后一部分，在主要词条的练习之后。我们希望教师在实际教学中也遵循这个顺序。这种做法看起来也许有些反直觉，但是有助于防止学生进行错误类比。

此处列出的补充词汇不必全数教给学生。绝对不应要求学生掌握所有的补充词汇。我们提供这些补充词汇，主要是因为它们有助于学生对所学词条的掌握。

主课文的练习

在这一部分，我们建议用一些练习方式，以帮助学生熟悉课文。

怎样使朗读更有效：为了帮助学生建立汉字字体和发音的联系，建议把课文投影在屏幕上并突显正在朗读的部分。为了让更多学生参与并确保课文的理解，我们建议念对话时分别让学生扮演说话者和翻译的角色。

我们还就课文内容提了一些问题，以此方法来检查学生对课文的理解，同时可以帮助学生练习听力及口语。

Suggested Integrative Activities

The activities in this section are typically used after the introduction of vocabulary items and grammatical elements for the purpose of integrating them. The activities are grouped under three headings: "Speaking and Listening," "Reading and Writing," "Grammar and Vocabulary."

Speaking and Listening

Some common activities under this category include:

Surveys

The data collected from the surveys are used for further follow-up activities, such as presentations.

Interviews

Students are asked to interview their language partners. Typically, the questions are given providing the necessary control and scaffolding while allow for a certain amount of creativity.

Presentations can be made based on the results of interviews.

Reading and Writing

Some common activities under this category include:

- Reading passages followed by comprehension questions.
- Written responses based on reading. One common format is responding to an e-mail message, which is a very realistic task.
- Supplementary readings. These are extensions of the text, with the same cast of characters and the same themes as in the text.

Grammar and Vocabulary

Most of the exercises here are designed to focus on discrete lexical and grammatical elements. The two most common types of questions are fill-in-blanks and sentence completions, which both direct attention to the targeted elements and encourage cognitive engagement. While the former tends to elicit fixed answers, the latter allows for some degree of creativity while maintaining sufficient control/scaffolding.

综合练习活动

这种练习通常在介绍过一定数量的生词和语法点以后进行，目的是对这些生词和语法点进行整合。练习分成三大类，即听说、读写、语法和词汇。

听说

一些常见的活动包括：

调查

调查得到的资料可用作后随活动，如报告。

采访

要求学生采访他们的语伴。采访的问题一般可以给出，这样可让学生发挥一定的创造力，也能保证必要的控制和支持。

可以让学生报告采访的结果。

读写

这里一些常见的练习包括：

- 阅读短文，然后回答问题。
- 根据所读短文写短文。一个很常见也很有用的任务是回复电邮。
- 补充阅读。这些是课文的延续，有同样的人物和同样的话题。

语法与词汇

这里的练习大多是用来凸显单个的词汇和语法成分。两种最常用的题型、既能让学生注意目标成分，也鼓励他们动脑筋，就是填空和完成句子。前者往往有固定答案，而后者在保持足够的控制和支持下允许学生发挥一定的创造力。

Sample Syllabus

Goals & Objectives

Students will gain listening, speaking, reading and writing skills in standard (Mandarin) Chinese, attaining approximately the **Intermediate High** to **Advanced Low** level on the ACTFL/ETS proficiency scale. Specifically, students will be able to achieve the following:

Listening   Able to understand paragraph-length utterances pertaining to a wide range of topics relating to daily life such as: Chinese festivals, traveling, health, environmental protection, money management, interviewing for a job, etc.

Speaking   Be able to handle successfully a wide range of task-oriented and social functions pertaining to such topic areas as those mentioned above, participating fully in casual conversations. Will be able to narrate, describe, compare and contrast in paragraph length.

Reading   Be able to identify key facts and details in descriptive material on daily life. Can discern linkages among sentences in connected texts. Be able to understand a wide range of authentic texts dealing with personal and social needs, and some texts dealing with public life.

Writing   Be able to write in paragraphs with appropriate connectors. Can describe one's own experiences, and certain events such as Chinese festivals. Can express one's own opinion on issues such as health, gender equality in the work place, environmental protection, etc.

Text & Materials

- *Integrated Chinese (Level 2, Part 2), Textbook* (Third Edition), Yuehua Liu and Tao-chung Yao, et al. Boston: Cheng & Tsui Company, 2010. Print and eBook versions available.
- *Integrated Chinese (Level 2, Part 2), Workbook* (Third Edition), Yuehua Liu and Tao-chung Yao, et al. Boston: Cheng & Tsui Company, 2010. Print and online versions available.
- *Integrated Chinese (Level 2, Part 2), Character Workbook* (Third Edition), Yuehua Liu and Tao-chung Yao, et al. Boston: Cheng & Tsui Company, 2010.
- Audio Recordings for *Integrated Chinese (Level 2, Part 2),* Third Edition. Boston: Cheng & Tsui Company, 2010. Available on CD or as downloadable MP3s from **www.cheng-tsui.com**.
- *Integrated Chinese* Companion Site: www.integratedchinese.com
- Tao-chung Yao's *Integrated Chinese* resource website: http://eall.hawaii.edu/yao/icusers/

Student Responsibilities

This information may vary according to your institution's policies.

Attendance: Attendance is mandatory. Absences without valid reasons will affect your grade. Students who are more than 15 minutes late to class will be regarded as absent for that session.

Class preparation and participation: All students are expected to prepare for class and participate actively in the day's language practice. Students' class participation and performance will be evaluated daily and a final score will be given at the end of each class using the following scale:

    4 = Well prepared with excellent performance
    3 = Gave some indication of good preparation
    2 = Participated, but displayed inadequate preparation
    1 = Present with almost no participation
    0 = Absent

3. Homework and assignments: **All homework and assignments must be turned in on the day due. Late homework and assignments will NOT be accepted even if they are submitted along with new homework.** You are expected to listen to the audio recordings and practice speaking EVERY DAY. Practice writing characters EVERY DAY! No language can be acquired overnight. The best way to build up your Chinese language proficiency is gradually, through constant practice.
4. Quizzes and tests: Every effort should be made to take quizzes and tests at the specified times. If you know you must miss a class ahead of time, tell the teacher before that class. Quizzes **cannot** be made up unless arrangements are made BEFORE your absence from class. No one is allowed to make up a missed test without a valid, written excuse.

Please keep in mind that each student's background, interests, learning style, difficulties, and goals are different. Please be patient with each other and do not hesitate to see one of the teachers for extra help or explanations.

Grading

Note: The percentage for each segment may vary according to the individual teacher's grading policy.

Final course grades will be based on the results of:

1. Attendance and Participation: 40%
2. Quizzes (10%) and Tests (10%):   20%
3. Homework and Assignments: 10%
4. Midterm (5% plus oral 5%) and Final (10% plus oral 10%):   30%

Final grade: 100–98=A+, 97–94=A, 93–90=A-, 89–87=B+, 86–84=B, 83–80=B-, 79–77=C+, 76–74=C, 73–70=C-, 69–67=D+, 66–64=D, 63–60=D-, 59 and below=F

Sample Daily Class Schedule
(Four Hours a Week)

List of Abbreviations:

CH: Culture Highlights, **CWB:** Character Workbook, **G:** Grammar, **L:** Lesson, **LP:** Language Practice, **RC:** Reading Comprehension, **SE:** Speaking Exercises, **T:** Text, **TB:** Textbook, **V:** Vocabulary, **WB:** Workbook, **WGE:** Writing and Grammar Exercises, **WP:** Words & Phrases

[Note: This schedule is based on a 16-week long semester. The class only meets four days each week. Each lesson will take 5 days to finish. There will be a short unit test after each lesson, except for L15 and L20. There will be a midterm exam and a final exam. Remember to allow extra time for breaks and holidays, depending on your school's schedule.]

Week 1 (Days 1–4)

Date	Class Activities	Homework Due	Preparation
Day 1	Introduction to the course; Background information sheets; Student roster; Classroom Expressions Review; Getting to know each other; Review IC2 Part1		
Day 2	Begin Integrated Chinese Level 2, Part 2 L11 Intro. to V (TB pp. 10–12) & T (TB pp. 2–9)		Study TB L11 T, V, CH (pp. 2–16)
Day 3	Review L11 V&T L11 G (TB pp. 17–20)	WB L11 LC (pp. 1–2) CWB L11 (PP. 1–11)	Preview WB L11 SE (pp. 2–3) Study TB L11 G (pp. 17–20)
Day 4	Review L11 G L11 WP (TB pp. 20–23) L11 Voc Quiz	WB L11 RC (pp. 3–8)	Study TB L11 WP (pp. 20–23)

Week 2 (Days 5–8)

Date	Class Activities	Homework Due	Preparation
Day 5	LP (ABCDEF) (TB pp. 24–26)	WB L11 WGE (A–H) (pp. 8–14)	Study TB L11 LP (ABCDEF) (p. 24–26)
Day 6	LP (GHIJK) (TB pp. 27–30) L11 Test	WB L11 WGE (I–L) (pp. 15–17)	Study TB L11 LP (GHIJK) (pp. 27–30)
Day 7	L12 Intro. to V&T		Study TB L12 T, V, CH
Day 8	Review L12 V&T L12 G	WB L12 LC CWB L12	Preview WB L12 SE Study TB L12 G

Week 3 (Days 9–12)

Date	Class Activities	Homework Due	Preparation
Day 9	Review L12 G L12 WP L12 Voc Quiz	WB L12 RC	Study TB L12 WP
Day 10	LP (ABCD)	WB L12 WGE (A–G)	Study TB L12 LP (ABCD)
Day 11	LP (EFGH)	WB L12 WGE (H–J)	Study TB L12 LP (EFGH)
Day 12	Review L12 Test		

Week 4 (Days 13–16)

Date	Class Activities	Homework Due	Preparation
Day 13	L13 Intro. to V&T		Study TB L13 T, V, CH
Day 14	Review L13 V&T L13 G	WB L13 LC CWB L13	Preview WB L13 SE Study TB L13 G
Day 15	Review L13 G L13 WP L13 Voc Quiz	WB L13 RC	Study TB L13 WP
Day 16	LP (ABC)	WB L13 WGE (A–G)	Study TB L13 LP (ABC)

Week 5 (Days 17–20)

Date	Class Activities	Homework Due	Preparation
Day 17	LP (DEFG) L13 Test	WB L13 WGE (H–K)	Study TB L13 LP (DEFG)
Day 18	L14 Intro. to V&T		Study TB L14 T, V, CH
Day 19	Review L14 V&T L14 G	WB L14 LC CWB L14	Preview WB L14 SE Study TB L14 G
Day 20	Review L14 G L14 WP L14 Voc Quiz	WB L14 RC	Study TB L14 WP

Week 6 (Days 21–24)

Date	Class Activities	Homework Due	Preparation
Day 21	LP (ABCD)	WB L14 WGE (A–G)	Study TB L14 LP (ABCD)
Day 22	LP (EFGH)	WB L14 WGE (H–K)	Study TB L14 LP (EFGH)
Day 23	Review L14 Test		
Day 24	L15 Intro. to V&T		Study TB L15 T, V, CH

Week 7 (Days 25–28)

Date	Class Activities	Homework Due	Preparation
Day 25	Review L15 V&T L15 G	WB L15 LC CWB L15	Preview WB L15 SE Study TB L15 G
Day 26	Review L15 G L15 WP L15 Voc Quiz	WB L15 RC	Study TB L15 WP
Day 27	LP (ABCD)	WB L15 WGE (A–H)	Study TB L15 LP (ABCD)
Day 28	LP (EFG)	WB L15 WGE (I–K)	Study TB L15 LP (EFG)

Week 8 (Days 29–32)

Date	Class Activities	Homework Due	Preparation
Day 29	Let's Review! L11–15	WB R1 Let's Review L11–15	Study Let's Review! L11–15
Day 30	Midterm Exam		
Day 31	L16 Intro. to V&T		Study TB L16 T, V, CH
Day 32	Review L16 V&T L16 G	WB L16 LC CWB L16	Preview WB L16 SE Study TB L16 G

Week 9 (Days 33–36)

Date	Class Activities	Homework Due	Preparation
Day 33	Review L16 G L16 WP L16 Voc Quiz	WB L16 RC	Study TB L16 WP
Day 34	LP (ABC)	WB L16 WGE (A–H)	Study TB L16 LP (ABC)
Day 35	LP (DEF) L16 Test	WB L16 WGE (I–K)	Study TB L16 LP (DEF)
Day 36	L17 Intro. to V&T		Study TB L17 T, V, CH

Week 10 (Days 37–40)

Date	Class Activities	Homework Due	Preparation
Day 37	Review L17 V&T L17 G	WB L17 LC CWB L17	Preview WB L17 SE Study TB L17 G
Day 38	Review L17 G L17 WP L17 Voc Quiz	WB L17 RC	Study TB L17 WP
Day 39	LP (ABCD)	WB L17 WGE (A–H)	Study TB L17 LP (ABCD)
Day 40	LP (EFG)	WB L17 WGE (I–K)	Study TB L17 LP (EFG)

Week 11 (Days 41–44)

Date	Class Activities	Homework Due	Preparation
Day 41	Review L17 Test		
Day 42	L18 Intro. to V&T		Study TB L18 T, V, CH
Day 43	Review L18 V&T L18 G	WB L18 LC CWB L18	Preview WB L18 SE Study TB L18 G
Day 44	Review L18 G L18 WP L18 Voc Quiz	WB L18 RC	Study TB L18 WP

Week 12 (Days 45–48)

Date	Class Activities	Homework Due	Preparation
Day 45	LP (ABCDE)	WB L18 WGE (A–G)	Study TB L18 LP (ABCDE)
Day 46	LP (FG) L18 Test	WB L18 WGE (H–J)	Study TB L18 LP (FG)
Day 47	L19 Intro. to V&T		Study TB L19 T, V, CH
Day 48	Review L19 V&T L19 G	WB L19 LC CWB L19	Preview WB L19 SE Study TB L19 G

Week 13 (Days 49–52)

Date	Class Activities	Homework Due	Preparation
Day 49	Review L19 G L19 WP L19 Voc Quiz	WB L19 RC	Study TB L19 WP
Day 50	LP (ABCDE)	WB L19 WGE (A–H)	Study TB L19 LP (ABCDE)
Day 51	LP (FGHI)	WB L19 WGE (I–K)	Study TB L19 LP (FGHI)
Day 52	L19 Test		

Week 14 (Days 53–56)

Date	Class Activities	Homework Due	Preparation
Day 53	L20 Intro. to V&T		Study TB L20 T, V, CH
Day 54	Review L20 V&T L20 G	WB L20 LC CWB L20	Preview WB L20 SE Study TB L20 G
Day 55	Review L20 G L20 WP L20 Voc Quiz	WB L20 RC	Study TB L20 WP
Day 56	LP (ABC)	WB L20 WGE (A–G)	Study TB L20 LP (ABC)

Week 15 (Days 57–60)

Date	Class Activities	Homework Due	Preparation
Day 57	LP (DEF)	WB L20 WGE (H–J)	Study TB L20 LP (DEF)
Day 58	Let's Review! L16–20	WB R2 Let's Review L16–20	Study Let's Review! L16–20
Day 59	Review for the final exam		
Day 60	Final Exam		

Don't forget to insert the holidays observed by your school into your schedule and adjust the dates accordingly.

Date	Holiday

Sample Daily Class Schedule
(Five Hours a Week)

List of Abbreviations:

CH: Culture Highlights, **CWB:** Character Workbook, **G:** Grammar, **L:** Lesson, **LP:** Language Practice, **RC:** Reading Comprehension, **SE:** Speaking Exercises, **T:** Text, **TB:** Textbook, **V:** Vocabulary, **WB:** Workbook, **WGE:** Writing and Grammar Exercises, **WP:** Words & Phrases

[Note: This schedule is based on a 15-week long semester. The class meets five days each week. Each lesson will take 6 days to finish. There will be a short unit test after each lesson, except for L15 and L20. There will be a midterm exam and a final exam. Remember to allow extra time for breaks and holidays, depending on your school's schedule.]

Week 1 (Days 1–5)

Date	Class Activities	Homework Due	Preparation
Day 1	Introduction to the course; background information sheets; student roster; classroom expressions review; getting to know each other; review IC2 Part 1		
Day 2	Begin Integrated Chinese Level 2, Part 2 L11 Intro. to V (TB pp. 10–12) & T (TB pp. 2–9)		Study TB L11 T, V, CH (pp. 2–16)
Day 3	Review L11 V&T L11 G (TB pp. 17–20)	WB L11 LC (pp. 1–2) CWB L11 (pp. 1–11)	Preview WB L11 SE (pp. 2–3) Study TB L11 G (pp. 17–20)
Day 4	Review L11 G L11 WP (TB pp. 20–23) **L11 Voc Quiz**	WB L11 RC (pp. 3–8)	Study TB L11 WP (pp. 20–23)
Day 5	LP (ABCDEF) (TB pp. 24–26)	WB L11 WGE (A–H) (pp. 8–14)	Study TB L11 LP (ABCDEF) (pp. 24–26)

Week 2 (Days 6–10)

Date	Class Activities	Homework Due	Preparation
Day 6	LP (GHIJK) (TB pp. 27–30)	WB L11 WGE (I–M) (pp. 16–19)	Study TB L11 LP (GHIJK) (pp. 27–30)
Day 7	Review **L11 Test**		
Day 8	L12 Intro. to V&T		Study TB L12 T, V, CH
Day 9	Review L12 V&T L12 G	WB L12 LC CWB L12	Preview WB L12 SE Study TB L12 G
Day 10	Review L12 G L12 WP **L12 Voc Quiz**	WB L12 RC	Study TB L12 WP

Week 3 (Days 11–15)

Date	Class Activities	Homework Due	Preparation
Day 11	LP (ABCD)	WB L12 WGE (A–G)	Study TB L12 LP (ABCD)
Day 12	LP (EFGH)	WB L12 WGE (H–J)	Study TB L12 LP (EFGH)
Day 13	Review **L12 Test**		
Day 14	L13 Intro. to V&T		Study TB L13 T, V, CH
Day 15	Review L13 V&T L13 G	WB L13 LC CWB L13	Preview WB L13 SE Study TB L13 G

Week 4 (Days 16–20)

Date	Class Activities	Homework Due	Preparation
Day 16	Review L13 G L13 WP **L13 Voc Quiz**	WB L13 RC	Study TB L13 WP
Day 17	LP (ABC)	WB L13 WGE (A–G)	Study TB L13 LP (ABC)
Day 18	LP (DEFG)	WB L13 WGE (H–K)	Study TB L13 LP (DEFG)
Day 19	Review **L13 Test**		
Day 20	L14 Intro. to V&T		Study TB L14 T, V, CH

Week 5 (Days 21–25)

Date	Class Activities	Homework Due	Preparation
Day 21	Review L14 V&T L14 G	WB L14 LC CWB L14	Preview WB L14 SE Study TB L14 G
Day 22	Review L14 G L14 WP **L14 Voc Quiz**	WB L14 RC	Study TB L14 WP
Day 23	LP (ABCD)	WB L14 WGE (A–G)	Study TB L14 LP (ABCD)
Day 24	LP (EFGH)	WB L14 WGE (H–K)	Study TB L14 LP (EFGH)
Day 25	Review **L14 Test**		

Week 6 (Days 26–30)

Date	Class Activities	Homework Due	Preparation
Day 26	L15 Intro. to V&T		Study TB L15 T, V, CH
Day 27	Review L15 V&T L15 G	WB L15 LC CWB L15	Preview WB L15 SE Study TB L15 G
Day 28	Review L15 G L15 WP **L15 Voc Quiz**	WB L15 RC	Study TB L15 WP
Day 29	LP (ABCD)	WB L15 WGE (A–H)	Study TB L15 LP (ABCD)
Day 30	LP (EFG)	WB L15 WGE (I–K)	Study TB L15 LP (EFG)

Week 7 (Days 31–35)

Date	Class Activities	Homework Due	Preparation
Day 31	Review		
Day 32	Let's Review! L11–15	WB R1 Let's Review! L11–15	Study Let's Review! L11–15
Day 33	More review for the midterm (or start midterm oral)		
Day 34	**Midterm Oral Exam**		
Day 35	**Midterm Written Exam**		

Week 8 (Days 36–40)

Date	Class Activities	Homework Due	Preparation
Day 36	L16 Intro. to V&T		Study TB L16 T, V, CH
Day 37	Review L16 V&T L16 G	WB L16 LC CWB L16	Preview WB L16 SE Study TB L16 G
Day 38	Review L16 G L16 WP **L16 Voc Quiz**	WB L16 RC	Study TB L16 WP
Day 39	LP (ABC)	WB L16 WGE (A–H)	Study TB L16 LP (ABC)
Day 40	LP (DEF)	WB L16 WGE (I–K)	Study TB L16 LP (DEF)

Week 9 (Days 41–45)

Date	Class Activities	Homework Due	Preparation
Day 41	Review **L16 Test**		
Day 42	L17 Intro. to V&T		Study TB L17 T, V, CH
Day 43	Review L17 V&T L17 G	WB L17 LC CWB L17	Preview WB L17 SE Study TB L17 G
Day 44	Review L17 G L17 WP L17 Voc Quiz	WB L17 RC	Study TB L17 WP
Day 45	LP (ABCD)	WB L17 WGE (A–H)	Study TB L17 LP (ABCD)

Week 10 (Days 46–50)

Date	Class Activities	Homework Due	Preparation
Day 46	LP (EFG)	WB L17 WGE (I–K)	Study TB L17 LP (EFG)
Day 47	Review **L17 Test**		
Day 48	L18 Intro. to V&T		Study TB L18 T, V, CH
Day 49	Review L18 V&T L18 G	WB L18 LC CWB L18	Preview WB L18 SE Study TB L18 G
Day 50	Review L18 G L18 WP L18 Voc Quiz	WB L18 RC	Study TB L18 WP

Week 11 (Days 51–55)

Date	Class Activities	Homework Due	Preparation
Day 51	LP (ABCDE)	WB L18 WGE (A–G)	Study TB L18 LP (ABCDE)
Day 52	LP (FG)	WB L18 WGE (H–J)	Study TB L18 LP (FG)
Day 53	Review **L18 Test**		
Day 54	L19 Intro. to V&T		Study TB L19 T, V, CH
Day 55	Review L19 V&T L19 G	WB L19 LC CWB L19	Preview WB L19 SE Study TB L19 G

Week 12 (Days 56–60)

Date	Class Activities	Homework Due	Preparation
Day 56	Review L19 G L19 WP L19 Voc Quiz	WB L19 RC	Study TB L19 WP
Day 57	LP (ABCDE)	WB L19 WGE (A–H)	Study TB L19 LP (ABCDE)
Day 58	LP (FGHI)	WB L19 WGE (I–K)	Study TB L19 LP (FGHI)
Day 59	Review L19 Test		
Day 60	L20 Intro. to V&T		Study TB L20 T, V, CH

Week 13 (Days 61–65)

Date	Class Activities	Homework Due	Preparation
Day 61	Review L20 V&T L20 G	WB L20 LC CWB L20	Preview WB L20 SE Study TB L20 G
Day 62	Review L20 G L20 WP L20 Voc Quiz	WB L20 RC	Study TB L20 WP
Day 63	LP (ABC)	WB L20 WGE (A–G)	Study TB L20 LP (ABC)
Day 64	LP (DEF)	WB L20 WGE (H–J)	Study TB L20 LP (DEF)
Day 65	Review		

Week 14 (Days 66–70)

Date	Class Activities	Homework Due	Preparation
Day 66	Let's Review! L16–20	WB R2 Let's Review! L16–20	Study Let's Review! L16–20
Day 67	Review for the final oral		
Day 68	Review for the final written		
Day 69	Final Oral Exam		
Day 70	Final Written Exam		

Don't forget to insert the holidays observed by your school into your schedule and adjust the dates accordingly.

Date	Holiday

General Principles and Useful Resources
总体教学原则及资源

Lesson Pace

Schedules vary from school to school, some being on a semester system while others are on a quarter system; some classes meet as few as three hours per week while others as many as five hours. It is, therefore, up to the individual school and instructor to decide how much material to cover in the school term.

While the two sample daily schedules provided in this handbook (one with 4 hours per week and the other with 5 hours, both on a semester system) do cover all ten lessons of Level 2 Part 2, teachers should not feel that all of the lessons have to be covered. Quite a few schools feel that eight lessons are all they can manage in a 15 or 16 week semester. This means that each lesson will take close to two weeks to finish, including the chapter tests and the midterm. The amount of instructional time for each lesson then is between 8–9 hours, if a five-day schedule is assumed. However, we do know that some schools finish all ten lessons in one semester.

Sequencing and Time Allocation

While the time taken to cover a lesson can vary from school to school, some general principles of time allocation and sequencing, both for a whole lesson cycle and within an instructional hour, can nonetheless be applicable.

The Lesson Cycle

The following is one possible option, with five hours allotted for each textbook lesson:

First hour: vocabulary and grammar (listening and speaking only)

- Warm up (Relate and Get Ready)

- Presentation and practice of vocabulary and grammar (listening and speaking)

教学进度

每个学校的学制不尽相同,有的是学期制(semester system),有的是学季制(quarter system)。每周的课时也因校而异,少的一周三节课,多的一周五节课,所以每个学校和教师必须根据自己的情况决定一学期或一学季的教学内容、进度。

手册中的两个课程表分别按每周四个课时和每周五个课时设计,一学年均为两学期,内容包括课本上册十课。但老师不必把十课都教完。不少老师觉得一个学期(或十五、十六周)顶多上八课,也就是说,把每课的测验和期中考试计算在内,一个学期平均下来每课将近用两周上完。如每周五节课的话,每课八到九个学时。我们知道,也有些学校一学期上完十课。

教学步骤和时间安排

虽然每课的教学时间因校而异,但有些教学步骤和时间安排的原则,如每课总的安排和课时的具体设计,对大家应该都是同样适用的。

每课的基本模式

以下是一种可能的安排法,每一课用五课时。

第一个课时:生词和语法(听和说)

- 准备 (Relate and Get Ready)

- 生词及语法的介绍和练习(听说)

- Recap
- Homework assignment

Second hour: text (reading Chinese characters)
- Review
- Reading vocabulary and dialogue
- Character writing practice
- Character structures (radicals etc.)
- Recap
- Homework assignment

Third hour: words and phrases
- Practice "words and phrases" of this lesson
- Vocabulary quiz
- Recap
- Homework assignment

Fourth hour: language practice
- Review
- Go over "Language Practice" of this lesson
- Communicative activity
- Recap
- Homework assignment

Fifth hour: review of both dialogues
- Comprehensive review
- Integrative communicative activity
- Check workbook answers

The Instructional Hour
- Warm up (pronunciation work, Relate and Get Ready, Cultural Highlights etc.)
- Feedback on homework assignments/tests

- 总结
- 布置作业

第二个课时：课文（看汉字）
- 复习
- 朗读生词和对话
- 汉字练习/习字
- 汉字结构（部首等）
- 总结
- 布置作业

第三个课时：词语
- 练习本课的词语
- 生词测验
- 总结
- 布置作业

第四个课时：语言练习
- 复习
- 让学生做本课的"语言练习"
- 交际练习
- 总结
- 布置作业

第五个课时：复习
- 总复习
- 综合交际练习
- 核对练习本答案

每个课时的安排
- 准备活动（发音练习、Relate and Get Ready、文化背景等）
- 作业解析

- Review of previously introduced materials
- Introduction and practice of new words and structures
- More controlled practice (pattern practice, teacher-student interaction)
- More open-ended communicative activities (student- student interaction)
- Integrative practice and overall review

For the suggested activities provided in this handbook, no length of time is specified. Teachers should be able to assess the optimum amount of time an activity should take. A judicious amount of repetition is necessary, but too much repetition will surely induce boredom. Therefore, it may not be a good idea to go through every student in the class for a given teacher-student interaction.

Pronunciation

Although some elementary Chinese classes start with concentrated practice of pronunciation before any lesson is introduced, it may not be a good idea to practice pronunciation outside of vocabulary. Doing that may be boring and hard to integrate with the teaching of vocabulary and grammar.

In order to make the practice of pronunciation more fun and meaningful, at the beginning teachers can bring in names of famous people and places in China as well as transliterations of familiar names of people and places.

Try not to use 1, 2, 3, and 4 to mark tones, as they are quite arbitrary. Also avoid using special terminology like 阴平 (high tone), 阳平 (rising tone), 上声 (low tone), and 去声 (falling tone); instead use terms like *high*, *rising*, *low*, and *falling*.

- 复习
- 介绍和练习生词以及新的结构
- 相对可控性练习(句型操练、老师和学生互动)
- 比较活的交际练习(学生和学生互动)
- 综合练习和总复习

手册中建议的练习没有指明具体的时间长度，老师可自行决定。适当的重复是必要的，但重复过多，学生会觉得乏味，所以老师和学生的互动练习，不必和每个学生都过一遍。

发音

有些初级中文课先集中练习发音，然后再进入正课内容，但总的来说，不宜脱离词汇 练习发音。一来乏味 ，二来不易与词汇和语法的教学结合起来。

为了使发音练习更有意思和有意义，开始可用中国的名人、名胜的名字和学生熟悉的人名地名。

尽量避免使用1、2、3、4来标声调，也不要用专业术语如阴平、阳平、上声和去声。High, rising, low 和 falling 这样的说法更形象易懂。

For ease of typing tone marks on a regular keyboard, the following tone marks can be adopted for doing homework and tests: 1 (high tone) ='-' (dash): 2='/'; 3='_' (underscore); 4='\'. e.g., 我爱中国= wo_ ai\ zhong- guo/. A Microsoft Word macro for converting these marks to official tone marks can be found at http://www-rohan.sdsu.edu/dept/chinese/newtonemarkconversion.txt

These marks also have the advantage of suggesting pitch contour in an iconic fashion. For demonstrating tone contours in class, hand-gestures can also be used.

English rising and falling intonation associated with questions and statements can be used to prompt the rising and falling tones in Mandarin.

The free acoustic analysis software WaveSurfer can be used to display tone contour instantly, either in class or by students at home: http://www.speech.kth.se/wavesurfer/

It may be a good idea to present the four tones as two pairs: high vs. low and rising vs. falling, instead of the traditional sequence of high, rising, low and falling.

Students can be encouraged to have a few standard phrases incorporating all four tones such as "我_爱\中-文/" (I love Chinese), or "我_去\中-国/" (I go to China).

在一般电脑键盘上，可用下列符号代表调号：1（high tone）= '-'（dash）；2= '/'；3= '_'（underscore）；4= '\'.e.g., 我爱中国= wo_ ai\ zhong- guo/. 下载下列软件便可将这些符号转换成正式调号：

http://www-rohan.sdsu.edu/dept/chinese/newtonemarkconversion.txt

这些符号的优点是形象，声调的升降起伏一目了然。老师也可在课堂上用手势示范不同的声调。

英语疑问句和陈述句的语调变化也可用来提示普通话的二声和四声。

免费的语音分析软件WaveSurfer可用来当场显示不同声调的曲线。可供老师在课上用，也可供学生在课后用：

http://www.speech.kth.se/wavesurfer

可一对一对地介绍四声，如一声和三声、二声和四声，不一定因循传统的一声、二声、三声、四声顺序。

可鼓励学生背诵含有四个声调的一两个句子，如："我_爱\中-文/"、"我_去\中-国/"。

It may also be a good idea to ask students to draw out the contours of the tones as they pronounce them. While tracing the contours of the high, rising and falling tones is quite straightforward, the third tone is in most instances short and low, instead of a short fall followed by a rising component. The full third tone, which contains a short fall followed by a rising portion, is rather limited in occurrence and therefore can be left out.

Some hard sounds for English-speaking students:
Seven initials: j, q, x, z, c, zh, r

Simple finals: o e (ê) i ü

Compound finals: ui, iu, ian, ü ê, üan

Teachers need to be prepared to work on pronunciation for the long haul and not expect to achieve perfect results at the beginning. Continuous work on the difficult spots such as tones and vowels like e, i, ü, and consonants like z, c, zh, j, q, may persist into the second year.

Some recent research results may be incorporated into the teachers' knowledge, such as Shi Feng, Wen Baoying: "Study of Language Transfer in Vowel Articulation by Chinese and American Students" (JCLTA, 42:2, May 2009), especially the following chart showing how English-speaking students are affected by their native language.

也可请学生在练习发音的同时，画出声调的形状。一声、二声和四声比较容易画，三声总的是短而低。全三声出现的几率很少，所以可以不教急促的下降然后上升的全三声。

对英语为母语的学生比较难的音有：

七个声母：j, q, x, z, c, zh, r

单韵母：o e (ê) i ü

复韵母：ui, iu, ian, ü ê, üan,

发音练习得持之以恒，不能指望学生一学就能掌握。一些难点如声调，某些元音如e, i, ü 和某些辅音如 z, c, zh, j, q, 可能要练到二年级。

有些近来的研究如石锋，温宝莹：中美学生元音发音中的母语迁移现象研究（JCLTA, 42：2，May 2009）可能对教学有参考作用，特别是下面一张英语影响学生发音的图：

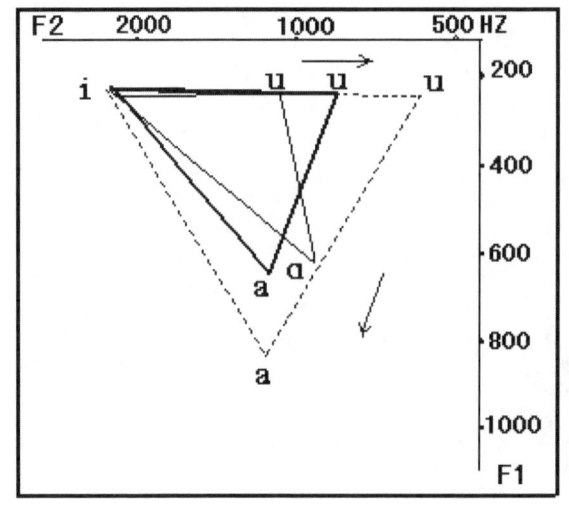

As can be seen from the chart on the previous page, American students' pronunciation is affected by their native language. The distance between vowels is less in English than in Chinese. When pronouncing the vowel sound "a," native English-speakers do not typically open their mouths as wide as is required in Chinese; similarly, when pronouncing "u," their tongues might not be sufficiently back in the mouth. Teachers can use this chart to demonstrate the differences between Chinese and English vowels.

Pinyin

There have been different Romanization systems over the years and *pinyin* is now the most widely-used system. There are 25 letters in *pinyin*, as "v" is not a distinctive phoneme. In Beijing speech, it is a variant of w. Generally speaking, *pinyin* spelling is more regular than in English. However, in order to simplify its written use, *pinyin* is not entirely phonetic. Some letters are not pronounced in the same way in every instance, for example, the vowel sound "o" varies from "song" to "ao." In some cases, the pronunciation of a sound is influenced by its surrounding sounds, such as the "a" in "ian" in such combinations as "xian," which becomes less open than when alone. There are also cases of one letter representing more than one sound, such as i, e, o, and u. There are also abbreviated spellings: ui(=uei), iu(=iou), un(=uen), ün(=üen) etc.

At the beginning, students may not be aware of the discrepancy between spelling and pronunciation. We recommend that students avoid reading off *pinyin* when they learn the pronunciation of words; it is better to imitate the teacher and audio recording.

Vocabulary

Although the separation between individual Chinese characters can be clearly seen, the boundaries between Chinese words made up of groups of characters are not so distinct as in alphabetic writing systems. However, students should still learn the differences between characters and words. Vocabulary items are words, not characters, even though some single characters function as words.

由上图可以看出，英语为母语的学生的发音受英语的影响，元音之间的距离小于汉语为母语者。发 a 时，口张得不够开；发 u 时，舌头偏前。老师可以在示范发音时，用此图显示英汉语元音的区别。

拼音

汉语有几种不同的注音符号系统，"汉语拼音"是现在最普及的一种。拼音共有二十五个字母。在北京话里，v 和 w 不具区别意义作用。一般来说，汉语拼音比英文来得有规律。但制定汉语拼音方案时，为了简便，拼写和发音并不完全一致。有些字母的发音不完全一样，如"song"和"ao"中的 o。有时一个音受周围的音影响，如"ian"中的"a"口型比单独发的"a"小。有的字母代表不同的音，如 i, e, o 和 u。有的拼写属缩略式的，如 ui (=uei), iu (=iou), un (=uen), ün (=üen) 等。

开始的时候，学生可能不会意识到拼写和发音之间不一致的情况，练习时最好避免指着拼音一个音一个音地念，最好让学生模仿老师和录音。

词汇

虽然单个汉字很容易辨别，但不像拼音文字，汉语的单词之间没有间隔。学生还是应该知道字和词的区别。词汇的单位是词而不是字，虽然某些字也是一个词。

Attention needs to be paid to both characters and words. Words are composed of individual characters and have their own independent meanings; the meaning of a word does not necessarily reflect the combination of the individual characters' meaning. Therefore, when introducing vocabulary items, it is not enough to focus only on the characters themselves. However, as characters are the building blocks of words and can be shared by related words, they should be examined to facilitate retention and the expansion of student vocabulary.

The order of vocabulary presentation does not need to follow that of the vocabulary list. The vocabulary list is organized by the order of appearance in the text, which may or may not be best for pedagogical purposes. The order used in this handbook often differs from the vocabulary list, and it can be adopted in class if one so wishes.

To introduce the meanings of new words, it is best not to solely rely on English glosses out of context. If presentation software is available, then try to use images as much as possible. Defining new words in Chinese can be phased in gradually. Although this practice may be more applicable at more advanced levels, it can be done to some extent even at the beginning level.

Students tend to rely on self-made flashcards with *pinyin*, simple English translations and little or no context. More vocabulary work should be done in class to counter this approach and cultivate better vocabulary learning strategies.

字和词都得重视。词由字组成，具有独立的意义，一个词的意义不一定是字意的直接组合，所以介绍生词时，把注意力只放在字上是不够的。反过来，字所代表的音节是词的构件，意义有关系的词可能有相同的字，所以介绍字，不仅能帮助学生记忆，而且对他们以后扩大词汇量会很有帮助。

介绍生词时不一定要按照词汇表的顺序。词汇表是以生词在课文出现的先后排列的，不一定适合教学的目的。《教师手册》内的词汇和课文中的排列顺序不同，可供上课参考。

介绍生词时，最好不要完全依赖脱离具体语境的英文翻译。如有简报软件(ppt)的话，尽量多用图片。可逐步用中文讲解生词。当然高年级用中文容易些，但在某种程度上，低年级也可以。

学生常常喜欢自己做生词卡，标上拼音和英文翻译，没有任何上下文。老师应在课堂上加强词汇练习，帮助学生找到更好的词汇练习方法。

For example, one way to learn vocabulary in context is to integrate it with pattern practice, right after a new word is introduced. To avoid being misled by *pinyin* spelling, new words can be first presented aurally without any *pinyin*, so that students can concentrate on the sounds. When there are good familiar sound clues in the new characters, *pinyin* can be totally or partially withheld and the sound clues used to indicate sound instead. For example, 吗 can be used to indicate the pronunciation of 妈, thus relating the new to the old. The same thing can be done to connect new and old characters in terms of shape and meaning, for example, brainstorming about characters with specific phonetic or semantic components. To help retention, the teacher can also try to reuse characters as much as possible and have them appear in as many contexts and new combinations as possible. However, care should be taken that the characters' meanings stay the same or vary only slightly in the new combinations.

Cheng & Tsui publishes a set of *Integrated Chinese BuilderCards* by Haidan Wang and Song Jiang, which present vocabulary in a more contextualized fashion. Vocabulary items from *Integrated Chinese* are listed with linguistically associated words, allowing more effective recall of definitions and contextual interpretation of unfamiliar words.

Characters

The distinctness of the Chinese written script may blur a fundamental difference that needs to be made between language and writing, i.e., between 语 and 文. Confusing the two may lead to undue emphasis on the written representation of language at the expense of language itself.

It is also worth mentioning at the outset that there is a widespread pictographic myth regarding the nature of Chinese characters, which simplistically assumes that all Chinese characters are based on pictures. In fact, pictographs are only one of four types of characters:

例如，一个通过语境来教生词的方法是把生词和句型结合起来，学了生词马上就用在句型里。为了避免拼音拼写的误导，开始要求学生集中听。如果生词中有学生很熟悉的声符，可以完全不用拼音，而利用声符。比如，"吗"字可用来提示"妈"，以旧带新。同样，可以利用学生学过的意符，举一反三，找出含有同样声符和意符的字。为了帮助记忆，老师可尽量在不同的语境和组合中重复用学生学过的字，但必须注意新的组合中的字的意思不变或相近。

Cheng & Tsui 出版王海丹、姜松设计的 *Integrated Chinese BuilderCards* 将词汇放在语境中，可供参考。相关的词汇同时列出，帮助单词的记忆和理解。

汉字

汉字的特殊形式可能模糊语和文之间的区别，导致重文轻语。

另需指出的是有个对汉字性质的普遍误解，认为汉字都是从象形字演变而来。实际上，象形字只是汉字所谓六书(本文举其中四个常用的)中的一种：

Pictographs:	日 月 水 火 人	象形：	日 月 水 火 人
Simple indicatives:	一 二 三 上 下	指事：	一 二 三 上 下
Compound indicatives:	信 明 林 森 家	会意：	信 明 林 森 家
Semantic-phonetic compounds:	清 吗 想 饭 背	形声：	清 吗 想 饭 背

Although some Chinese characters did originate from pictographs, they actually constitute a very small portion of the characters in use. The other two types of characters representing meanings directly, i.e., the simple and compound indicatives, likewise constitute a small percentage. Most characters are of the fourth type, i.e., "semantic-phonetic compounds," with a meaning and a sound component.

虽然一些汉字的确起源于象形字，但它们只占了总数的一小部分，另两类即指事和会意同样比例不大。大部分的汉字属于第四类，即形声字。

Along with the pictographic myth, there also seems to be a related bias favoring the semantic components at the expense of the phonetic, which arguably are of greater importance in the transmission of information than the meaning components. Although some sound clues may not indicate the accurate pronunciation (both in terms of tones and initials) due to historical sound changes, semantic components only suggest the category of meaning for each character. The phonetic components should be pointed out to students whenever they present themselves, even from the beginning of their studies.

除了误认为汉字都是象形的以外，很多人还重意符轻声符，其实后者更重要，因为声符比意符能传递更多的信息。虽然因为汉语语音的变化，声符可能在声调和发音上不一定完全准确，但意符只表示字的义类，对词的意义不能提供更多的信息。从一开始学汉语的时候，就应该对学生指出生字中的声符。

Instead of using the sometimes confusing term "radical," it may be simpler and more understandable to use the terms 意符 "semantic component" and 声符 "phonetic component" to refer to the character components.

形容字的构件时，用"意符"和"声符"可能比用"部首"简单易懂。

Instead of treating characters in isolation, we should alert students to connections between the characters they have learned in terms of meaning, structure, and pronunciation whenever possible.

应该尽量提醒学生学过的汉字哪些在意思、形状和发音上是有关联的。

Character writing should not be restricted to mechanical practice. It is also important to cultivate students' ability to analyze characters and identify components. Apart from hand-writing characters, they should also be able to do the following:

Identify components: ex. 姓= 女+ 生

Provide context: ex. 姓=我姓王

In addition to demonstrating stroke order of characters selected by the teacher, eStroke (www.eon.com.hk/estroke/, demo version available) can also be used to prepare animated displays of stroke order and components and included in computer presentations, for use in class or for students' own use.

Grammar

It is not a good idea to learn grammar simply for its own sake. Grammatical explanations should be simple and to the point, focusing on the most basic cases and those directly relevant to the current lesson. More complex grammatical structures are spread out over a few lessons instead of being taught all at once, to avoid cognitive overload for students.

The basic principle is to lecture less and practice more. Learning to use the language is more important than learning grammatical rules and terminology. Students should be encouraged to use analogies (举一反三). This is especially important for teaching grammar to students who are not that well versed in the grammar of their native language.

Practice

Practice should not be purely mechanical. Students should be engaged cognitively as much as possible, and there should be room for creativity even in strictly controlled exercises, with a good balance between control and creativity. Completing sentences, fill in-the-blanks, and answering questions according to the students' own situations are all formats that allow some creativity and yet stay within the scope of targeted structures.

练习汉字不应该光是机械重复，应该培养学生分析汉字的能力。除了手写汉字，学生还应该能：

找出字的构件，如：姓= 女+ 生。

知道怎么造句，如：姓=我姓王。

eStroke（www.eon.com.hk/estroke/）可用来通过动画的形式演示字的笔顺和构件。可供老师作成投影片在课上用，也可供学生在课下自己用。

语法

应该避免为了学语法而学语法。语法解释应该简单明了，例句应该是最基本的，并和课文直接有关。为了易于学生消化接受，比较复杂的结构我们分成几课讲而不是一下子讲完。

我们的基本原则是精讲多练。学习对语言的运用比学习语法规则和术语更为重要。应该多给学生一些例句，并鼓励学生自己造句，举一反三。对于那些对母语语法都不太熟悉的学生来说，多解释不如多模拟。

练习

练习不应该纯粹是机械性的，应该尽量让学生动脑。即使是有范围控制的练习，也可以活一点。完成句子，填空和按照真实情况回答问题，这些形式都既有范围控制又能使学生有创造性。

When students work in pairs or small groups, they should be given sufficient support (scaffolding) and specific parameters. Before a task, modeling of the structure, clear instructions, and time limits should be provided, as well as the expected demonstrable outcome. During the task, the teacher can facilitate the activity by providing assistance. After the task, some students should be asked to perform the task and the teacher should provide any necessary feedback.

学生们跟语伴或在小组中练习时，应得到足够的支持和具体的指导。开始前，应有示范、清楚的说明和时间限制，以及所要达到的结果。练习中，教师应给于必要的协助。完成后，应选几个学生作汇报；教师应提供必要的反馈。

Texts/Dialogues

Classroom instruction should be driven by the focal structures and functions of the lesson, rather than by the dialogues or text passages. Therefore, there is no need to start with the dialogues or follow their sequence. The dialogue or main text can in fact be introduced after the key elements have been practiced, as an integrative review.

课文／对话

课堂教学应围绕每课的重点结构和功能，而不是对话或课文，所以没有必要按照对话的顺序按部就班地上。对话或主要课文可以在每课重点练习完后，作为综合练习介绍。

The text may be presented using transparencies or slideshows. Students can take turns reading the dialogue and instructors can provide feedback on pronunciation.

课文可先用透明幻灯片或电脑投影片介绍对话，学生可轮流朗读对话，老师纠正发音。

Apart from doing the exercises in the workbook, teachers can also devise additional questions to test student comprehension and to give students an opportunity to make use of the new words and structures.

除了《学生练习本》里的作业，老师还可自行设计问题来测试学生的理解，让学生练习生词和结构。

Being able to recite dialogues from memory does not necessarily mean students will be capable of using the content spontaneously. What is more important is to be able to use the words and structures in new contexts.

学生能够背诵对话并不意味他们真正掌握了内容，重要的是能活用生词和语法。

The English translation at the end of the lesson can be used to do "back translations" – that is, to translate the English back into Chinese, with the original Chinese text as built-in feedback.

可以让学生把每篇课文后的英译反译成中文，和原文对照，起到反馈的作用。

The dialogues can be cut into pieces, which are then reassembled by students, to test their comprehension and elicit some limited form of controlled production.

对话可分成几段让学生重新组合，来检查理解和进行有限的模拟对话。

The Uses of Presentation Software

Slideshow software (ex. Microsoft PowerPoint®) are now used ubiquitously to make presentations. These computer-based presentations can also be used to advantage in the language classroom, as long as they are used judiciously. Some of the strengths of slideshows are:

- Greater amount of information presented (compared with chalkboards)

- Ease of incorporating multimedia

- Ease of sharing

Typing vs. Hand-Writing Characters

More and more people, including native Chinese, exclusively type characters instead of hand-writing them. In addition to being a necessary skill to acquire, typing Chinese characters also has the following pedagogical benefits:

- Reinforcement of *pinyin* skills

- Intensive character recognition

- Increased awareness of word separations, due to faster and more accurate word-based input

- Ease of delivery/dissemination/record keeping

- Easier integration with audio-enabled testing in language labs

Some common input methods are listed below, along with their download sites:
- Microsoft IME: comes with Windows software

- Google Input: www.google.com/ime/pinyin/

- Sogou input: pinyin.sogou.com/

Although many people in China now use the computer exclusively to produce characters, there is still some advantage to hand-writing characters. There may be what is popularly called "muscle memory" involved in the learning of characters. Hand-writing characters also forces the students to attend to details that can otherwise be overlooked.

简报软件的使用

幻灯片播放软体(例如Microsoft PowerPoint®)现今普遍被运用在简报的制作上。只要善加操作,这些电脑多媒体软件也能令语言学习更生动。一些幻灯片创作播放软体的优点有:

- 信息量大

- 容易结合多媒体

- 容易分享

打字和手写汉字

越来越多的人,包括中国人,用电脑打字而不是手写,所以打字技能十分有用,而且也有助于学习:

- 加强拼音能力

- 加强汉字识别能力

- 加强词汇意识,尤其是用以词为单位的输入法

- 易于交流和保存

- 易于在语言实验室结合音响来测试

下列是常用的一些输入法下载网址:

- 微软IME: Windows 系统软件本身包含

- 谷歌输入法:www.google.com/ime/pinyin/

- 搜狗输入法:pinyin.sogou.com/

虽然电脑打字越来越普遍,但是学习手写汉字还是有益的、必要的。首先,手写("肌肉记忆")能帮助学生记住汉字,其次手写能使学生注意容易忽视的细节。

The Use of English and Translation

The use of English should be limited but not eliminated. English is necessary for giving instructions and explanations and can be helpful in clarifying concepts and word meanings. The judicious use of some English may also lessen student anxiety.

Translation, long considered undesirable for the language classroom, may also be judiciously used, such as for the following purposes:

- Student comprehension can be tested more thoroughly, rather than through spot checks alone
- Students can be requested to use targeted vocabulary and sentence structures

Teacher Talk

There are some characteristics of teacher talk that are important to bear in mind, such as the form teachers' questions can take and how negative feedback is given.

Teachers' questions can be used for soliciting the correct answers which the teacher already knows or for obtaining information that the teacher does not already know. The former category of questions is called "display questions" and the latter is "reference questions."

While there are situations where display questions are unavoidable, the use of reference questions should be encouraged whenever possible, as they are genuinely communicative.

Although negative feedback is part of learning, there is more than one way of giving negative feedback, some of which might not be perceived as negative. For example, teachers can ask students to expand and clarify their answers: Is this what you meant? Did you mean to say…?

使用英语和翻译

课堂上应尽量少用英语，但说明要求和讲解时，英语还是必要的。适当地运用一些英语能减轻学生的焦虑。

翻译练习长期被认为不适合运用于外语教学，但如目的清楚，运用得恰到好处，能收到很好的效果。如：

- 能较彻底地检查学生的理解，而不只是抽查
- 能要求学生必须使用需要掌握的词汇和结构

教师用语

须注意教师课堂用语的特征，如发问和给出负面反馈的形式。

老师的问题可分为两种。一种是所谓的呈现性问题，即答案是已知（封闭）的。另一种是答案是未知（开放）的，即所谓征询性问题。

呈现性问题有时不可避免，但应尽量使用征询性问题，因为后者更具有交际功能。

纠错是教学不可或缺的一部分，但纠错的形式多种多样，有直接的，有委婉的。例如，老师可请学生扩展和澄清答案：你的意思是？你是说这个吗？

For realistic video teaching demos, the DVDs by Nyan-Ping Bi and Yuehua Liu titled "Teaching Demonstrations for Beginning Chinese" (Foreign Language Teaching and Research Press) are available from Cheng & Tsui at: www.cheng-tsui.com/store/products/teaching_demonstrations_beginning_chinese.

Seating Arrangements

If logistics allow, classroom seating can be arranged in such as way that students can see each other, which helps create a friendlier atmosphere.

Selected Readings on Chinese and the Teaching of Chinese

On Chinese character formation:

DeFrancis, John. *The Chinese Language: Fact and Fantasy,* University of Hawai'i Press, 1984.

Wu, Jianhsin. *The Way of Chinese Characters,* Cheng & Tsui Company, 2009.

Zhou, Youguang. *The Historical Evolution of Chinese Languages and Scripts*, (Pathways to Advanced Skills Series, vol. 8), Ohio State University National East Asian Languages Resource Center, 2003.

For teaching strategies and tools:

Everson and Xiao, eds. *Teaching Chinese as a Foreign Language: Theories and Applications,* Cheng & Tsui, 2011.

Selected Web Resources

The following web resources are up-to-date at the time of printing. If the links are no longer working, you can try searching for them using keywords.

***Pinyin*:**

Pinyin Practice: pinyinpractice.com/wangzhi/
An interactive website on *pinyin* reading and ear-training by Alan Peterka at the University of Iowa.

具体教学示范，请参考毕念平和刘月华的 "Teaching Demonstrations for Beginning Chinese": www.cheng-tsui.com/store/products/teaching_demonstrations_beginning_chinese.

座位的安排

如果情况许可，可将座位摆得让学生们可以互相看得见，以打造一种温馨的氛围。

汉语和汉语教学参考文献

关于汉字的结构：

DeFrancis, John. *The Chinese Language: Fact and Fantasy,* University of Hawai'i Press, 1984.

Wu, Jianhsin. *The Way of Chinese Characters,* Cheng & Tsui Company, 2009.

Zhou, Youguang. *The Historical Evolution of Chinese Languages and Scripts*, (Pathways to Advanced Skills Series, vol. 8), Ohio State University National East Asian Languages Resource Center, 2003.

一般教学策略和工具的论文集：

Everson and Xiao, eds. *Teaching Chinese as a Foreign Language: Theories and Applications,* Cheng & Tsui, 2011.

网上参考资料

下述链接在本书付印时尚有效，如过时的话，可用关键词查找。

拼音：

Pinyin Practice: pinyinpractice.com/wangzhi/
互动式拼读拼音和听力训练，作者 University of Iowa, Alan Peterka.

WaveSurfer: www.speech.kth.se/wavesurfer/
A free acoustic analysis software program that can display tone contour instantly.

Characters:
eStroke: www.eon.com.hk/estroke/
Software with animated displays of stroke order and component parts.

www.csulb.edu/~txie/azi/page1.htm
A free animated character site.

Integrated Chinese Companion Site:
The companion site for *Integrated Chinese* has a variety of resources that teachers can use in the classroom. At www.integratedchinese.com teachers can find course-related slides, vocabulary, and grammar exercises, as well as an online Image Gallery with the illustrations and photographs from the textbooks.

Cheng & Tsui is planning to add more supplementary exercises in upcoming revisions to the companion sites. There are *Integrated Chinese*-specific resources available through www.cheng-tsui.com as well. An online version of the workbook is already available for all levels of *Integrated Chinese*. Students and teachers can access all exercises and audio from any computer connected to the Internet, with immediate feedback available for most activities, as well as classroom management capabilities for teachers. This new option also allows students to record exercises and submit them to the teacher electronically—which is especially effective for individual pronunciation practice.

WaveSurfer: www.speech.kth.se/wavesurfer/
免费语音分析软件，能即时显示声调曲线。

汉字：
eStroke: www.eon.com.hk/estroke/
用动画呈现笔顺和字的部件的软件。

www.csulb.edu/~txie/azi/page1.htm
免费汉字动画。

中文听说读写网站：
中文听说读写网站上有一系列教师上课时可用的资源。在 www.integratedchinese.com 可以找到课件幻灯片、词汇语法练习、以及含有课本上的插图和照片的图片库。

Cheng & Tsui 计划不断把补充练习放到 *Integrated Chinese* 相关网址上 www.cheng-tsui.com 上也有专为 *Integrated Chinese* 设计的资源。*Integrated Chinese* 各册的《学生练习本》已有网上版，学生和教师可从任何联网的电脑上获取所有的练习和录音，并能在做大多数练习时得到即时的反馈，以及为教师提供的课堂管理功能。这个新的功能可让学生将作业录音后传给老师，这对检查学生发音尤其有效。

LESSON 11

Chinese Festivals 中国的节日

Chapter Structure

- **Lesson Focus**
- **Priorities**
- **Focal Themes Teaching Suggestions**
- **Sequencing and Suggestions for Key Grammar and Vocabulary**
- **Exercises for the Main Text**
- **Suggested Integrative Activities**
  Speaking and Listening
  Reading and Writing
  Grammar and Vocabulary

Lesson Focus
本课重点

本课语言功能请参考本课第一页上的学习目标。若新内容超过学生负担，应进行筛选。下面是我们的建议。

学生应掌握的最基本文化知识与语言功能是，能说出几个中国重要的传统节日的日期、食物、以及过春节的一些习俗。老师可按学生情况决定介绍多少细节。

Function
1. 能说说中国有哪些传统节日。
2. 过节吃什么东西。
3. 过节做什么事。
4. 能用中文拜年。
5. 能用中文祝人成功、健康。
6. 能谈谈自己住的地方/环境怎么样（如以上都能完成，并仍有时间。）

Priorities
取舍

如学生年龄小，不必练习"为…干杯"。

"以茶代酒"中的"以"是文言，学生理解其意思即可，不必要求会用，也不必练习，因为在这个阶段，对他们来说可能太难。

"嘛"如果学生掌握不了，也不必强求。

如果觉得学生负担太重，可不必练习"倒计时"。不过如果介绍"倒计时"，可用美国纽约时代广场每年12月31号晚上一起倒计时做引导。

Focal Themes Teaching Suggestions
重点主题教学建议

为了增加学习的趣味性并加深印象，可在中国春节(农历年)期间教授本课。那时可让学生上网寻找春节的习俗，应景的图像与影片。老师也可与学生一起制作春节贺卡，学以致用。

1. 说说中国有哪些传统节日。

    先复习年月日，再用有农历的月历指出农历的年月日(可用实物或投影)。可利用月历上的颜色(红色)来凸显农历的节日，并可让学生说出当天是农历几月几号。

    提问句式举例：

    今天是农历的几月几日？
    (请问)X节是农历的几月几日？
    春节是农历的哪一天？(正月初一)
    除夕是哪一天？(春节的前一天晚上)

    示范一、两次后，就可让学生互相问答。

    本课也提到美国节日感恩节，因为感恩节跟春节和中秋节一样，是家人团聚的日子。问答举例：

    中秋节跟美国的什么节很像？(跟感恩节很像)
    为什么？(都是一家人团圆的节日/大家都回家跟家人团圆)
    感恩节是哪一天？(十一月的第四个星期四)

    做阶段总结或复习时，可做本章后面 Suggested Integrative Activities 中跟节日有关的练习，尤其是 "Basic information about important festivals." 另外可做课本的
    Language Practice E: "Name that Holiday," Language Practice F: "Don't Get the Wrong Food."

2. 过节吃什么东西。

    可用实物或图片介绍各个节日的食物：

    问答句式举例：

    Q: 这是什么？
    A: 这是元宵 / 粽子 / 月饼。
    Q: 过什么节吃元宵 / 粽子 / 月饼？
    A: 过元宵/端午/中秋节吃元宵 / 粽子 / 月饼。
    Q: 元宵什么样？
    A: 白白的、圆圆的。

Q: 年夜饭一定要有什么？
A: 得有鱼，但鱼不能都吃了。北方人还吃饺子。
Q: 为什么？
A: 因为"年年有鱼"的"鱼"跟"年年有余"的"余"发音一样，"余"有"剩下（钱）"的意思。"饺子"像以前的钱，也是希望新年有钱的意思。

3. 过年/过节做什么。

   可用图片或视频介绍各个节日的庆祝活动。可利用词语或图片，先做"连连看"游戏。在这个基础上做口语练习，然后集中练习/复习春节的活动，例如：

   中国人过春节以前得做什么？(打扫房子，准备好吃的东西)
   除夕做什么？(回家跟家人团圆，忙着做年夜饭，然后家人一起吃年夜饭，看春[节]晚[会])
   晚上12点做什么？(12点一到，就放鞭炮，给家人拜年)
   正月初一做什么？(穿新衣服/鞋，出门给人拜年，小孩给大人拜年，大人给小孩红包…)

   最后可用 Language Practice J: "Don't Miss Out!" 做复习或检查。

4. 怎么拜年、拜年的时候说什么

   先应该强调介词"给"和表拜年方式的状语：怎么给家人朋友拜年？(打电话/发短信/写卡片给…拜年；小孩给大人拜年)。可做本章后面 Suggested Integrative Activities 中 Grammar and Vocabulary 中的部分练习。

   学生都会说"新年快乐"，不必练习，应多多鼓励学生说其他的祝贺词语，如："恭喜发财"、"新年好"、"过年好"、"祝你在新的一年里身体健康/学习进步/找工作顺利/事业成功。"等。

   提醒学生"恭喜发财"前不能加"祝(你)"，"新年好""过年好"前一般也不说"祝(你)"。可做 Language Practice G: "Happy New Year to You All!" 练习。中可做本章后面 Suggested Integrative Activities 中 "Say the right thing!" 的练习。

5. 怎么祝人成功、健康

   可做 Language Practice H: "Well-Wishing" 以及本章后面 Suggested Integrative Activities 中 "Say the right thing!" 的练习。

6. 自己住的地方/环境怎么样(为本年级第一、二课的内容；如以上1–5各项学生都能完成，并仍有时间时可复习)

   可先以单句问答(参考本章后面 Suggested Integrative Activities 中 "How is your living environment?")，然后再引导学生串成段落(可参考本章后面 Suggested Integrative Activities 中 Grammar and Vocabulary 中最后一题 "My Place")。

Sequencing and Suggestions for Key Grammar and Vocabulary
重要的语法和词汇的顺序与教学建议

> 1. 结束；2. 继续；3. 本来；4. 舅舅、舅妈；5. 感情；6. 幸福；7. 环境；8. 奇怪；9. 意思；10. 顺利；11. 进步；12. 成功；13. 浪费；14. 传统；15. 拜年；16. 恭喜；17. 热闹；18. 存现句；19. 有 vs. V着；20. Adj/V + 着 + V；21. 量词重叠；22. (先)…再；23. V起来；24. V得/不出来；25. 介词"以"；26. 嘛

1. 结束

More examples:	暑假昨天结束了。 昨天下午我们开会开到五点钟才结束。 这个学期上个星期就结束了，可是我们的工作还没有结束。
Q&A Practice:	这个学期什么时候结束？ 这个学年什么时候结束？ 学期结束以后你打算做什么？
Other combinations:	结：结果、结业、结算

2. 继续

Character:	两字均有"纟"旁；可用来帮助记忆。
More examples:	他已经学了两年中文了，下个学期会继续学下去。 昨天我们的会没有开完，今天要继续开。
Q&A Practice:	下学期你会继续学中文吗？
Other combinations:	继：继父、继母 续：续杯、续水

3. 本来

Chinese gloss:	原来
More examples:	这个学期我本来想选一门电脑课，可是我的指导老师不同意。 去年夏天我们本来想去云南旅游，可是我舅舅建议我们去哈尔滨。
Completion:	他本来想坐火车去旅游，可是_____。 我本来_____，可是选那门课的人太多了，就没选。

guided completion using the pattern 我本来想___，可是___：

make a reservation at a restaurant	but can't get seats
go to Harbin	but do not have time
go traveling with friends	but nobody wants to go with me

4. 舅舅、舅妈

Chinese gloss: 舅舅是妈妈的哥哥或弟弟；舅妈是舅舅的太太。

Q&A Practice:
舅舅是什么人？
舅妈是什么人？
你有舅舅吗？你有几个舅舅？

Other combinations: 舅：大舅、二舅、小舅

5. 感情

Character: "感情"两个字的意符均为"心"。

More examples:
王先生和王太太结婚四十年了，感情一直很好。
我是在纽约长大的，所以对纽约很有感情。

Collocation: 孩子对父母的感情、妈妈对儿子的感情

Other combinations:
感：感觉、感想
情：爱情、亲情、友情

6. 幸福

Usage: 注意区别"幸福"与"快乐"：周末快乐、新年快乐、*周末幸福、*新年幸福

Q&A Practice: 你觉得有钱的人都很幸福吗？

Collocation: 幸福的生活、幸福的家庭

Other combinations:
幸：幸运、有幸
福：福气、口福、眼福、全家福

7. 环境

Q&A Practice: 我们学校附近的环境怎么样？

Collocation: 住房环境、家庭环境、校园环境、自然环境

Other combinations:
环：N环、环保、环城路
境：家境、语境

8. 奇怪

More examples:
昨天弟弟问了一个很奇怪的问题，我不知道怎么回答。
他是个很奇怪的人，夏天穿毛衣，冬天只穿一件衬衫。
奇怪！现在是五月，怎么下起雪来了？

Other combinations:
奇：奇石、奇才
怪：怪人、怪事

9. 意思

Character: "意思"两个字的意符均为"心"。

Meaning: "意思"的意思有好几个，如以下例句所示。

More examples:	这个字我没学过，是什么意思？ "美国"我觉得可以有"美丽的国家"的意思，虽然本来不是这个意思。 那个电影我看过，我觉得没什么意思。 A：小林，这是给你的生日礼物，是我的一点小意思。 B：让你为我花了那么多钱，真不好意思。 A：我们都是朋友，别不好意思！
Other combinations:	意：好意、大意、会意、三心二意

10. 顺利

Character:	"顺"的意符为"川"。
More examples:	祝你明年工作顺利！ 他本来想自己打工挣钱交学费，可是找工作一直不太顺利。
Other combinations:	顺：顺便、顺水 利：便利、利己、利人

11. 进步

More examples:	祝你学习进步！ 上个学期她在中国留学，所以她的中文有了很大的进步。
Q&A Practice:	这学期你学中文进步大吗？
Other combinations:	进：进口、上进 步：同步、步步高

12. 成功

Character:	"功"的声符为"工"。
Grammar:	可以是动词、形容词。
More examples:	钱教授想用新的办法解决这个经济学问题，可是没有成功。（动词） 弟弟的工作一直很顺利，我为他的成功感到高兴。 舅妈不但做菜做得好，而且是一位很成功的律师。（形容词--定语） 雪梅父母的事业一直很成功。（形容词--谓语）。
Q&A Practice:	你觉得在学校学习好，将来事业就会成功吗？

13. 浪费

Grammar:	可以是动词、名词或形容词。
More examples:	别浪费电！（动词） 你怎么一张纸上就写一个字？这是很大的浪费。（名词） 在餐馆点的菜应该吃完，要不然就太浪费了。（形容词）
Q&A Practice:	你觉得我们生活中什么浪费得最多？
Collocation:	浪费钱、浪费时间
Other combinations:	浪：热浪、海浪 费：费时、费事、费钱

14. 传统

Grammar:	可以用作名词和形容词，可分别练。
More examples:	中国人有过年放鞭炮的传统。（名词）
	在北京，很多人住在小区里，传统的房子越来越少了。（形容词-定语）
	王爷爷王奶奶比较传统，不希望儿子搬出去住。（形容词-谓语）
Q&A Practice:	中国（美国、你们国家）有哪些传统节日？
	你觉得学习传统文化重要吗？/传统文化对你重要吗？
Completion:	母亲 (mǔqīn, "mother") 节的传统礼物是____。
	你常常听（美国、你们国家）的传统___吗？
Q&A Practice:	在中国，过春节拜年、放鞭炮、贴"福"字是一个文化传统。请你说说美国（你们国家）过什么节，有什么文化传统。
	我们学校有什么有意思的传统？
Fill in blanks:	在美国，感恩节下午全家一起看_____是个传统。
	我们家过新年的传统是_____。
Collocation:	传统文化、传统节日
Other combinations:	传：传人、传话、传说、传言、传真、传教

15. 拜年

More examples:	老师，给您拜年！祝您在新的一年里，身体健康，事事顺利！
	今天是中国新年，我要打电话给舅舅拜年。
Q&A Practice:	中国人什么时候拜年？
	中国人拜年的时候说什么？
Other combinations:	拜：拜天、拜地、礼拜

16. 恭喜

Q&A Practice:	朋友有了新工作，你怎么恭喜他？
Collocation:	恭喜发财！
Other combinations:	喜：喜欢、喜事、喜酒

17. 热闹

Pronunciation:	"闹"字在这里是轻声。
Grammar:	形容词，也常作名词。课本没有介绍名词用法，但理解和使用都不难，可以考虑包括进去。
More examples:	中国人最热闹的节日就是中国新年。（形容词-定语）
	过年一家人团圆吃年夜饭，大人聊天，小孩跑来跑去，真热闹。（形容词-谓语）
	舅妈和舅舅不一样：舅舅喜欢热闹，可是舅妈喜欢安静。（名词）
	有的人很喜欢看热闹，我不喜欢。（名词）
Q&A Practice:	你们国家什么节日最热闹？
	纽约每年十二月三十一号哪儿最热闹？

Completion:	在中国，春节晚上很多人到外面去＿＿＿＿，所以很热闹。 我的同屋很喜欢热闹，每个星期五晚上他都请朋友来宿舍＿＿＿＿＿＿＿＿，害得我很晚才能睡觉。
Collocation:	怕热闹、喜欢热闹、看热闹
Other combinations:	闹：闹新房、吵闹、闹钟

18. 存现句

Grammar:	提醒学生不要受英语影响在处所前加"在"。
Presentation tip:	用实物布置教室来练习巩固存现句： 桌子上放着什么？（桌子上放着一本书、两枝笔…） 椅子上挂着什么？（椅子上挂着一个包、一件衣服…） 墙上挂着什么？（墙上挂着一个钟。） 墙上贴着什么？（墙上贴着一张红纸。） 红纸上写着什么？（红纸上写着一个"福"字／"春"字。）

19. 有 vs. V 着

More examples:	手里有一杯茶	手里拿着一杯茶
	桌子上有一本书	桌子上放着一本书
	教室里有二十个学生	教室里坐着二十个学生
	教室里有一位老师	教室里站着一位老师
	衣架上有一件大衣	衣架上挂着一件大衣
	墙上有一张照片	墙上贴着一张照片
	黑板上有一个字	黑板上写着一个字

Preferred mode of practice:	两者语序相同，因此应该将它们联系起来。二者相比，前者容易些，因为只用一个动词"有"；后者用不同的动词，而且还得加上"着"。建议先练前者，后练带"V 着"的存现句。

20. Adj / V + 着 + V

Explanation:	这种结构中的"着"跟我们前面学的表示动作、状态持续的"着"用法不同，我们把"Adj/V+着+V"作为一个句型教给学生。"V1+着+V2"的连动式，V1与V2的关系与意义有很多种。在 Adj/V+着+V 中，"着"后的动词（一般后边还有宾语）表示原因。我们目前学过的可以用于这种结构前一部分的动词和形容词还很少，所以重点练习书上给的"忙"、"急"、"哭"就可以了。
More examples:	例一：　　快过年了，妈妈忙着打扫屋子。（为什么"忙"？因为"打扫屋子"。） 课本例一：…忙着准备考试。（为什么"忙"？因为"准备考试"。） 例二：　　小王急着回家。（为什么"急"？因为"要回家"。） 课本例二：他急着去见朋友…（为什么"急"？因为"要见朋友"。）

Completion:	我姐姐每个周末都忙着_____，没有时间陪我看电影。 快八点了，我急着_____，没吃早饭。 妈妈因为工作，要去中国旅行，小红哭着要_____去。
21. 量词重叠 Explanation:	量词重叠使用表示"由个体组成的全体中毫无例外"的意思。"孩子们个个都很高兴"的意思是"所有的孩子都很高兴"。再如： 　　我昨天去公园照了很多照片，张张都照得很漂亮。 　　王刚上个周末买了五条裤子，条条都是名牌。 有些名词具有量词的功能，如"人"、"天"、"年"、"月"等也可以重叠： 　　我在学生餐厅天天吃中国饭。 　　小李年年去北京学中文，他的中文现在好极了。
Grammar:	应该注意，量词重叠跟"每"用法不完全相同。在主语的位置上，二者区别不明显。如上述各例的"张张"、"条条"、"天天"、"年年"都可以用"每张"、"每条"、"每天"、"每年"来替换。但是在宾语位置上，只能用"每"，不能用量词重叠形式： 　　　　妹妹认识我的中文书上的每一个字。 不能说：*妹妹认识我的中文书上的个个字。 　　　　这次考试，你应该复习学过的每一个生词。 不能说：*这次考试，你应该复习学过的个个生词。 量词重叠和"每"的不同实际上更为复杂，现阶段不宜多讲。 Transformation using reduplication of measure words to replace "每"： 我们每天都上中文课➔ 他每年夏天都去中国➔
22. （先）…再… Explanation:	这个结构里的"再"和前面学过的副词"再"意思不同，表示一个动作出现以后，另一个动作才出现，即，先做什么，然后做什么。
More examples:	老师每天先给我们复习前一天学的，再教新的东西。 明天的电影是五点钟，我们先看电影再吃晚饭。 张明的哥哥想先在美国学两年中文，再去中国找工作。
Completion:	开晚会的时候，我们先吃饭，然后再_____。 上中文课的时候，我们先_____，然后再学课文。
23. V起来 Meaning:	从某个方面或角度说或看，常以对比形式出现，如"说起来容易，做起来难"，所以形容词前常不带修饰语。

Q&A Practice:	你的新电脑用起来方便吗？
	你的牛仔裤看起来很漂亮，穿起来舒服吗？
Completion:	北京烤鸭吃起来很_____，可是做起来_____。
	对家长来说，尊重孩子的选择说起来_____，做起来_____。
	汉字____起来很美，可是____起来很难。
	这个歌____起来很好听，可是____起来很不容易。
Collocations:	听起来(很好听)、唱起来(不容易)、住起来(很舒服)、打扫起来(很花时间)、汉字学起来(很有意思)

24. V得出来／V不出来

Meaning:	表示有能力通过感官判断、分辨等。常用的动词包括"看"、"听"、"闻(wén, "smell")"、"吃"、"喝"、"摸(mō, "touch")"等。
Q&A Practice:	她是加拿大人还是美国人，你听(她说话听)得出来吗？
	冰箱里的清蒸鱼放了三天了，坏了没有？你闻得出来吗？
	这个家常豆腐放没放味精，你吃得出来吗？
Fill in blanks:	舅舅和舅妈把时间都放在事业上，_____事业对他们很重要。
	这是中国绿茶还是日本绿茶，你_____吗？
	她们姐妹长得太像了，很多人_____谁是姐姐，谁是妹妹。

25. 介词"以"

Explanation:	介词"以"有很多意思，本课学的"以"与"用"近似，"以茶代酒"意思是"用茶代替酒"。

26. 嘛

Explanation:	语气助词，用于陈述句末尾，意思比较明显，表示说话人认为"理应如此"，有"显而易见"的语气。语气词是汉语特有的词类，表示的意思有时很细微，学生不太容易掌握。如果学生掌握不了，也不必强求。
More examples:	我是你的哥哥，你没有钱就跟我要嘛，客气什么。
	你问我小王的妹妹为什么在美国不容易找到工作？很清楚，因为她的英文不好嘛。
	A: 我不想在这个饭馆吃饭，这里的菜太油。
	B: 你不喜欢这个饭馆早点告诉我嘛，害得我开了这么长时间的车。
Fill in blanks with	"嘛"、"吗"、"吧"：
	明天是春节，中文老师请我们去他家吃饺子，你去____？
	周末没事，我们去购物中心买衣服____！
	A: 这件衣服太贵了！
	B: 你看，是名牌____，当然贵了。

Completion: Isn't that obvious?
　　　　　　　_____ 吃元宵嘛！
　　　　　　　_____ 吃年夜饭嘛！
　　　　　　　_____ 看春晚嘛！
　　　　　　　_____ 说中文嘛！

Exercises for the Main Text
主课文的练习

认读课文：可用幻灯片显示课文，让学生轮流扮演对话中的角色及其口译员。老师可用鼠标跟踪、凸显生词及难点。可借此机会纠正学生们的发音，并检查他们对所学内容的理解状况。

问答：课文认读完毕后，老师可就课文提问，以此方法来检查学生对课文的理解状况，同时可以帮助学生练习听力及口语。

Questions about the text:
- 柯林、雪梅为什么在中国？
- 他们是在哪儿过的春节？他们是跟谁一起过的春节？
- 雪梅的舅舅做什么工作？她的舅妈呢？
- 雪梅的舅舅、舅妈想要孩子吗？为什么？
- 他们住的小区环境怎么样？
- 他们的公寓有几房、几厅、几卫？
- 把"福"字、"春"字倒贴是什么意思？
- 除夕那天雪梅的舅舅舅妈忙着做什么？
- 现在很多家庭在哪儿吃年夜饭？
- 雪梅他们为什么不在餐馆吃年夜饭？
- 他们年夜饭吃了些什么？
- 为什么中国人过年要吃鱼？鱼为什么不能都吃了，要剩下一些？
- 雪梅怎么给爸爸妈妈拜年？她怎么给朋友拜年？
- 拜年的时候说什么？
- 过年的时候还做什么？
- 什么节吃粽子？什么节吃月饼？什么节吃元宵？
- 中秋节像美国的什么节日？为什么？

Suggested Integrative Activities
综合练习活动

Speaking and Listening

1. Basic information about important festivals:

   - 元宵节是哪一天？
   - 中国人过元宵节吃什么？元宵什么样？
   - 端午节是哪一天？
   - 中国人过端午节吃什么？
   - 中秋节是哪一天？
   - 中国人过中秋节吃什么？
   - 中秋节跟美国的什么节很像？为什么？
   - 感恩节是哪一天？
   - 美国人过感恩节一定得吃什么？

2. Interview each other:

   a. What are the holidays like at your home?
      - 你们家过什么节？
      - 这个节日是什么时候？
      - 这个节日你们怎么过？
      - 这个节日有什么传统的食物？
      - 你会回家跟家人团圆一起过这个节吗？

   b. How is your living environment?
      - 你住在校内还是校外？
      - 你住的地方大不大？有几房几厅？
      - 家具新不新？
      - 你的房间乱不乱？干净不干净？
      - 住起来舒服不舒服？
      - 附近环境好不好？吵不吵？

3. Say the right thing!: "Well-wishing."

   a. Let's have a toast:
      - 祝（您/你）学习＿＿＿！
      - 祝（您/你）身体＿＿＿！
      - 祝（您/你）事业＿＿＿！
      - 为＿＿＿＿＿＿＿＿干杯！
      - 为＿＿＿＿＿＿＿＿干杯！

b. Toasting without alcohol:

吃饭的时候，中国人喝酒祝你身体健康，你不喝酒，但也得祝他身体健康，你怎么办？

举例：

中国朋友(举起酒杯)：	祝你身体健康！
你(举起茶杯)：	我以茶代酒，也祝你身体健康！
中国朋友(举起酒杯)：	祝你工作顺利！
你(举起茶杯)：	_____
中国朋友(举起酒杯)：	祝你事业成功！
你(举起茶杯)：	_____
中国朋友(举起酒杯)：	为你的身体健康干杯！
你(举起茶杯)：	_____
中国朋友(举起酒杯)：	为你的工作顺利干杯！
你(举起茶杯)：	_____
中国朋友(举起酒杯)：	为你的事业成功干杯！
你(举起茶杯)：	_____

Reading and Writing

1. Suppose you are the intended recipient of the email below. Read the message and then write a response (Interpersonal):

我下个星期就可以回美国了，可是我的中国朋友要我在上海多住几天，这样就可以去他家过春节了。你觉得中国的春节有意思吗？有人说春节那几天的电视节目特别好看，是真的吗？还有，中国人为什么吃年夜饭一定要有鱼？这些都是我想知道的事情。你比我更了解中国，请你告诉我应不应该去那位朋友家过春节。谢谢！

2. Read the passage and answer the questions:

我舅舅和舅妈跟别人不一样。别人家的年夜饭什么菜都有，舅舅舅妈家的年夜饭只有三样菜：红烧鱼、清蒸鱼、糖醋鱼。你可别以为他们过年吃鱼，为的是"年年有余"，年夜饭的三盘鱼，他们总是吃得一点儿也不剩的。元宵节，别人都吃元宵，他们不吃。端午节，别人都吃粽子，他们也不吃。他们吃什么呢？还是吃鱼！他们爱吃鱼，是因为他们做的鱼味道特别地道，另外他们也认为吃鱼对健康特别有好处。结婚二十多年了，他们过年过节一直都只吃鱼。

True/False:
( ) 1. Uncle and Aunt have fewer dishes for the Chinese New Year's Eve dinner than most others.
( ) 2. Because Uncle and Aunt eat up all their fish dishes at the New Year's Eve dinner, they can't save any money at the end of the year.
( ) 3. Uncle and Aunt eat fish for the Lantern Festival and Dragon Boat Festival.
( ) 4. Even though their fish dishes are not always delicious, they know they are good for their health.
( ) 5. Both Uncle and Aunt seem like very unconventional people.
( ) 6. They have had the same dietary preference for at least twenty years.

3. Complete the following sentences:

- 中秋节是农历_____。
- 农历_____是_____节。
- 我听说北京的景点很多，早就_____。
- 听得出来，雪梅的舅舅和舅妈_____。
- 雪梅的舅舅舅妈没有孩子，把时间都放在_____上。
- 老师，我给您拜年，_____！_____！
- 美国的感恩节有点像_____。
- 给你拜年了！祝你在新的一年里，_____！

4. Complete the following piece, "My place":

我住的地方环境_____，是一套_____的公寓。家具不太多，卧室里____一张床，床的旁边____着一张书桌，书桌前边____一__椅子。客厅里____沙发，靠墙是电视机。饭厅里___一___饭桌和四___椅子。公寓不_____，但是住起来很_____。

Grammar and Vocabulary

1. Match the festivals with the right dates:

农历_____是_____节。
- 八月十五   端午
- 五月初五   中秋节
- 正月初一   元宵节
- 正月十五   春节

2. Match the festivals with the right foods:

_____节吃_____。
- 中秋节   鱼、饺子、年夜饭
- 元宵节   粽子
- 春节   火鸡
- 端午节   月饼
- 感恩节   元宵

3. Match the festivals with the right activities:

- 春节   拜年
- 端午节   看花灯
- 元宵节   放鞭炮
- 春节   赛龙舟
- 中秋节   给/拿红包

- 端午节　　　　　看春晚
- 春节　　　　　　赏 (shǎng, "admire") 月

4. Fill in the blanks with words that are closest in meaning to those given in the parentheses:

学期___（完）了，柯林___（想好）到北京___（接着）学中文，___（可是）林雪梅想在北京实习和找工作。去北京前，他们先___（坐飞机去）到杭州雪梅家看___（爸爸和妈妈），在杭州___（小住）了几天以后，来到了北京雪梅的___（妈妈的哥哥/弟弟）家。

5. For which kind of person are the following methods of delivering a New Year greeting most appropriate?

Example: 发短信给同学拜年
- 发电邮给____拜年
- 打电话给____拜年
- 去舅舅家给____拜年
- 写卡片给____拜年

6. What method of delivering a New Year greeting is most appropriate for the following people?

Example: 打电话给他拜年
- _____给爸爸妈妈拜年
- _____给朋友拜年
- _____给男朋友拜年
- _____给女朋友拜年
- _____给同学拜年

7. Fill in the blanks (one character per blank):

- 农历__月十五是元宵节。
- 农历__月十五是中秋节。
- 农历五月__五是端午节。
- 农历八月十__是中秋节的前一天。
- 中秋节看月__，吃月__，是家人__圆的日子。
- 春节/过年的时候要__鞭炮，很热__。
- 这几年很多人喜欢__短信__朋友拜年。
- 春节大人给小孩红__。
- 门上__着一张红纸，纸上写__一个幸福的"福"字，可是贴__了。
- 年年有__和年年有__的发音一样。
- __年好！
- __喜发财！
- 中秋节快__！

LESSON 12
Changes in China 中国的变化

Chapter Structure

- Lesson Focus
- Priorities
- Focal Themes Teaching Suggestions
- Sequencing and Suggestions for Key Grammar and Vocabulary
- Exercises for the Main Text
- Suggested Integrative Activities
  - Speaking and Listening
  - Reading and Writing
  - Grammar and Vocabulary

Lesson Focus
本课重点

本课语言功能请参考本课第一页上的学习目标。若新内容超过学生负担，应进行筛选。下面是我们的建议。

Function
1. 能说在大城市里看到的人、事、物。
2. 能简单说南京保留了什么古迹。
3. 能由1,2扩展简单说说南京（或本国或其他国家的城市）的变化。
4. 能用"没想到"、"竟然"等词语表达出乎意料之外的情况。

Priorities
取舍

若学生负担太重，可不必介绍练习"可"、"啊"等词语。"脚步"的用法比较受限制，可以不练习。

Focal Themes Teaching Suggestions
重要主题教学建议

1. 说说在大城市里看到的人、事、物，如：

    一般大城市有很多人，很多车，很多建筑；
    到处都是新盖的大／高楼，大街上挤满了汽车；

    可用 Language Practice D: "What Do You See?" 做练习或检查。

    可先帮学生复习一年级第19课的内容来说说北京这个大城市，然后再进入本课主题城市南京：

    北京是中国的首都，也是政治、文化中心，有很多名胜古迹，好吃的饭馆、小吃也多得不得了。去北京旅游的游客肯定都会尝尝北京烤鸭。

    南京以前也是首都，也是政治中心，也有很多名胜古迹，好吃的小吃也很多。去南京旅游的游客肯定都会尝尝南京板 (bǎn) 鸭。

    如果老师认为需要加强，可让学生选一、两个亚洲，美洲或欧洲的城市做类似的叙述练习。

2. 简单说说南京有哪些古迹，保留了哪些传统的建筑、特色小吃等。

    可用南京夫子庙的图片或影片来介绍：夫子庙的建筑，在夫子庙能尝到什么好吃的小吃，玩什么好玩儿的…。可分组用Language Practice G: "Visiting a Popular Tourist Destination" 做练习。

3. 简单说说城市的变化。

    可用以下范句：

    一边是(一栋栋)高楼大厦，一边是(一座座)传统建筑
    旧房子不见了，路两旁都是又高又新的大楼
    路上都是车／挤满了车，大街上开了很多新商店

    学生年轻，涉世经验不多，不太能想象城市四、五十年前是什么模样，要他们谈城市变化，难度稍高。因此建议尽量使用历史图片／影片来引导练习，如可用北京高楼跟胡同的照片或影片提示来做对照练习，再针对南京的旧貌新貌做练习。另可用 Language Practice F: "Taking a Stroll Down Memory Lane" 做阶段整理复习。

4. 怎么用"没想到"、"竟然"等词语表达出乎意料之外的情况。

    建议练习时，"没想到"、"竟然"两词同时出现在句子中，加深学生印象。可用 Language Practice A: "This Is Totally Unexpected!" 做辅助练习。

Sequencing and Suggestions for Key Grammar and Vocabulary
重要语法和词汇的顺序与教学建议

> 1. 变化／变；2. 来得／不及；3. 拍；4. 陌生；5. 熟悉；6. 想象；7. 对面；8. 特色；
> 9. 保留；10. 不管；11. 脚步；12. 难过；13. 完全；14. 的确；15. 要不是；16. 从来；
> 17. 看来；18. 尽可能；19. 竟（然）；20. 补语"过"；21. 语气助词"啊"；22. 以A为B；
> 23. "一"+量词重叠形式；24. 副词"可"（是）

1. 变化/变

Grammar: "变化"可用作谓语动词和宾语。"变"只能做谓语动词，后边可有宾语或补语，常接补语"成"。

More examples:
最近十年这个城市有很大的变化。
去过中国的人都说中国变化得很快。
这是你的车吗？怎么变了颜色？（＋宾语）
那孩子长大了，完全变了样子。（＋宾语）
三年不见，小王变得越来越会说话了。（＋补语）
你看，这件衣服洗了以后变成什么样子了，完全不能穿了。

Q&A Practice:
你们州，春天还是秋天天气变化比较大？
红色和黄色在一起，会变成什么颜色？

Other combinations:
变：变天、变脸、女大十八变、变暖
化：美化、绿化、现代化

2. 来得/不及

More examples:
现在六点二十了，去看六点半的电影已经来不及了。
A: 你的飞机是八点钟的，你现在去机场一定来不及了。
B: 没问题，来得及，王朋开车送我去机场。

Q&A Practice:
考试前一天复习功课来得及吗？
早上七点起床出门上课来得及吗？

Other combinations: 及：及时

3. 拍

Character: "拍"的声符为"白"。
Meaning: 还有用手拍的意思。

Q&A Practice:
你旅游的时候常用手机还是照相机拍照？
你比较喜欢看谁拍的电影？

Collocation: 拍电影、拍录像、拍手

4. 陌生

Character:	注意区别；"陌"与"拍"两个字的声符和意符。
More examples:	对我来说，这是个陌生的地方，我从来没来过这儿。
	好几天没有练习写中文日记了，所以我觉得不少汉字有些陌生了。
	他们虽然是陌生人，可是对我都很客气。
Q&A Practice:	你会跟陌生人说话吗？
	你在陌生的地方会紧张吗？

5. 熟悉

More examples:	我本来对北京很熟悉，可是五年没去了，北京变得陌生了。
	他虽然是我的同学，可是我对他并不熟悉。
Q&A Practice:	你对我们这个城市熟悉吗？
	你对我们学校的环境熟悉吗？
Other combinations:	熟：熟人、熟路

6. 想象

More examples:	中文没有我以前想象的那么难。
	A: 我没去过纽约。
	B: 那么你想象中的纽约是个什么样的城市？
Other combinations:	想：空想
	象：印象

7. 对面

Q&A Practice:	马路对面有没有商店？
	我们上课这栋楼的对面是图书馆，电脑中心，还是运动场？
Collocation:	马路对面、宿舍对面、图书馆对面、河对面
Other combinations:	对：对手、对角、对过
	面：前面、后面、上面、下面、正面、反面

8. 特色

More examples:	这家餐馆很有纽约的特色。
	她的帽子是在东京买的，很有日本特色。
Q&A Practice:	我们这个城市有什么特色？
	美国哪个城市的建筑很有特色？
Collocation:	特色菜、特色火锅 (guō)
Other combinations:	特：特点、特长、特区

Lesson 12 • Changes in China

9. **保留**
   - More examples:
     南京有很多高楼，可是也保留了不少传统的建筑。
     我们的城市很热闹，可是也保留了几个很安静的公园。
     我们的看法不一样，所以我保留我的意见。
   - Other combinations:
     保：保护、保安
     留：留学

10. **不管**
    - More examples:
      不管你怎么忙，都要回家跟父母一起过年。
      今天晚上的饭是年夜饭。不管你怎么爱吃鱼，都不能把鱼吃完。懂吗？
    - Completion:
      不管你喜不喜欢，你都得_____。
      不管_____，我们都要好好学。
    - Other combinations:
      管：主管、管理

11. **脚步**
    - More examples:
      妈妈要回来了，我听到了她的脚步声！
    - Collocation:
      脚步声、时间的脚步
    - Other combinations:
      脚：三脚架、四脚蛇 (shé)、小脚
      步：进步、退 (tuì) 步、同步、五十步笑百步
      "脚步"的用法比较受限制，可以不用对话练习。

12. **难过**
    - More examples:
      这个学期一结束我就要毕业了。一想到这儿，我又高兴又难过。
      母亲节那天我忘了给妈妈打电话，让我难过了好几天。
      别难过了！这次考试没考好，还有下次考试呢。
    - Q&A Practice:
      别人忘了你的生日，你会难过吗？
    - Other combinations:
      难：难看、难吃、难受、难学

13. **完全**
    - Meaning:
      有强调的意思。表示否定意义时，同 "一点都不/没"，可用复述、替换的方法练。
    - Completion using "完全" to replace the underlined parts:
      天明的爸爸对南京的变化<u>一点都不</u>_____。
      雪梅刚来美国的时候，对新的环境和生活<u>一点都不</u>____。
      去哈尔滨的机票<u>都</u>_____，我们只能坐火车去了。
    - Other combinations:
      完：完工、完事、完成
      全：全国、全校、全身、全天、全日

14. 的确

Meaning: 表示赞同或肯定，是"真的"，"确实像所说那样"的意思，常用来肯定前面的话。

Preferred mode of practice: 最简单的练习是让一个学生说一句话，再让另一个学生用"的确"重复，表示同意：

"True indeed!" (agreeing using 的确)

Example:
老师： 你们觉得昨天热吗？
学生 A： 昨天很热。
学生 B： 昨天的确很热。
老师： 你觉得中国融入了世界是件好事吗？
学生 A： 我觉得是件好事。
学生 B： 我同意，_____。

A: 在上海，有时我以为我在美国呢。
B: _____是这样，上海到处是美国快餐店、_____和_____。
A: 南京的很多景点很有名。
B: 南京的景点_____，特别是_____。
A: 中国春节的时候很热闹。
B: _____，到处可以看到墙上贴着___和___字，有很多人放___，晚上全家吃___，饭后看_____。

15. 要不是

Meaning: 表示与事实相反的假定情况，意思是"如果不是那样的话"，可先让学生复述：
他朋友不喜欢吃肉，所以他没点牛肉饺子。(implied: 要不是他朋友不喜欢吃牛肉，他一定/可能会点牛肉饺子。)
今天下午下雨了，要不然我们一定会去外面打球。(implied: 要不是今天下午下雨，我们一定会去外面打球。)

Q&A Practice: 要不是老师告诉你云南有很多少数民族，你会知道吗？
要不是老师告诉你他今年五十八了，你看得出来吗？

Completion: 要不是表哥当导游，天明他们肯定不会看到那么多_____，吃到那么多_____。
要不是我学习了中国地理，不会知道云南_____。

16. 从来

Grammar: 多用于否定式。也可用于肯定句，表示"一直都"的意思。

Q&A Practice: 你上过中国哲学课吗？
你吃过粽子吗？

Lesson 12 · Changes in China

Completion:	海南是中国最南边的一个省，冬天很暖和，从来_____。 衣服不打折，我从来_____。 A: 没想到我叔叔、舅舅、阿姨那么不尊重他们儿子女儿的选择。 B: 为什么？ A: 因为我爸爸妈妈从来都_____。

17. 看来

Meaning:	同"看起来"。
Completion:	舅舅、舅妈和柯林有说不完的话，看来他们对柯林_____。 南京的很多景点的建筑很有中国特色，比如说夫子庙。看来南京还是保留很多_____。 今天上午考试后我看见我同屋了，他很高兴，看来_____。

18. 尽可能

Grammar:	如果上下文清楚的话，不需要具体说尽可能"做什么"。如： A: 明天的晚会，事儿多，你帮帮我吧！ B: 没问题，我尽可能早点儿到。 A: 你能不能上网帮我查一下资料？ B: 对不起，我今天很忙。我尽可能吧。
Completion:	A: 我饿了，能不能给我们找一家有云南特色的小吃店吃一点东西？ B: 这里变化得很大，很多有特色的小吃店都搬走了。我_____。 A: 这台电脑用起来不方便，你能不能帮我看看？ B: 我对这台电脑也不熟悉，我_____。 --- 我星期一到星期五没有时间运动，周末_____。

19. 竟(然)

Grammar:	副词，表示出乎意料。
More examples:	小张的弟弟不喜欢跟数字打交道，竟(然)要选经济专业。（"数学"没教） 这次考试我没有准备，没想到竟(然)考了95分，太高兴了！ 在雪梅家吃年夜饭的时候，雪梅妈妈做的清蒸鱼很好吃，柯林竟(然)把一条鱼都吃完了。
Completion:	没想到上课的时候她竟然_____。 有些学生竟然不知道感恩节_____。
Preferred mode of practice:	建议练习时，"没想到"和"竟然"都出现在句子中，加深学生印象。可用 Language Practice A 做辅助练习。

20. 补语"过"

Explanation: 动词"过"做补语，表示动作完成。应该注意跟动态助词"了"的区别："过"前的动词所表示的动作应该是已知信息(听说双方都知道的)。

① A: 小李病了，住院了，咱们去看看他吧。
　 B: 我上午去过了，你找别人跟你去吧。
② A: 你什么时候去找你的指导教授讨论选课的事？
　 B: 我吃过早饭就去。
③ 不知道为什么，汉字我写过就忘，真急死我了。

因为"了"与"过"都有"完成"的意思，所以上述句子中，例①的"过"可以删掉，只用"了"；其余两个例子中的"过"可以用"了"替换。
但是如果动词不表示已知信息，就只能用"了"：
第十一课我们学了54个生词，真多，可是不太难。
李友的生日舞会请了很多朋友。
这两个句子里的"了"不能用本课学的"过"替换。
另外，"过"可以是动态助词，也可以是动词。"过"为动词时，可以做趋向补语，如"我们的车开过校园，在宿舍前边停了下来。"也可以做结果补语，如本课所学。"过"做结果补语时还表示其他意思。所以老师在课本或其他材料里遇到"过"时，应该仔细辨识，弄清楚其意义和功能。
动态助词"过"和表示完成的结果补语"过"不仅意思不同，而且形式上也不同。最明显的，第一，动态助词"过"必须念轻声，而表示结果的"过"可以重读；第二，动态助词"过"后不能用"了"，而表示完成的"过"后可以用"了"。
"过"比较难，可以只给学生简单说明，不必着重练习。

21. 语气助词"啊"

Explanation: "语气助词"啊"有很多用法，本课教了四个用法。
a.　用于感叹句的末尾，表达感情、评价；
b.　用于叙述句的末尾，作用是解释；
c.　用于疑问句的末尾，表示疑问；
d.　用于祈使句、命令句，可以缓和语气。

可以让学生解释下面句子中"啊"属于哪一种用法：
① 今天真冷啊，我不想去打球了。
② 什么，你找小张啊？等一下。
③ 这个房子在路边，车很多啊。
④ 别走啊，小林马上就来了。
⑤ 你唱歌唱得真好啊，我不能跟你比，我根本不会唱歌。
⑥ 你什么时候去中国学中文啊？
⑦ 小心点啊，外边太黑了！
⑧ 去中国城的路多难走啊，我找不到，还是你开车吧。

22. 以A为B

Pronunciation: "为"读第二声。

书面语,"以"有"把"的意思,"为"有"作为、当做"的意思,如:"以学生为中心"、"以赚不赚钱为标准"。学生明白就可以了,不必要求会用,因为学生掌握的词语还太少。

23. "一"+量词重叠形式

Usage: 虽然"'一'+量词重叠形式"也表示比较多的物体,但是和"很多"不同。"很多"只表示数量,而"一+量词重叠形式"的功能在于描写,描写很多个体呈现在眼前。

Preferred mode of practice: 描写事物比较难,学生也不常用到,了解其他意思,知道和"很多"不同就可以了。当然能做一些填空练习更好。

Completion:
看见孩子们_____笑脸,我非常高兴。(张)
桌子上放着_____冰水和可乐,还有几盘菜。(杯)
海边_____小船都空着,人都到哪儿去了?(条)

24. 副词"可(是)"

Explanation: "可是"是连词也是副词。连词"可是"表示转折:"虽然大家都说那个电影好,可是我不喜欢"。
副词"可是"也有不止一个用法,本课的"可(是)"的作用是加强语气。在IC 2-1的第8课曾经出现过这个"可",本课继续练习。

Variation: 经常只说"可"。

Preferred mode of practice: 如前所述,语言中表示语气的成分往往比较虚,不太好解释,学生也不容易掌握。本课的"可"也是这样。我们可以用填空或完成句子的方式让学生体会,考试中一般不必出现。

Completion with 可(是):
你妈妈要来了?我很怕她,我_____。(不想跟她见面)
A: 我觉得学哲学很有意思,你学哲学吧。
B: _____,不想学太难了,再说我不觉得哲学有意思。
A: 你知道我妹妹怎么了?她为什么哭了?
B: 这事_____,你问问你姐姐吧。(我不知道)

Exercises for the Main Text
主课文的练习

认读课文:可用幻灯片显示课文,让学生轮流扮演对话中的角色及其口译员。老师可用鼠标跟踪、凸显生词及难点。可借此机会纠正学生们的发音,并检查他们对所学内容的理解状况。

问答:课文认读完毕后,老师可就课文提问,以此方法来检查学生对课文的理解状况,同时可以帮助学生练习听力及口语。

Questions about the text:
- 张天明和丽莎为什么到中国去？
- 他们为什么来南京？
- 张天明的姑妈是张天明爸爸的什么人？
- 你的表哥可能是谁的儿子？
- 丽莎到中国以前想像的中国是什么样子？
- 南京有什么变化？
- 南京最有中国特色的地方是什么？那儿有什么？
- 南京有什么外国的东西？
- 张天明的爸爸对现在的南京熟悉吗？为什么？

Suggested Integrative Activities
综合练习活动

Speaking and Listening

1. Pair activity: with a partner, describe your favorite city and talk about what kind of city you would like to visit:

- 你最喜欢美国的哪个城市？
- 你是什么时候去那个城市的，是怎么去的？
- 你对那个城市熟悉吗？
- 那个城市里有没有很多外国商店？
- 那个城市高楼大厦多，还是传统建筑多？
- 那个城市最近二十年有没有很大的变化？
- 如果你旅游，你一般想去陌生的地方还是熟悉的地方？
- 如果你去陌生的地方旅游，希望不希望有人给你当导游？
- 你比较喜欢安静的城市还是热闹的城市？
- 你最想在哪个城市待一段时间？为什么？
- 如果你现在在一个大城市工作，你会开车上班还是骑自行车上班？

2. Jeopardy: work with your partner and challenge each other to come up with questions or statements that will elicit the responses below.

- 我现在就申请，我想还来得及。
- 不用来上海接我，我坐高铁去南京，又快又方便。
- 找不到那个中学就算了，不用再找了。
- 我同意你的看法，可是我担心有中国特色的东西会越来越少了。
- 我也听说过那句话，"吃"真的是老百姓生活中最重要的事儿。
- 可是我还是更喜欢吃中国饭。
- 我想他一定会很难过。

3. Monopoly

可用中文自己设计一个类似"大富翁"(Monopoly) 游戏的简单地图：
- 在哪儿盖房子/盖楼；
- 哪儿有服装店/快餐店/银行/小吃店；
- 哪儿有庙/公园/景点/名胜古迹…

Reading and Writing

1. Suppose you are the intended recipient of the email below. Read the message and then write a response (Interpersonal):

爸爸：今天表哥开车带我们去找您以前上过的中学。您说过，那儿是个非常安静的地方，有一条小河，您的中学就在小河边，是一座传统建筑，河边有很多大树。我们今天看到了那条小河，可是河边的大树和传统建筑都已经没有了。那儿变成了一个很大的购物中心，门前人山人海，大街上挤满了汽车。您要我们找的地方对您来说其实是个完全陌生的地方。不知道您会为南京的变化感到高兴还是难过。您能谈谈您的看法吗？

天明

2. Read the passage and answer the questions:

看来这几年南京的变化的确很大，有了不少新盖的高楼，可是还是保留了很多传统建筑。很多人认为中国的城市应该有中国特色，可是我担心，城市里一两百年的传统建筑太多了，能盖高楼的地方就很少了。再说，中国的大门已经打开了，中国融入世界了，有中国特色的建筑其实就没那么重要了。南京最有中国特色的是夫子庙。如果我们把夫子庙里的那些餐馆搬到高楼里去，餐馆里的饭菜不也一样好吃吗？

True/False:
( ) 1. The writer agrees that Nanjing has changed a great deal.
( ) 2. The writer complains that there are too many tall buildings in Nanjing.
( ) 3. The writer believes that a Chinese city should look distinctly Chinese.
( ) 4. According to the writer, traditional architecture has become less important because China has melded with the wider world.
( ) 5. According to the writer, not even the Temple of Confucius is indispensable.

3. Write a composition where you pick a place and describe how it has changed over time. It can be your hometown or your parents' hometown. You can also provide pictures that show off the old aspects of the place you chose, as well as the new aspects.

Grammar and Vocabulary

1. **The right measure!** 可用图片与文字进行"连连看"游戏来复习一、二年级介绍过的量词:

- 一栋大厦/高楼
- 一座建筑
- 一种声音(本课)
- …

2. **Antonyms.** 反义词练习 / 复习:

- 新←→
- 安静←→
- 熟悉←→

3. **Fill in the blanks:** (以为、就、原来、渴、高兴、难过、熟悉、一、饿、道理、陌生、一边、一边、要不然)

- 昨天我们____吃过早饭,表哥____带我们去一家法国服装店买衣服。
- 妈妈告诉我那儿现在非常热闹,可是那儿_____是一个很安静的地方。
- _____你给我发了电子邮件,我还以为中文考试是在下个星期呢。
- 两年前我搬到这儿的时候,这是一个完全_____的地方,可是现在我对这儿已经很____了。
- 我们快找一家餐馆吧,我可是又____又____了。
- 没想到这位小姐是您的女儿!我还_____她是您的妹妹呢。
- 你看,这个城市_____是高楼大厦,_____是传统建筑。
- 你说得很好,我觉得挺有_____的。
- 你把这件事告诉她,不知道她会_____还是_____。

4. **Complete the sentences:**

- 我上个月才申请去中国留学,原来以为来不及了,_____。
- 我想去以前常去那个购物中心,可是_____。
- 我以为我对这个城市很熟悉,_____。
- _____,所以我们很想找一位导游。
- 很多以前骑自行车上班的人现在都开车了,所以_____。
- 听说美国快餐并不健康,可是为什么_____?
- 法国服装店里的衣服特别贵,可是_____。
- 一个现代化的城市,不但要有高楼大厦,而且_____。

LESSON 13

Travel 旅游

Chapter Structure

- **Lesson Focus**
- **Priorities**
- **Focal Themes Teaching Suggestions**
- **Sequencing and Suggestions for Key Grammar and Vocabulary**
- **Exercises for the Main Text**
- **Suggested Integrative Activities**
  Speaking and Listening
  Reading and Writing
  Grammar and Vocabulary

Lesson Focus
本课重点

有关本课语言功能方面的问题，请参考本课第一页学习目标。如果新内容的学习对学生负担过重，老师应对所教授的内容进行筛选。下面是我们的几点建议。

因为第十课的内容是中国地理，也可上完第十课后直接上本课。

Function
1. 能利用第十课学过的中国地理，重点介绍云南。
2. 能简单谈谈自然风景美的地方。
3. 除了欣赏自然风景外，能说游客一般可能还希望做什么。
4. 能讨论参加旅行团／旅游团有什么好处。
5. 能简单介绍中国火车的硬卧、软卧。
6. 能说出(出国)旅行前的准备；旅行时的"食"、"行"、"计划"。

Priorities
取舍

与学习目标无直接关系的词语，可不必练习。如，分别、分享、逗、灯笼、来往、房东等等。至于云南各个景点地名，若学生负担太重，可酌情删减，如大理三塔。

Focal Themes Teaching Suggestions
重要主题教学建议

1. 复习中国地理，重点介绍云南。

   用挂图或电脑打出中国地图，复习中国重要的省、市、河流。让学生找出云南省的位置(在中国的西南部)，最好用云南地图或旅游宣传短片加深印象。再让学生说说云南风景美跟地形有没有关系(云南有高山，有河流，所以风景很美)。

2. 谈谈自然风景美的地方。

   从1扩展，引导学生说出自然风景优美的地方，除了有山，有水以外，还可能有什么？(有树，有花，有石头…；树又大又多又绿，花很多很美，石头又大又多，千奇百怪，很特别…)。可用 Language Practice E: "A Nature Lover" 巩固与扩展。

3. 游客可能还希望做什么。

   从2引导学生说说旅游时除了看风景以外，游客可能还希望做什么。比如：看看传统建筑，拍拍照，了解一下当地的风俗习惯，买纪念品，了解那个地方的饮食，尝尝地方小吃(复习第三课：四川菜又麻又辣；广东菜一般比较清淡；上海菜甜甜的。新加：云南菜酸酸的、辣辣的)等等。可用 Language Practice F: "What Kind of Tourist Are You?" 巩固或检查。

4. 讨论参加旅行团／旅游团有什么好处。

   好处：不必自己订旅馆，买机票/景点门票；不用担心三餐；有导游介绍景点的风景、文化…。

   坏处：得付导游小费；比较不自由；购物太浪费时间；团费贵…。

   接下来说旅行团团费一般包括什么：交通、旅馆、三餐、景点门票。提醒学生这些是分类项目。口语可说，包括坐车的钱，住旅馆的钱，去餐馆吃饭的钱，看景点时买门票的钱…。可用 Language Practice C: "A Frugal Traveler" 辅助。

   另外，关于旅行团的"导游"方面，可练习说什么是"好导游"：人好，性格开朗，不会忘这忘那、不会丢三拉四、(复习第六课)，幽默，能介绍景点／文化／风俗习惯…

5. 简单介绍中国火车的硬卧、软卧。

   对从来没去过中国、在中国坐过火车的学生，要他们主动提供这方面的讯息比较困难。因此建议老师直接用图片或短片介绍，再让学生练习。相关内容：价格、车厢、软卧几人一间，上中下铺、好处、坏处…

6. 出国旅行前的准备，包括以下几个方面：

办护照，办签证，订机票，订旅馆，租车(复习一年级)，计划／研究路线，决定参加旅行团或是自助游…。

词语介绍或练习时可分类进行：

"食"：吃方便面，买盒饭，在餐车／餐馆吃，在家庭旅馆吃家常菜…。
"行"：飞机 vs. 火车 vs. 船：好处 vs. 坏处

订机票：跟旅行社、航空公司，上网订(复习一年级19课)；单程／往返票，靠走道／窗户的位子。

Sequencing and Suggestions for Key Grammar and Vocabulary
重要语法和词汇的顺序和教学建议

> 1. 印象；2. 深；3. 留(下)；4. 报名；5. 参加；6. 包括；7. 硬；8. 软；9. 拥抱；10. 幽默；11. 逗；12. 风俗；13. 习惯；14. 故事；15. 古老；16. 讲；17. 来往；18. 分别；19. 分享；20. 之前；21. 只好；22. 亲；23. 千万；24. 不过；25. 多项定语；26. 比较句总结；27. 由数字构成的成语(固定短语)

1. 印象

Explanation: "A对B的印象"，"A给B(留下)的印象"，学生常会弄不清谁是A谁是B。可用翻译的方法，帮助学生建立起中英文的对应关系：

David's impression of Susan:	David 对 Susan 的印象
Tianming's impression of Nanjing:	天明对南京的印象
Xuemei's uncle and aunt's impression of Ke Lin:	雪梅的舅舅和舅妈对柯林的印象。请学生注意，颠倒过来，换一种说法，A和B也变了：A对B的印象==B给A的印象：提醒学生记住这个转换公式：
Susan's impression on David:	Susan 给 David(留下)的印象
Nanjing's impression on Tianming:	南京给天明(留下)的印象
Ke Lin's impression on Xuemei's aunt and uncle:	柯林给雪梅舅舅舅妈的印象 以上两种说法都很常见，学生容易混淆，要多练几次。

Q&A Practice:	你对你同屋的第一个印象怎么样？/你同屋给你的第一个印象怎么样？ 南京的什么给天明和丽莎留下了很深的印象？
Other combinations:	印：脚印、手印、打印机 象：图像、想象

2. 深

Character:	"深"的意符为"氵"。
More examples:	很深的爱 河里的水很深。 舅舅和舅妈的感情很深。 姐姐新买的车颜色很深。
Other combinations:	深：深入、深颜色、深情

3. 留（下）

More examples:	我的同屋毕业的时候，给我留下了好几本书。 她要我给她打电话，可是忘了留下她的手机号码。 南京给天明留下了很深的印象。
Other combinations:	留：留学、留学生

4. 报名

More examples:	我想暑假去北京学中文，可是还没有报名。 如果你想下个月去加州旅游，现在就得报名了。 很多高中毕业生想申请这个大学，已经有很多人报名了。
Other combinations:	报：报到、报告

5. 参加

More examples:	第一次去中国旅游，还是参加旅游团比较方便。 他每个学期都参加中国留学生的活动，所以她的中文进步很快。
Q&A practice:	你参加什么校内或校外活动？
Other combinations:	参：参赛

6. 包括

Variation:	在台湾不少人把"括"念作"guā"。
More examples:	我的房租每月八百美元，包括水电费，可是不包括电话费。 我们班一共有九个人去过中国，包括我自己。
Q&A practice:	你的房租包括水电费吗？
Other combinations:	包：包吃、包住、包机

7. 硬

Character:	"硬"的意符为"石"。

More examples:	我宿舍里的床太硬，睡起来。 我爸爸做的饭有点儿硬，没有妈妈做的饭好吃。 他说话的态度很硬，不是一个很客气的人。
Q&A practice:	梨，你喜欢吃硬的还是软的？ 硬卧比软卧舒服，价钱呢？
Other combinations:	硬：硬座、硬汉、硬水、硬件、硬性

8. 软

More examples:	这个枕头很漂亮，可是对我来说太软了一点儿。 那个女孩子说话的声音很软。
Q&A practice:	米饭你喜欢吃硬一点的还是软一点的？
Other combinations:	软：软座、软件、吃软饭

9. 拥抱

Character:	两个字的意符均为"扌"；"拥"的声符为"用"；"抱"的声符为"包"。
More examples:	我们三年没见面了，所以这次一见面就拥抱起来。 我忘不了我们一起旅游的那几天，忘不了他给我的拥抱。 中国人见面一般不拥抱。
Q&A practice:	你每次回学校前和你父母说再见时，会跟他们拥抱吗？
Other combinations:	拥：拥护 抱：抱孩子、抱歉、抱团

10. 幽默

Etymology:	为英语"humor"译音。
More examples:	小张人很幽默，大家都喜欢跟他在一起。 他工作的时候不开玩笑，但是我们都知道他是个非常幽默的人。 他觉得自己是个说话很幽默的人，可是我一点都听不懂他的幽默。
Q&A practice:	你觉得哪个演员最幽默？

11. 逗

Character:	"逗"的声符为"豆"。
Grammar:	可做形容词和动词。
Meaning:	用作形容词时意为"有趣"或"很幽默"；动词的意思为"tease"。
More examples:	老王今天没上班，在家里逗小狗玩儿。（动词） 你别逗这个孩子了，她都要哭了。 妹妹刚才还在哭，哥哥一句话，把她逗笑了。 舅妈说话很逗，常常让我们哈哈大笑。（形容词）

12. 风俗
More examples: 结婚的时候请客吃饭是中国很多地方的风俗。
中国人过年的时候给孩子红包,这个风俗历史很久了。

Q&A practice: 美国的感恩节有什么风俗?
Other combinations: 俗:俗话、俗语、俗气

13. 习惯
Grammar: 可做动词和名词。
More examples: 我刚来美国的时候不喜欢吃美国饭,可是现在已经习惯了。(动词)
他有很多不好的生活习惯。(名词)

Q&A Practice: 你有睡觉前躺在床上看书的习惯吗?
Other combinations: 习:习俗、习气

14. 故事
Character: "故"的声符为"古"。
More examples: 中文有很多四个字的短语 (phrase) 都有一个有趣的故事。
你在中国工作了三年,给我们讲个中国的故事吧。

Q&A Practice: 小时候你爸爸妈妈常常讲什么故事给你听?
Other combinations: 故:故宫 (gōng)、故人

15. 古老
More examples: 中国是一个古老的国家,但是也是一个年轻的国家。
这座古老的建筑有三百多年的历史了。

Q&A Practice: 世界上哪个文化最古老?
Other combinations: 古:古人、古城、古玩

16. 讲
Collocation: 讲话、讲故事、讲道理、讲课

17. 来往
Meaning: "往"的意思是"去"。
More examples: 我们以前是很好的朋友,可是他搬到纽约去以后,我们就很少来往了。
已经半夜了,没想到马路上还有这么多来来往往的游客。

Q&A Practice: 很多家长反对孩子跟什么样的人来往?

18. 分别
Meaning: 可作副词,意思是"不是一起(做某事)"。
Completion: A: 你们是一起去机场的吗?
B: 不,我们是＿＿＿＿＿＿。

A: 昨天是李小红的生日，你们给她买了些什么？
B: 我和小王分别_____。
A: 你们两个呢？
C: 我们没有给她买东西，我们分别_____。
"分别"也可作为动词，可不练。
明天你们就要分别了，你们的心情怎么样？
你和你的男(女)朋友分别以后，想不想他(她)？

19. 分享

Usage: 英文可以说: "I share your pain"，但中文不能说："我分享你的痛苦"。向学生指出"享"是"享受"的意思，所以分享的内容必须是愉快或正面的。常用介词"和"或"跟"引导。

Q&A Practice:
如果你种 (zhòng, "plant, grow") 了很多的黄瓜，你愿意和别人分享吗？
你常常跟你的爸爸妈妈分享你的快乐吗？
你愿意和别人分享研究资料吗？

Collocation: 分享经验、成果 ("accomplishment, positive result")

20. 之前

Grammar: 请学生注意中英文词序的不同，"之"是"的"意思，所以在名词后。
毕业之前=毕业(的)以前，"before graduation"
睡觉之前=睡觉(的)以前，"before going to bed"
2000年之前=before the year 2000
"毕业之前"和"毕业以前"意思一样。"⋯之前"好像离前面名词表示的时间更近。

Q&A Practice:
睡觉之前，你喜欢做什么，不喜欢做什么？
毕业以前，你还得选几门课？
你旅行之前，常常查很多的资料，看很多的书作准备吗？
"之前"的反义是"之后"：
大家都以为应该吃饭之后吃水果，但最近的研究资料说其实吃饭之前吃水果对身体更有好处。

21. 只好

Chinese gloss: "没有别的办法，"有退而求其次的意思。

Completion:
硬卧票比较便宜，可是都卖完了，我们只好_____。
我们今年夏天要去很远的地方旅行，可是我爸爸不喜欢坐飞机，所以我们只好_____。
我们的旅馆在高山上，不能用手机，也不能上网，只好_____。
旅馆里的每个菜都很辣，我们吃不下去，只好_____。

22. 亲

More Combinations: 亲眼、亲自、亲耳、亲手、亲身："亲眼"、"亲耳"、"亲手"不难练，提醒学生眼=看，耳=听，手=作。"亲自"，"亲身"稍微抽象些。"亲自"是不让别人代劳，"亲身"强调直接经验。

Completion: 填空或完成句子
这件衣服是她妈妈____做的，所以她特别喜欢。
这次去中国，天明和丽莎____看到了中国的变化。
他下个学期要去中国留学，我____听他说的。
指导教授____给他打电话，告诉他得到了奖学金。
这件事是我____做的，所以印象特别深。

23. 千万

Composition: 注意本词的构成，有强调的意思。
Usage: 用于祈使句，敦促提醒的意思。
Completion: 去外国旅行，千万不能忘了____。
如果你不喜欢买东西的话，下次找旅游团，千万____。
他不喜欢别人问他家里的事，你千万____。
明天会很冷，你出去千万____。

24. 不过

Meaning: 有两个意思。一个意思同"但是"，"可是"，但语气没有那么强。另有"只不过"的意思。课文出现的是第二个意思。

Q&A Practice: 昨天的功课很容易，你花了多少时间就作完了？
你的宿舍离教室很近，走多少时间就到了？

Completion: 这台电脑很便宜，我花了____。
你别生气，他不过____，不是真的。

25. 多项定语

Explanation: 一个名词前可以出现几个定语，这种结构在书面语中更常见。本课学的是第一个定语为数量词语，后面是描写性的词语：

一件很漂亮的T恤衫　　　一个小红苹果
一盘很香的清蒸鱼　　　两座很有特色的公寓
三条纯棉的裤子　　　　一些很健康的孩子

也就是说，一般来说，如果名词前有数量词又有描写性的定语时，数量词要放在前面。但如果要突出描写性的短语，或为某种表达的需要，也可以把它放在数量词的前边：
前面是很有特色的两个公寓，我们去看看吧。
但是现阶段不必教这个用法，也不必讲。

Suggested mode of practice:	将下面文字投影于屏幕上，让学生自己或与同学翻译成英语。学生从练习的过程中体会两种语言的异同。全班讨论各人／各组之翻译，并认可非洋泾浜英语后，再将中文原文撤去，让学生由翻译好的英语再翻回中文。

一辆又旧又挤的火车
两碗香香的辣辣的方便面
三个人口集中的城市
两个面积接近的国家
一个正在买纪念品的游客
几个自然条件不好的城市

26. 比较句总结

Grammar: 从一年级开始我们已经学过几种表示比较的方式。比较句不是一种句型，而是意义上相关的一类句子：

A跟B差不多／一样…；
A比B…；
B没有A…；
B不如A…

因为说话中常用，所以一般汉语教材都把它列为语言点。本课列出以下几种比较句：
比较异同的：表示两个或几个事物相同或不同。句型为：跟/和…一样/不一样(+adj./V)：

①这两件衣服的样子、长短一样，只是颜色不同。
②我昨天看的房子和今天看的一样安静，租哪个，要看哪个租金能更便宜一点。
③小李跟她妹妹一样，觉得昨天的电影不好看。

在这种句子中，"一样/不一样"后边可以出现的动词限于"喜欢、觉得、愿意、想"等表示心理活动的一类。

比较不同的：表示两个或几个事物之间不同。
用"比"字：A+比+B+adj./V(心理活动)

①我姐姐比小张的姐姐大。
②我姐姐比小张的姐姐大一点儿。
③我姐姐比小张的姐姐大得多。
④我姐姐比小张的姐姐大多了。
⑤学生活动中心比图书馆近。
⑥图书馆比学生活动中心远。
⑦那个男孩子比我弟弟喜欢游泳。

注意"不比"的意思。A不比B大：A=B，或A<B)：

⑧老张不比老李有钱。

意思可能是：老张和老李一样有钱。或者：老张没有老李有钱。建议不练习或强调"不比"。
注意提醒学生不要把用"比"的句子和用"跟"的句子混起来用。因为表示比较时，学生更容易、更喜欢用"比"，说出"小李比小张一样高"这样的句子。
用"没有"：A+没有+B+ adj./V（心理活动）

①小张的姐姐没有我姐姐大。
②学生活动中心没有图书馆远。
③我没有你喜欢打球。

用"没有"比较，多用"大"、"远"、"长"一类正向形容词。但是形容词前有"那么"或有上文中出现了某些非正向形容词时，用什么形容词就比较自由了。比如一般不说：

*我姐姐没有小张的姐姐小。
但是说下面的句子就没有问题：

①我姐姐没有小张的姐姐那么小。
②图书馆没有学生中心那么近。

用"不如"：A+不如+B+ adj./V（心理活动）

①小张的姐姐不如我姐姐大。
②学生活动中心不如图书馆远。

"不如"后边可以没有形容词：

③我觉得打球不如看电影。（好）
④A: 你觉得写短信方便还是写邮件方便？
　B: 写邮件不如写短信。（方便）

用"不如"时，形容词一般也是正向的。
可用 Language Practice D: "Should we travel by train?" (p. 100) 辅助练习。

27. 由数字构成的成语（固定短语）

Explanation: 汉语有很多固定短语，多为四字形式，也称之为四字格。固定短语中有一部分结构凝结得非常紧，四个字不能随便用其他字替换，整个短语的意思不是由四个字的意思简单相加而成，这种固定短语有些叫成语。有一些成语还有历史渊源，有历史故事、典故等等。但是固定短语和成语的界限已经不那么容易划分清楚。
在固定短语中，有一些由两个数字和另外两个字（很多是一个词）构成。有些数字含有一定的意义。比如书上举了一些例子。再如：

一…半…：表示"少"（一男半女、一时半会、一知半解）
三…四…：有贬义（丢三落四、说三道四、不三不四、朝 (zhāo) 三暮 (mù) 四）
七…八…：表示杂乱无章（乱七八糟、七上八下、横 (héng) 七竖 (shù) 八）
千…百…、千…万：表示"多"。
九…一…：表示对比悬殊（九死一生、九牛一毛）

有些字没学过，老师应该能解释。这些让学生了解就可以了。

Exercises for the Main Text
主课文的练习

认读课文：可用幻灯片显示课文，让学生轮流扮演对话中的角色及其口译员。老师可用鼠标跟踪、凸显生词及难点。可借此机会纠正学生们的发音，并检查他们对所学内容的理解状况。

问答：课文认读完毕后，老师可就课文提问，以此方法来检查学生对课文的理解状况，同时可以帮助学生练习听力及口语。

Questions about the text:
- 张天明跟朋友去哪儿旅游？
- 云南在哪儿？
- 为什么选择去云南？
- 他们是怎么去云南的？他们是什么时候去云南的？
- 他们是从哪儿出发的？
- 张天明他们旅游得怎么样？我们怎么知道的？
- 张天明对什么的印象很深？
- 他们为什么不坐软卧？
- 他们游览了云南的什么景点？
- 他们住的家庭旅馆怎么样？
- 丽江的什么给他们留下很深的印象？

Suggested Integrative Activities
综合练习活动

Speaking and Listening

1. Pair activity: suppose you and your partner visited Yunnan last month and are now planning to vacation in Harbin soon. Discuss with your partner your last trip to Yunnan, as well as your trip plans for Harbin.

- 上次去云南旅游，什么给你留下比较深的印象，云南的风景还是那儿的导游？
- 云南有些什么特色？
- 我们坐火车去云南买的是硬卧票。你觉得硬卧有什么好处，有什么坏处？
- 我很喜欢餐车上的午饭，你呢？
- 你更喜欢石林还是丽江？为什么？
- 如果我们下个月分别从北京和上海出发去哈尔滨，我们在什么地方见面呢？
- 你希望我们找个什么样的导游？
- 我觉得我们应该参加有"购物"的旅游团，还是自助游？
- 我原来打算在哈尔滨住家庭旅馆，可是你为什么不喜欢家庭旅馆呢？
- 我对哈尔滨不太熟悉，你能不能上网看看哈尔滨有些什么好玩的地方？

II. Jeopardy: work with your partner and challenge each other to come up with the questions or statements that will elicit the responses below.

- 还是买软卧票吧，硬卧太吵，睡不好觉。
- 不用把照片寄给我了，放在博客上我就能看到了。
- 可是，要是你的火车比我早到几个小时，怎么办呢？
- 我没睡好，因为上铺的人一直打呼噜。
- 我跟你的口味不一样，我还是喜欢吃方便面。
- 对不起，我不同意，我觉得自助游更方便。
- 不过我觉得自然风景比民族风俗更有意思。
- 不一定，有的能上网，有的不能上网。

III. Be a tour guide! 简单介绍一下云南的：

- 地理、地形
- 山、河、风景
- 建筑、城市
- 人、服装
- 饮食、味道
- 故事

IV. Plan a trip to China!

- 怎么选择旅游景点：去中国的什么地方旅游？为什么选这个地方？
- 走什么路线？
- 坐火车 / 坐飞机 / 坐船的好处与坏处；简单比较中国和美国的火车座位或卧铺
- 参加旅行团 / 不参加旅行团 / 自助游的好处与坏处；打算不打算参加旅行团
- 有导游有什么好处 / 没有导游有什么好处
- 出国旅行前应做什么准备

Reading and Writing

1. Suppose you are the intended recipient of the email below. Read the message and then write a response (Interpersonal):

妈妈：我们来云南旅游已经三天了。昨天我们游览了石林，那儿的石头千奇百怪，几乎每一块石头都有一个故事。今天我们到了有名的古城丽江，城里的茶馆，门旁都挂满了红灯笼，漂亮极了。您几个星期前在电子邮件里说云南的自然条件不好，建议我们去四川旅游，可是很多人都说这里的旅游点非常有特色，跟四川的完全不一样。另外，我们也觉得很安全。真希望你们不要为我们担心，而且建议您和爸爸明年来中国旅游的时候，也来云南看看。怎么样，这个主意不错吧？

天明

2. Read the passage and answer the questions:

我做导游做了五年了，觉得很多游客不理解我们这些当导游的。旅游景点一般都有一些卖纪念品的商店。我们把游客带到那些店里，希望他们多买东西。很多游客以为我们这样做完全是为了我们自己多赚钱，有的游客甚至抱怨说到这些商店来购物是浪费时间。游客买纪念品确实对导游有一些经济上的好处，但是纪念品对游客来说也是有益的。比如，游客游览了大理三塔以后买一些那里的纪念品，很多年以后这些纪念品还会帮他们想起这次旅游。所以，我们导游带游客买纪念品并不完全都是为了我们自己。

True/False:
( ) 1. The writer changed his job after working as a tour guide for five years.
( ) 2. The writer thinks that tour guides are often misunderstood.
( ) 3. According to the writer, it is a waste of time for tourists to visit souvenir shops at tourist spots.
( ) 4. The writer admits that tour guides benefit financially from taking tourists to souvenir shops.
( ) 5. The writer thinks that a souvenir helps preserve the memory of a vacation.
( ) 6. The writer suggests that tourists shouldn't complain about being taken to souvenir shops.

3. Go online and find travel ads, using keywords such as 团费 (tour group fee)、包食宿 (food and lodging included)、免费 (free)、etc. Answer the following questions:

- Whose ad is it?
- What are the destinations?
- What are the selling points?
- What contact information is provided by the ad?

4. Design an ad for a travel agent: 引导学生分组设计制作旅游宣传海报或旅游景点简介广告。挑选自己所熟悉或喜爱的景点，可为城市或国家公园等等，用图画或照片剪贴配上适当文字凸显该景点的特色。图片文字处理后，各组可上台展现出所制作文宣，口语介绍该景点。

Grammar and Vocabulary

1. Fill in the blanks:（亲手、分别、亲耳、逗、比、抱怨、没有、风俗、分享、亲眼、印象、亲自）

- 硬卧_____软卧舒服，可是软卧_____硬卧那么容易找人聊天。
- 我们明天_____从南京和昆明坐飞机去北京。
- 我是二十年前去云南的，可是我对那儿还有很深的_____。
- 真的，这是我_____听他说的，他说他_____看到小王把小李的车开回家了。
- 这是我_____做的菜，你要_____尝一尝才知道好吃不好吃。
- 把你的照片都放到博客上吧，这样我们都可以_____你的快乐。
- 姐姐的男朋友说话很幽默，常常_____得我们哈哈大笑。
- 除了美丽的自然风景，我们对少数民族的_____也很感兴趣。
- 老师给我们很多功课，可是没有一位同学_____。

2. Compare! Use different kinds of comparison patterns to express the following:

(A比B adj.； A不如B (adj.)； A没有B adj.； A跟B 差不多)

- 王明21岁　　　　　　李天18岁
- 昨天86°C　　　　　　今天70°C
- 姐姐喜欢看电影　　妹妹不太喜欢看电影

3. Complete the sentences:

- 我们这次旅游的导游没有上次的导游幽默，可是_____。
- 云南的自然风景跟四川很不一样，所以_____。
- 这次旅游团的团费包括火车票和旅馆，可是_____。
- 上铺比中铺和下铺安静一点，可是_____。
- _____，没想到没有人在车站接我们。
- _____，可是牌子上有一个名字写错了。
- _____，所以我在每个旅游点都买了不少纪念品。
- 你不是说把你的照片放在博客上吗？怎么_____？

Lesson 14: Life and Wellness 生活与健康

Chapter Structure

- Lesson Focus
- Priorities
- Focal Themes Teaching Suggestions
- Sequencing and Suggestions for Key Grammar and Vocabulary
- Exercises for the Main Text
- Suggested Integrative Activities
  - Speaking and Listening
  - Reading and Writing
  - Grammar and Vocabulary

Lesson Focus
本课重点

有关本课语言功能方面的问题，请参考本课第一页学习目标。如果新内容的学习对学生负担过重，老师应对所教授的内容进行筛选。下面是我们的几点建议。

Function
1. 能谈谈自己怎么锻炼身体／运动。
2. 能谈谈怎么注意饮食让身体健康。
3. 能谈谈什么生活习惯对身体健康(没)有好处。

Priorities
取舍

与本课语言功能无紧要关系的词语如"夫妻"、"表演"、"科学"、"可见"等可略过。

学生语言功能基本掌握后，老师再帮助学生练习词语句式，如"否则"（可用 Language Practice E: "Giving Your Advice" 做练习），"只要…就…"。

为避免引起某些学生的不自在或反感，有关胖瘦问题与减肥方面的话题和词语，请老师酌情处理。如果学生可接受，则可以谈。

Focal Themes Teaching Suggestions
重要主题教学建议

1. 谈谈自己怎么锻炼身体 / 运动。

   可以问答引导学生说出自己怎么运动 / 锻炼身体：

   你常常运动/锻炼身体吗？
   你一般什么时候锻炼身体？早晨还是晚上？为什么？
   你大多在什么地方锻炼身体？运动中心、健身房、还是公园？
   你做什么运动？
   你喜欢快动作的运动还是慢动作的运动？（举例）
   你觉得什么运动的动作很美？
   你每次VOV/V多长时间/多久？ (V=verb; O=object)
   你每个星期/每个月锻炼身体锻炼几次？/锻炼几次身体？
   你多久运动一次？/锻炼一次身体？
   你多长时间/几天没锻炼身体了？
   你偶尔也V(O)吗？ (V=verb; O=object)
   什么能让一个人 / 一个城市显得很有活力？

   表示动作持续时间和频率的肯定、否定形式需要特别练习。

   可用 Language Practice F: "To Exercise or Not to Exercise" 来巩固。也可用网络上的教学影片，简单介绍太极拳。学习中间，可让学生舒展筋骨，小试一番。

2. 说说怎么注意饮食对身体健康有好处。

   可在黑板或屏幕上列出"多，少，不/别"等副词，让学生提供个人的建议：

多	少	不/别
多吃青菜、水果	少吃(肥)肉	做菜的时候，别放味精
多喝水	少喝咖啡/茶	别喝酒
多注意营养…	少喝甜的饮料	别乱吃东西…
做菜的时候，	少放油/盐…，	不放味精

   为了鼓励学生参与或增加学习趣味性，可让学生分组竞争，看哪组提的建议最多最好。

   最后学生将搜集到的讯息，成段说出，作为阶段总结。可用 Language Practice G: "It's Good for Your Body" 做复习或检查。

3. 说说什么生活习惯对身体健康没有好处。如：吸烟、生气、紧张、压力大、熬夜/开夜车等等。讨论范句举例如下：

关于饮食：
你每天吃几顿饭？
你会乱吃东西、乱喝东西吗？
不吃早饭，影响不影响学习？
要是营养不良，怎么补充营养？…

关于生活习惯
你平常早睡早起、晚睡早起、早睡晚起还是晚睡晚起？
晚睡早起会不会睡眠不足 (zú)？
睡眠不足你的眼睛会变成熊猫眼吗？…
你什么时候必须开夜车 / 熬夜？

关于胖瘦/减肥
瘦等于身体健康，对吗？
注意饮食等于减肥，你同意吗？
丽莎觉得只要身体健康就好，胖瘦并不重要，乱减肥对身体没有好处。你同意她的看法吗？

Sequencing and Suggestions for Key Grammar and Vocabulary
重要语法和词汇的顺序与教学建议

1. 锻炼；2. 散步；3. 排队；4. 成为；5. 出门；6. 动作；7. 表演；8. 身材；9. 营养；10. 注意；11. 重视；12. 科学；13. 必须；14. 否则；15. 方面；16. 熬夜；17. 随便；18. 偶尔；19. 即使；20. 补充；21. 等于；22. 可见；23. 与；24. 使；25. 显得；26. 活力；27. 只要…(就)…；28. 有的…有的…；29. 口语双音节→书面语单音节

1. 锻炼

Character:	"锻"字的意符为"钅"；"炼"字的意符为"火"。"锻"与"炼"的意思跟冶炼有关。
More examples:	有些人喜欢冬天在河里游泳，锻炼身体。 小钱知道那个城市的自然条件比较差，可是她说去那儿工作可以锻炼自己。
Q&A Practice:	你一般什么时候锻炼身体，早晨，中午，下午还是晚上？ 你喜欢在哪儿锻炼，家里，公园还是健身房？

2. 散步

More examples:	中国很多老人都有到公园散步的习惯。 A: 老张，你去哪儿？ B: 哪儿也不去，今天天气好，出来散散步。
Other combinations:	步：进步、退步、同步

3. 排队

More examples:	很多人想看这个电影，我买票的时候，排队排了半个小时。 早上很多退休老人来到公园。他们先排成队，然后开始跳舞。
Q&A Practice:	做什么得排队？
Other combinations:	排：排名、排球

4. 成为

Usage:	书面语。口语用"成"。
More examples:	爸爸退休了，太极拳成为他最喜欢的运动了。 一千多年前中秋节就成为中国人的重要节日了。
Other combinations:	成：成人、成年

5. 出门

More examples:	这是你的学生证，出门的时候别忘了！ 今天我吃过早饭出门的时候，找不到汽车钥匙了。

6. 动作

Character:	"动"字的意符为"力"。
More examples:	我哥哥打网球的动作很漂亮。 对我来说，跳舞的动作太难了。
Q&A Practice:	看什么球赛，你希望电视里能看到慢动作？
Other combinations:	动：动画、自动、手动

7. 表演

Grammar:	可以是动词，也可以是名词。
More examples:	你们俩跳舞的动作太美了，能不能给我们再表演一次？（动词） 上个周末我们请她来我们小区表演瑜伽。（动词） 他在电视上说的话不是真的，只不过是在表演。（动词） 上周我去看了一个非常有意思的表演。（名词）
Q&A Practice:	在很多人面前表演，你会紧张吗？
Other combinations:	演：演出、演员、公演

8. 身材

Character: "材"字的声符为"才"。

Q&A Practice: 你注意自己的身材吗?
哪个演员的身材好?

Collocation: 很美的身材、漂亮的身材

9. 营养

More examples: 你最近好像很累,要注意营养,补充睡眠啊。
医生说我们应该多吃豆腐,豆腐很有营养。

Q&A Practice: 你平常怎么注意营养?

Collocation: 营养品、营养食品

10. 注意

Character: "注"字的声符为"主"。

More examples: 大家读课文的时候,请注意发音。
这两个字意思不一样,可是发音完全一样,你们一定要注意。
他打太极拳不太注意动作,所以他的动作不太漂亮。

Q&A Practice: 学中文的时候,你最注意什么,发音、语法还是汉字?
出国旅游应该注意什么?

Other combinations: 意:好意、心意、三心二意

11. 重视

Character: "视"字的意符为"礻"。

Grammar: 一般作为及物动词,一般要点明重视的事物。

Meaning: "视"是"看","重视"是觉得什么很重要的意思。"重视健康"就是"to view health as very important or to attach great importance to health."

Q&A Practice: 美国大学(我们学校)是不是太不重视外语教育了?
你重视不重视饮食健康?

Completion: 我们的城市很重视_____,不重视_____。
教育孩子,家长应该重视_____。

Other combinations: 重:轻重、重要、重点
视:轻视、电视、近视、远视

12. 科学

Grammar: 可以是名词,也可以是形容词。
我弟弟今年高中毕业了,可是他还不知道他在大学里会学文学还是学科学。(名词)
很多人说早饭应该比晚饭吃得多,我觉得这种看法不见得科学。(形容词)

Other combinations:	科：文科、理科、医科、商科 学：文学、医学

13. 必须
More examples:	你昨天晚上熬夜了，所以今天必须早点睡。 练习瑜伽的时候必须注意每一个动作。 医生说，除了每天锻炼以外，还必须注意饮食。
Other combinations:	必：必要、不必

14. 否则
Character:	注意"否"字构成为"不"+"口"。
Meaning:	同"要不然"，语气更正式些。
Q&A Practice:	快十点了，我们要不要明天早上再给老师打电话？否则这么晚打电话会不会影响她休息？ 跟朋友吵架，应该道歉吧？否则两个人可能再也不是朋友了，对吧？
Completion:	爸爸，南京的变化很大，你去最好带一张地图或者先问问表哥，否则_____。 你一定得注意锻炼和饮食，否则_____。
Other combinations:	否：是否、可否、能否、否定、否决

15. 方面
More examples:	王先生每天早上都打太极拳，可是饮食方面不太注意，所以他的身体不太好。 南京一方面盖了很多高楼，另一方面也保留了很多传统建筑。
Q&A Practice:	你希望政府注意哪些方面的问题？
Other combinations:	方：中方、美方、前方、后方

16. 熬夜
Character:	"熬"字的意符为"火"。
More examples:	明天有考试，可是我还没开始复习。今天晚上要熬夜了！ 你两只眼睛怎么都变成了熊猫眼？是不是昨天又熬夜了？
Q&A Practice:	你有熬夜的习惯吗？ 你熬夜的时候喝茶还是喝咖啡？
Other combinations:	熬：熬汤

17. 随便
Grammar:	介绍"随便"时，针对本课语言功能，应着重练习其副词用法。可用 Language Practice C: "Are You Accommodating?" 做辅助。

Lesson 14 · Life and Wellness   49

Meaning:	不加限制，不受拘束, at will；任何，无论，对应的英文常是—ever 结尾的词：随便什么时候=whenever, 随便哪儿=wherever, 随便什么=whatever, 随便谁=whoever, 随便怎样=however 等。
Q&A Practice:	你的东西客人可以随便用吗？ 上课的时候可以随便吃东西吗？
Completion:	A: 我明天下午来找你行吗？ B: 我明天一天都有空，你随便_____。 A: 星期五晚上的音乐会，我穿牛仔裤去可以吗？ B: 不是很正式的音乐会，你随便_____。

18. 偶尔

More examples:	我每天都在小区里散步，可是偶尔也去健身房锻炼身体。 我一般吃得很清淡，所以常常吃广东菜，不过偶尔也去四川餐馆。
Other combinations:	偶：偶然、偶发

19. 即使

Usage:	可告诉学生更口语化的说法是"就是"或"就算"，以指出语体的不同。"即使"引出的一般是比较夸张或极端的假设情况，常和"也"等副词搭配。
Completion:	上海的房子很贵，雪梅的表姐即使_____，也_____。 那家饭馆的素菜_____很好吃，即使_____也_____。 即使没有去过中国的人也知道中国_____。 即使是_____也知道一加一等于二。

20. 补充

Character:	"补"字的意符为"衤"。
More examples:	医生告诉我多吃蔬菜和豆腐，补充营养。 除了每个星期的功课以外，老师还给我一些补充练习。 你昨天晚上熬夜了，所以今天必须早点睡，补充一下睡眠。
Other combinations:	补：补衣服、补觉、补习、补考 充：充电

21. 等于

Chinese gloss:	"和什么一样"。
Suggested mode of practice:	可从简单的算术练起。
Q&A Practice:	五加五等于几？ 二十三减三等于多少？
Completion:	给孩子很多的钱不等于_____。 一个人爱开玩笑_____他很幽默。

22. 可见
Preferred mode of practice:
需要有一定的语境才能练习，但不难理解，用起来也不会太难。
完成句子：
你说你昨天没复习，可是你今天考得_____，可见你很聪明。
听说那个山城冬天常常下雪，可见是_____的好地方。

23. 与
Grammar: 和"和/跟"一样，既是连词，又是介词。
More examples: 运动与健康、家庭与社会、意见与建议
指导与帮助、质量与价格、卫生与健康
Usage: 书面语。

24. 使
Grammar: "使/让/叫+名词+动词/形容词…"这种句式叫兼语句或递系式。
"使/让/叫"后的名词是它们的宾语，同时是后边的动词的主语。
Usage: 在口语中多用"让/叫"。
大学生活使/让/叫他变了很多，他现在不怕在很多人面前说自己的看法了。
老师教得很好，使/让/叫我的中文进步得很快。
小张的生日舞会开得非常成功，使/让/叫参加的人都很高兴。
我的父母常常说，一定要使/让/叫我们受到良好的教育。

"让/叫"还有另外的意思：
还有指使、容许或听任等意思。
小李让/叫你明天早一点去机场接他。
你让/叫我在哪儿等你？
他为什么不让/叫我进房间？
我妈妈不让/叫弟弟玩电脑游戏，怕影响他的学习。
当介绍"使"时，用 Language Practice A: "The Domino Effect" 做辅助。

25. 显得
Explanation: 意思类似"看上去"（学生没学过，可介绍），但比"看上去"更正式。课本122页出现了两个句型：显得+形容词和显得+主谓结构。第一个比较简单，第二个是"使什么显得"的意思。"显得屋子很小"即"使屋子显得很小"。
Completion: 1. 显得+形容词
他昨天晚上准备考试熬了一夜，今天早上两只熊猫眼，显得___。
要是北京多保留一些传统建筑，城市就会显得_____。
2. 显得+主谓结构
Q&A Practice: 你觉得如果家具少一些，会不会显得房间大一点？
快到吃午饭的时间了，如果不请客人吃饭，会不会显得我们不够客气？

26. 活力

More examples: 她今年六十五岁了，可是每天都打太极拳，显得很有活力。
你穿红色的衬衫显得很有活力。
这个城市的经济比较有活力。

Collocation: 有活力、没有活力

Other combinations: 活：生活、鲜活

27. 只要…（就）…

Q&A Practice: 衣服只要舒服，我就喜欢。样子好看不好看、是不是名牌，我不在乎。

Completion: A: 你要租什么样的房子？
B: 只要环境好_____。房子_____没关系。
只要你每天锻炼，你的身体_____。
暑假只要飞机票不是太贵，_____。

28. 有的…，有的…

More examples: ①我有很多朋友，他们的爱好很不同。有的喜欢打球，有的喜欢唱卡拉OK，有的只想在家里看书。
② A: 你的衣服很好看，是在哪儿买的？
B: 有的是在老家买的，有的是去纽约的时候买的，还有的是来这儿买的。
③ A: 你觉得大学的课有意思吗？
B: 有的课有意思，有的课，比如金融，我觉得没有意思。

29. 口语中双音节 → 书面语单音节

Explanation: 口语中有些双音节的连词、副词、能愿动词等，在书面语中常常用作单音节的。再如：

需要 → 需
但是 → 但
可是 → 可

应注意，不是所有的双音节连词、副词、能愿动词等都可以用单音节。而且要注意某个单音节词所表示的意思。如"因"只表示"因为"，不表示"因此"；"可"有时表示"可以"，有时表示"可是"，要看上下文。所以学生只能一个一个学，不能随意类推。

Exercises for the Main Text
主课文的练习

认读课文：可用幻灯片显示课文，让学生轮流扮演对话中的角色及其口译员。老师可用鼠标跟踪、凸显生词及难点。可借此机会纠正学生们的发音，并检查他们对所学内容的理解状况。

问答：课文认读完毕后，老师可就课文提问，以此方法来检查学生对课文的理解状况，同时可以帮助学生练习听力及口语。

Questions about the text:
- 丽莎住在哪儿？
- 丽莎为什么没住留学生公寓？
- 丽莎需要付房租吗？
- 她一般怎么锻炼身体？
- 她对什么也有兴趣？
- 她是怎么注意饮食的？
- 什么是良好的生活习惯？
- 李文有什么不好的生活和饮食习惯？
- 要想身体健康，除了锻炼身体以外，还必须注意什么？

Suggested Integrative Activities
综合练习活动

Speaking and Listening

1. Pair activity: with a partner, discuss your health and workout routines:

- 你注意不注意身体健康？
- 你觉得早上锻炼身体好还是下午锻炼身体好？为什么？
- 你最喜欢那种锻炼身体的办法，散步、跑步、瑜伽、打太极拳、游泳还是打球？为什么？
- 在你的家乡，退休老人对什么运动最感兴趣？
- 要想身体健康，除了多运动以外，还应该注意什么？
- 什么样的饮食才是健康的饮食？
- 有人说，早餐要好，中餐要饱，晚餐要少。你觉得这句话有科学道理吗？
- 你功课多的时候，会不会熬夜开夜车？
- 要是你很晚才睡觉，你第二天会不会有"熊猫眼"？
- 你常常运动/锻炼身体吗？
- 你大多在什么地方锻炼身体？运动中心、健身房、还是公园？
- 你做什么运动？

- 你每次VOV/V多长时间/多久？(time duration, affirmative, habitual)
- 你每个星期/每个月运动几次？
- 你每个星期/每个月锻炼身体锻炼几次？/锻炼几次身体？(frequency, habitual)
- 你多久运动一次？/锻炼一次身体？(general questioning for frequency) (V or VO)
- 你多长时间/几天没锻炼身体了？(time duration, negative)
- 你喜欢动作快的运动还是动作慢的运动？（举例）你觉得什么运动动作很美？
- 你偶尔也V(O)吗？

2. Jeopardy: work with your partner and challenge each other to come up with the questions or statements that will elicit the responses below.

- 太好了，这样我每天都可以跟你爸爸妈妈练习太极拳了。
- 别客气，你也帮了我的忙，我的英文水平提高了不少。
- 对，他们都是退休老人。
- 你说得很对，我也觉得瑜伽的动作跟太极拳有点像。
- 可是到健身房去锻炼，感觉会更好。
- 是的，年轻人更喜欢打球、游泳那样的运动。
- 可是很多医生都说，瘦一点比胖一点好。
- 我同意，但是一点肉也不吃不一定对身体有好处。
- 谁愿意熬夜啊？可是我下个月要考研究生，不开夜车不行啊。

3. **How's your math?** 作为课堂调剂（也能与其他学科结合），老师不妨暂时充当数学老师，做些简单的加减运算。老师先示范，边写边用中文说，如：

   （写）1+1=2,（说）一加一等于二；
   （写）3-2=1,（说）三减二等于一。

接着老师写，学生说。也可让一名学生上前做小老师写，其余学生说。
Language Practice B: "How's Your Math?" 提供了一些练习。

Reading and Writing

1. Suppose you are the intended recipient of the email below. Read the message and then write a response (Interpersonal):

爸爸妈妈：你们都好吗？丽莎在李文家已经住了三个星期了，不但不必付房租，而且可以更多地了解一般中国人的生活。她每天早上出去散步的时候，都能看见很多人打太极拳。那些人说打太极拳是锻炼身体的好办法。你们对太极拳有兴趣吗？要是你们有兴趣，我可以从北京买一套太极拳的录像带回来，让你们一边看一边学。还有，李文的父母常说，早餐要吃好，午餐要吃饱，晚餐要吃少。你们认为这样说有科学道理吗？

天明

2. Read the passage and answer the questions:

谁都希望自己的身体健康。可是怎么才能使自己身体好呢？很多人都认为锻炼身体最重要。他们常常跑步、游泳、打球，甚至每天都去健身房。另外一些人觉得饮食最重要。他们吃很多青菜、水果，很少吃肉。锻炼身体对不对呢？对。注意饮食对不对呢？也对。可是，除了注意锻炼身体和注意饮食以外，我们还必须注意睡眠，最好每天睡八个小时。一个每天都熬夜的人，即使花很多时间锻炼身体，吃很多青菜、水果，身体也不会是非常健康的。

True/False:
(　) 1. The writer wishes to know who really wants to stay healthy.
(　) 2. The writer tries to dissuade people from going to the gym too often.
(　) 3. The writer agrees that one should eat more fruits and vegetables and less meat.
(　) 4. The writer does not believe that exercise and a good diet will necessarily lead to good health.
(　) 5. According to the writer, those who often have to burn the midnight oil should exercise more and eat more fruits and vegetables.

3. New Year Resolutions: write down at least five healthy life habits that you want to start employing in the new year. You can use the following format:

- 多_____
- 少_____
- 不_____

4. Composition on life and health:

结束本课前，应让学生练习段落组织：将所做过的口语练习串成段落，叙述自己的生活、饮食习惯，并给予建议或评论如何能保持或让身体健康。单元测试亦可用此方式进行口试或笔试。或让学生做出健康小手册，图文并茂，表达自己的意见。

Grammar and Vocabulary

1. Fill in the blanks: (有的…，有的…、注意、了解、偶尔、等于、即使、千万、显得、随便、等于)

- 他今年六十岁了，可是因为每天锻炼，所以_____很年轻。
- 你一定要_____饮食，千万不要_____乱吃东西。
- 今天是星期六，同学们_____去打球，_____去游泳。
- 和一个中国家庭住在一起，可以更好地_____中国人的生活。
- 我常常打球，_____也打打太极拳。
- 瘦并不_____身体健康，胖也并不_____身体有病。
- 熬夜对健康没有好处。_____你工作很忙，也_____不要开夜车。

2. Translate the sentences into Chinese, using 使, 叫, or 让:

- What the teacher just said enabled me to see the problems in my Chinese pronunciation.
- I couldn't find the middle school that I attended twenty years ago, and it made me very sad.
- Dad told me he would buy me a new car next year. That made me happy for quite a few days.
- The teacher asked me to tell you that you didn't do well on yesterday's examination.
- I am seventeen years old, but my parents do not allow me to drive.

3. Explain in Chinese the following words and phrases:

- 熬夜：
- 偶尔：
- 开夜车：
- 熊猫眼：
- 否则：

4. Use two syllable words to replace the underlined one syllable words:

- 昨晚回家<u>前</u>忘了去买菜。
- 咱们<u>边</u>吃<u>边</u>谈。
- 我想去中国留学，<u>但</u>没有时间。
- 我想出去旅游，<u>可</u>我没钱。

5. Use spoken style words to replace the underlined written style words:

- 健康<u>与</u>运动
- 每天锻炼<u>使</u>我身体健康。
- <u>即使</u>你没有时间，也应该注意饮食。
- 你应该少吃甜的，<u>否则</u>你会胖起来。

6. Complete the sentences:

- 为了_____，她决定明年去北京留学。
- 由于_____，所以他不必付房租了。
- _____，使校园显得非常有活力。
- 如果你不重视饮食，_____。
- 我觉得你不用花钱去健身房，因为_____。
- 很多女孩子不但很注意身体健康，而且_____。
- 有的人认为胖瘦并不重要，_____。
- 你昨天开夜车了，所以你必须_____。

LESSON 15

Gender Equality 男女平等

Chapter Structure

- Lesson Focus
- Priorities
- Focal Themes Teaching Suggestions
- Sequencing and Suggestions for Key Grammar and Vocabulary
- Exercises for the Main Text
- Suggested Integrative Activities
  - Speaking and Listening
  - Reading and Writing
  - Grammar and Vocabulary

Lesson Focus
本课重点

有关本课语言功能方面的问题，请参考本课第一页学习目标。如果新内容的学习对学生负担过重，老师应对所教授的内容进行筛选。下面是我们的几点建议。

Function
  1. 能简单说出在家庭里，夫妻之间怎么取得平等
  2. 能简单说说在工作上，男女怎么取得平等
  3. 能简单说说二十世纪中国妇女的社会地位有了什么变化
  4. 能用中文报告球类运动比赛分数与输赢

Priorities
取舍

若学生对课文内容有些微词，可不必练习"气管炎"、"妻管严"部分。

Focal Themes Teaching Suggestions
重要主题教学建议

1. 说说在家庭里，夫妻之间怎么取得平等。

   此部分可分段处理。可先让学生说出"家务"有哪些，平常帮不帮助做家务：

洗碗、洗衣服、买菜、做饭、打扫屋子、整理房间…

然后再练习以下这些词语：

互相体贴，互相照顾，一起做家务，带／教育孩子

可用 Language Practice C: "Do You Know Any Model Couples" 辅助练习。

2. 说说在工作上，男女怎么取得平等，如：

   工作机会一样，互相帮助，同工同酬

   可简单用中文解释"同工(不)同酬"是什么意思。

3. 简单说说二十世纪中国妇女的社会地位有了什么变化。

   可按课文的介绍，让学生练习根据时间顺序复述：

   1950年以前，中国妇女的社会地位和家庭地位都比男的低得多。
   1950年以后，女孩子逐渐和男孩子一样有受教育／工作的机会。社会地位有了很大的提高。

   改革开放以后，在工作上，又出现男女不平等的现象。不过，在城市家庭里，男女还算平等。

   如果学生对中国的情况不熟悉，可让他们用类似的模式说说自己国家男女平等／妇女地位这些年有些什么变化。可用 Language Practice F: "How Has Women's Social Status Changed" 做辅助。

   应提醒学生"男女平等"的否定说法是"男女不平等"，而"重男轻女"的否定说法是"不重男轻女"。若学生对社会、家庭以及职场上的男女平等不平等的情况不太了解，可让他们问家人的看法，然后在班上报告。

4. 用中文报告球类运动比赛分数与输赢

   建议复习一年级第18课美式足球部分的内容。让学生说出美式足球与本课提到的国际足球有什么不同：包括上场人数，比赛时间与比赛方式。老师用事先准备好的足球比赛结果，打成幻灯或投影。如，昨天xx队与yy队比赛，结果＃比＃，xx队赢了，yy队输了。可让学生挑选自己喜爱的球类运动、球队，上网查询最近该球队的战绩。按老师示范的模式，用中文向全班同学做简单的报告。可用 Language Practice G: "Such a Fan!" 做辅助。

Lesson 15 · Gender Equality

Sequencing and Suggestions for Key Grammar and Vocabulary
重要语法和词汇的顺序与教学建议

> 1. 妇女；2. 平等；3. 重男轻女；4. 地位；5. 逐渐；6. 机会；7. 以来；8. 改革开放；
> 9. 情况；10. 出现；11. 现象；12. 市场；13. 职业；14. 工厂；15. 单位；16. 企业；
> 17. 收入；18. 薪水；19. 同工同酬；20. 公平；21. 超过；22. 困难；23. 相信；24. 消息；
> 25. 讨厌；26. 队员；27. 骄傲；28. 不得了；29. 输；30. 赢；31. 成绩；31. 比分；
> 32. 大男子主义；33. 家务；34. 妻子；35. 气管炎；36. 妻管严；37. 互相；38. 体贴；
> 39. 表现；40. 模范；41. 丈夫；42. 由；43. 某；41. 毕竟 vs. 到底；42. 拿…来说(吧)；
> 43. 看你说的；44. 表示肯定的"是…的"；45. 表示结果意义的"过来/过去"

1. 妇女

Usage:	可作集体名词：中国妇女；也可作单个名词：两位妇女。
Collocation:	家庭妇女、职业妇女、妇女儿童

2. 平等

More examples:	中国历史上男人和女人的地位是不平等的。
	无论是男生还是女生，找工作的机会应该是平等的。
Q&A Practice:	你觉得在美国男女平等吗？

3. 重男轻女

Q&A Practice:	你觉得美国有重男轻女的现象吗？
Other combinations:	重__轻__：重理轻文、重农轻商

4. 地位

More examples:	他在我们公司工作三十年了，在公司里的地位很高。
Q&A Practice:	什么人的社会地位很高？
Collocation:	地位很高，地位很低

5. 逐渐

Chinese gloss:	慢慢地、渐渐
Usage:	书面语。
Completion:	秋天了，天气逐渐地_____。
	他以前老生病，后来他每天早上跑步，身体逐渐地_____。
	中国妇女的地位逐渐地_____。
	最近三十年中国的_____逐渐地融入了世界。

6. 机会
   Q&A Practice: 哪儿的工作机会比较多？
   你希望不希望有出国留学的机会？
   Collocation: 工作的机会、留学的机会、挣钱的机会

7. 以来：
   Q&A Practice: 这个学期开学以来，你回过几次家？
   中国改革开放以来，南京发生了哪些变化？
   Preferred mode of practice: "从…到现在"，可通过复述的方法让学生练，如，"从八十年代到现在=八十年代以来"。
   从2005年到现在＝
   从去年一月到现在＝

8. 改革开放
   Q&A Practice: 中国的改革开放是什么时候开始的？
   Other combinations: 改：房改、医改
   革：革命、文革

9. 情况
   More examples: 他说今年大学毕业生找工作很难，我不了解这方面的情况。
   现在很多家长对自己孩子交朋友的情况不太清楚。
   Q&A Practice: 最近你的学习情况怎么样？

10. 出现
    More examples: 我这个学期的学习本来很顺利，可是最近出现了一些问题。
    因为经济不好，有的城市出现了大学毕业生找不到工作的现象。
    Collocation: 出现…问题，出现…现象，出现…情况

11. 现象
    Q&A Practice: 改革开放以后又出现了什么现象？
    Other combinations: 象：气象

12. 市场
    Collocation: 菜市场、服装市场、金融市场、市场管理
    Other combinations: 市：超市、夜市

13. 职业
    More examples: 我喜欢医生这个职业，所以我打算大学毕业后上医学院。
    如果你想当职业运动员，你就必须有特别棒的身体。

Lesson 15 • Gender Equality

Q&A Practice:	你最喜欢哪一个职业篮球队？
	选择专业的时候，应该不应该考虑对将来选择职业有没有帮助？
Other combinations:	职：职员、职工、职位

14. 工厂

Other combinations:	厂：家具厂；食品厂；厂房

15. 单位

Chinese gloss:	工作的地方
Q&A Practice:	你想在什么单位工作？
Collocation:	企业单位、事业单位

16. 企业

More examples:	工厂和公司都是企业单位。
Other combinations:	企：国企、外企
	业：工业、商业、轻工业

17. 收入

Q&A Practice:	什么职业的收入高？
Other combinations:	入：入口、进入

18. 薪水

Character:	注意"薪"字里的"新"声旁。
Chinese gloss:	工资
Q&A Practice:	什么工作的薪水高？
Other combinations:	薪：高薪；月薪；年薪

19. 同工同酬

Chinese gloss:	做同样的工作得同样的薪水
Q&A Practice:	美国做到同工同酬了吗？
Other combinations:	酬：报酬、酬金、课酬

20. 公平

More examples:	没有男女平等，就不会有社会的公平。
	我的很多同学都去中国留学了。我也申请了，可是学校不同意。这不公平！
Q&A Practice:	职业球员的工资比科学家的工资高得多，你觉得这公平吗？

21. 超过
More examples: 我们学校女生人数超过男生。
几年前，中国超过日本，成为世界上第二经济大国。
Other combinations: 超：超级、超市、超长、超大、超高

22. 困难
Grammar: 可用作名词或形容词。
More examples: 你最近上课不爱说话，是不是学习上有什么困难？（名词）
小王想打工挣钱付学费，因为最近他父母经济上比较困难。（形容词）
你不会说中文，去中国工作有点儿困难。（形容词）

23. 相信
More examples: 你说什么？这个学期的中文课没有考试？我不相信。
他从来不随便乱说话，我相信他。
Q&A Practice: 有人说中国经济会很快超过美国，你相信不相信？
Other combinations: 信：自信、信服

24. 消息
More examples: 网上的消息不一定都可靠。
她本来说一到纽约就给我打电话，没想到到现在还没消息。
别急，我一听到她的消息就马上告诉你。

25. 讨厌
More examples: 我最讨厌这里的冬天，差不多每天都下雪！
我的同屋人很好，性格也挺开朗，可是我讨厌她夜里给朋友打电话。
李太太喜欢养狗，可是李先生讨厌狗在家里跑来跑去。
Q&A Practice: 你最讨厌下面哪一种情况：有人在你旁边吸烟，有人用手机打电话的声音太大，还是有人在古建筑上随便乱写乱画？

26. 队员
Q&A Practice: 篮球队有几个队员？
足球队有几个队员？
姚 (yáo) 明以前是哪个队的队员？
Other combinations: 队：球队、男队、女队
员：服务员、球员、工作人员、员工、学员、教员

Lesson 15 • Gender Equality 63

27. 骄傲
More examples: 你最近学习进步很快，不过千万别骄傲。
我们学校的球队昨天赢了世界冠军队，我们都觉得非常骄傲。
她觉得自己比谁都漂亮，所以骄傲得不得了。

28. 不得了
口语，在形容词后做补语，有"非常非常"、"不一般"的意思。
不难掌握，可用替换的方法练习。

Rephrase: 非常非常骄傲
非常非常讨厌
非常非常干净
太幽默了

Q&A Practice: 昨天晚上的篮球比赛怎么样？
学校餐厅的饭好吃吗？
你这个学期的课轻松吗？
你觉得中国改革开放经济上的成绩大吗？

29. 输
More examples: 昨天的比赛我们打得不好，所以输了。
输了一场球赛没关系，还有下一场呢。
Other combinations: 输：输球、输钱

30. 赢
Character: 注意赢里的"贝"部。
More examples: 你知道吗，我们的篮球队刚刚竟然赢了意大利队！
他们是世界冠军队，我们要想赢这场比赛是非常困难的。
Other combinations: 赢：赢球、赢钱

31. 成绩
Q&A Practice: 你这个学期哪门课的成绩最好？
如果参加比赛，你觉得比赛的成绩、输赢重要不重要？
Collocation: 学习成绩、比赛成绩

32. 比分
More examples: 今天的比赛的比分是88比66。
Other combinations: 比：比赛、一比一
分：学分、分数

33. 大男子主义
Other combinations: 主义：社会主义、资本主义、三民主义、女性主义

34. 家务
Chinese gloss: 家事

Q&A Practice: 你们家谁做家务做得多？
Other combinations: 务：公务、商务

35. 妻子
Chinese gloss: 太太
Usage: 不可做称谓。

36. 气管炎
Other combinations: 管：食管、水管
炎：发炎、鼻炎、脑炎、中耳炎

37. 妻管严
Chinese gloss: 妻子管得严
Other combinations: 严：严父、严师

38. 互相
Character: 注意"互"字的字形。
More examples: 小王和小李常常在一起学习，互相帮助。
张先生四川菜做得好，张太太广东菜做得好，他们互相学习，现在张先生的广东菜和张太太的四川菜也做得不错了。
Variation: 也可以说"相互"

39. 体贴
More examples: 现在很多丈夫非常体贴太太。

40. 表现
Grammar: 可以是动词或名词。作动词时，一般有补语"出(来)"，宾语常常是双音节的抽象名词。学生学过的抽象名词有限，可先单独练习一下：表现出…的兴趣，表现出…的样子。

学生互相问答：

你不高兴的时候，会不会马上表现出来？
你紧张的时候，会表现出什么样子？
如果你爸爸妈妈看到你的新电脑，他们会不会表现出很大的兴趣？
把一本经济和运动的书放在你同屋面前 (in front of)，他/她会对哪本书表现出更大的兴趣？

以上的"表现"均为动词。下面的是名词，不必练习：
你爸爸(或哥哥)在做家务方面的表现好不好？

Lesson 15 • Gender Equality

41. 模范
Collocation: 模范教师、模范家庭、模范妻子
Other combinations: 模：模特、名模、模子 (múzi)
范：范文、师范

42. 丈夫
Chinese gloss: 老公、先生
Other combinations: 夫：夫妻

43. 由
Usage: 书面语，不止一个意思。本课学的"由"，是"归"的意思（fall under [someone's responsibility, etc.], be up to someone）。

Q&A Practice:
如果你去中国留学，学费、生活费由谁负担？（父母　学校　自己）
你学什么专业由谁决定？（自己　父母　教授）
你暑假如果去实习可能由谁安排？（自己　学校　朋友）

44. 某
Grammar: 代词，代替一个不确定或不想明确说的人、机构或日期。
Other Combinations: 某人、某单位、某校、某公司
某小姐、某位先生、某年、某日、某某某

45. 毕竟 vs. 到底：
Explanation: 表示追根究底后的结论，"到底"更加口语：
你姐姐毕竟/到底比你有经验，出去旅游的事，你还是多听听她的意见吧。
你们毕竟/到底是学生，给你们太多的自由，不见得是好事。
我毕竟/到底已经二十岁了，你别把我看成小孩子了。
"到底"还用来追问，这个用法是"毕竟"没有的：
A: 大家都说你拿了小李的银行卡，你到底拿了没有？
B: 我当然没拿，我怎么会做那种事呢？
你一会说同意我的意见，一会说不同意，你到底是同意还是不同意？

46. 拿…来说(吧)
Meaning: "to take something as an example".
Preferred mode of practice: 造句前，先通过英译汉掌握这个结构。
Translation: Take Nanjing's traditional architecture as an example →
Take women's status as an example →

Completion: 我这个星期天天都很忙，就拿昨天来说(吧)，_____
_____。
我们去中国的每个地方都很有意思，拿云南来说(吧)，_____
_____。

47. 看你说的
Meaning: 表示对方说话夸张了。
Usage: 口语，不必特别练。

48. 表示肯定的"是…的"
Explanation: 我们学过"我是昨天来的"这种表示句子焦点的"是…的"，本课学的是表示肯定语气的"是…的"：
① 你别着急，你这次考试成绩是不会影响毕业的。
② 不好的事情是会过去的，不用担心。
③ 你要明白，父母是为你好的。
"是…的"中可以用形容词，如果用的是动词，前面要用"会、能"等能愿动词。
注意不要把这种"是…的"和表示焦点的"是…的"(我是昨天来的)混起来。

49. 表示结果意义的"过来/过去"
Explanation: 趋向动词"过来/过去"在动词后可以表示方向：他向我走过来。本课学的"过来/过去"不表示方向，而表示结果："过来"表示由不正常的状态转为正常的状态，"过去"相反：

醒过来/睡过去　　　活过来/死过去
醒过来/晕(yūn)过去　　救(jiù)过来　　　明白过来

今天早上我的狗不知道为什么好像快要死了的样子，医生花了两个小时才把它救过来。
爸爸跟我讲了很多道理，我才明白过来我做错了。

Exercises for the Main Text
主课文的练习

认读课文：可用幻灯片显示课文，让学生轮流扮演对话中的角色及其口译员。老师可用鼠标跟踪、凸显生词及难点。可借此机会纠正学生们的发音，并检查他们对所学内容的理解状况。

问答：课文认读完毕后，老师可就课文提问，以此方法来检查学生对课文的理解状况，同时可以帮助学生练习听力及口语。

Questions about the text:
- 在历史上，中国妇女的社会地位怎么样？
- 后来发生了什么变化？
- 改革开放以后，又出现了什么现象？
- 现在妇女的地位怎么样？
- 中国现在还有男女不平等的现象吗？
- 男人和女人同样有受教育和工作的机会吗？
- 社会上还有"同工不同酬"的现象吗？
- 运动员的薪水是由什么决定的？
- 雪梅的舅舅怎么体贴舅妈？
- 雪梅的舅妈什么不喜欢中国男足？

Suggested Integrative Activities

综合练习活动

Speaking and Listening

1. Survey: walk around the classroom and ask your classmates the following:

- 你觉得在美国(你的国家)男女平等吗？
- 你家重男轻女吗？
- 在你家男的(做家务做得多)还是女的做家务做得多？
- 你的爸爸是"模范丈夫"吗？
- 你的妈妈是"模范妻子"吗？

Record the results:

- 有几位同学认为在美国(他们的国家)男女不平等？
- 有几位同学认为他们家不重男轻女？
- 几位同学的家里男的做家务多？
- 有几位同学认为他/她的爸爸是"模范丈夫"？
- 有几位同学认为他/她的妈妈是"模范妻子"？

2. Pair Activity: Suppose you and your partner are the president and athletic director of a university. What information would the president be interested in about the athletic programs? Here are some of the questions the president may want to ask:

- 女足比男足的成绩好，女足队员和男足队员的奖学金一样多吗？
- 女运动员的卫生间够吗？
- 学校为女足比赛做的广告够吗？

3. Discuss the following questions with a partner and then report his or her views to the class:

- 有人不喜欢"妻管严"这个词，你呢？为什么？
- 妻子需要不需要管丈夫？
- 丈夫需要不需要管妻子？
- 夫妻之间怎样才能互相体贴、互相照顾？

4. Model Wife/Husband

可让男女同学分成两组，讨论心目中的"模范妻子"与"模范丈夫"。之后将两方的意见综合成"模范夫妻"。也可用 Language Practice D" My Ideal Spouse" 做引导练习。

5. Be a Sportscaster!

如果学生对球赛感兴趣，建议老师选出一小段篮球或美式足球比赛画面，静音，让学生尝试做简单的球评播报比赛实况：

- 现在比分＃比＃，xx队赢＃分
- 某某某打／踢得不错／跑得很快／…
- 比赛还剩下＃分钟…
- 比赛结束了，结果＃比＃，xx队赢了

Reading and Writing

1. Suppose you are the intended recipient of the email below. Read the message and then write a response (Interpersonal):

李文，你好。我有个问题，今天吃早饭的时候忘了问你，刚才想起来了，所以给你发一个电子邮件。昨天我们班上的一位同学说我们的钱老师是qiguan yan，说完就笑起来了。我不知道qiguan yan 是什么意思，上网去找了一下，才知道是一种病。可是我不理解，为什么钱老师生病了，那位同学会笑呢？这是不是太不客气了？还有，钱老师病了，要是我去看他，应该带一束花还是带些水果比较合适呢？

丽莎

2. Read the passage and answer the questions:

怎样才是真正的男女平等呢？有人说，男女应该是平等的，因为男人能做的事，女人也能做；女人能做的事，男人也能做。但是真的是这样吗？我认为不一定。比如，搬家的时候，丈夫能搬一个书架，妻子一般来说只能搬比较轻的家具；而做家务的时候，一般来说妻子做饭做得比丈夫更好，洗碗洗得比丈夫更干净。所以我认为，男女应该是平等的，但是男人跟女人是不一样的。

True/False:
- ( ) a. The writer is doubtful that men and women can do all things equally well.
- ( ) b. The writer is doubtful that men and women can become truly equal.
- ( ) c. The writer argues that men and women have different strengths and weaknesses.
- ( ) d. The writer believes that men and women are different but mutually complementary.
- ( ) e. The writer discusses men and women's roles in the family, rather than in society.

3. Memorandum of Understanding: after you have met with the university president (see speaking exercise 2 above), write a memorandum of understanding summarizing what you and the president discussed and agreed upon.

Grammar and Vocabulary

1. Fill in the blanks with vocabulary from this chapter:

- _____: 重视男的，不重视女的
- _____: 做同样的工作，得到的薪水也一样
- _____: 慢慢地、一点儿一点儿地
- _____: 一个男人不做家务，觉得在家里自己比妻子重要

2. Fill in the blanks:

- 出现____
- 互相____
- 重___轻___
- ____主义
- 模范____
- 注意____
- ___比___

3. Explain in Chinese the following words and phrases:

- 妻管严：
- 互相学习：
- 同工不同酬：
- 认为：
- 逐渐：
- 薪水：

4. Spell out the following abbreviations:

- 女足
- 男足
- 女篮
- 男篮

5. **Complete the following sentences:**

- 你昨天说和我一起去看女足比赛，现在又说可能没时间。你到底_____？
- 她毕竟练过半年的瑜伽，我刚开始练，所以她的动作_____。
- 只要你经常锻炼、多注意饮食，你的身体就会逐渐_____。
- 我的朋友都很喜欢旅游，每年都去国外玩。就拿小张来说，去年_____。

Lesson 16: Environmental Protection and Energy Conservation
环境保护与节约能源

Chapter Structure

- **Lesson Focus**
- **Priorities**
- **Focal Themes Teaching Suggestions**
- **Sequencing and Suggestions for Key Grammar and Vocabulary**
- **Exercises for the Main Text**
- **Suggested Integrative Activities**
  - Speaking and Listening
  - Reading and Writing
  - Grammar and Vocabulary

Lesson Focus
本课重点

在本课中，不是所有的生词和语法点都一样重要。本课语言功能请参考第一页上的学习目标。若本课新内容超过学生负担老师应根据实际情况作适当的筛选。下面是我们的建议。

Function
1. 能简单描述一个干净无污染的环境。
2. 能谈谈平常怎么保护环境／环保。
3. 能说出自己平时怎么节约能源。
4. 能说出传统能源有哪些，绿色能源有哪些，绿色能源有什么好处。
5. 能利用"V1的V1, V2的V2"的句式叙述一个场景/画面中的行为活动。

Priorities
取舍

在不影响学习目标的前提下，老师可不着重练习"中国政府规定"那一部分的内容。若觉得"后果不堪设想"太难，也可不练。为了避免学生负担太重，关于双音节动词和形容词的重叠方式，也不必详细给学生讲。

Focal Themes Teaching Suggestions
重要主题教学建议

1. 描述一个干净无污染的环境。

风景好，有山，有水／河，有树，有花⋯；
水／河很清／干净，树又多又绿，花很多很美⋯（以上为复习）
没有什么车，没有什么垃圾，空气新鲜，没有什么污染⋯（进入本课）

我们现在住的地球呢？还是这样吗？

可用 Language Practice C: "Paradise on Earth" 来辅助。

2. 说出自己怎么保护环境／环保，包括以下几方面：

　　a. 少开车，多走路，多骑(自行)车，多坐公共汽车
　　b. 不随便乱扔垃圾，多回收
　　c. 不随便乱扔空瓶子，应该回收
　　d. 上餐馆吃饭，自己带筷子／餐具，不用一次性筷子／餐具
　　e. 不买瓶装水，自己带水喝
　　f. 买菜／买东西自己带包，不用塑料袋
　　g. 少砍树

为加深印象与加强学习效果，也可让一名会画画儿的学生，画出学生说出的内容。最后可用整黑板的图画，来帮助学生复习或串接句子，理出顺序，形成段落。

尽量鼓励学生说出自己的情况，并帮助整理、分项、扩展。如：学生只说"多骑自行车"，就可提醒帮助学生说出"少开车，多走路，多骑(自行)车，多坐公共汽车"。又如，若学生说出"自己带包"，就引导学生说出"买菜／买东西自己带包，不用塑料袋"。

由于受英语影响，许多学生会说"带自己的包"与"带自己的水"，老师应提醒学生注意。另外，为了避免困扰，建议做此部分练习时，问答只用"怎么环保"或"怎么保护环境"其中一种说法。等学生熟悉后，再两者交互使用。

这一阶段的语言掌握后，再扩展，提高语言质量。

例一：少开车，多走路，多骑(自行)车，多坐公共汽车有什么好处？
　　　（少开车，多走路，多骑(自行)车，多坐公共汽车可以减少空气污染。）
例二：不买瓶装水，自己带水喝为什么能保护环境？
　　　（不买瓶装水，自己带水喝可以减少白色污染来保护环境。）

可利用 Language Practice E: "Do Your Part to Reduce Pollution" 来辅助。

3. 说出自己怎么节约能源，包括以下几方面：

　　a. 少开车，多走路，多骑(自行)车，多坐公共汽车
　　b. 随手关灯
　　c. 节约用水

d. 夏天少开空调，冬天少开暖气
e. 夏天空调温度别开得太低；冬天暖气温度别开得太高

学生掌握后，可提高难度，练习

我平常随手关灯，来节省能源，保护环境。

我从小地方做起，比如节约用水，夏天少开空调，这样来节约能源，保护环境。

节约能源/保护环境，我从小地方做起：比如…"

可用 Language Practice F: "Become a Conservation Advocate" 做练习

若进行顺利，老师可顺便介绍练习

节约能源	从每个人做起 从家庭做起 从我做起 从今天做起	…

4. 说出传统能源有哪些，绿色能源有哪些，绿色能源有什么好处。

可用图片引导，让学生告诉老师传统能源有哪些，绿色能源有哪些。可用 Language Practice D: "Energy Sources" 做练习。

然后讨论学生绿色能源有什么好处：

绿色能源(是)取之不尽(的)。
利用绿色能源发电不会造成污染。(水污染、空气污染、环境污染)

在讨论节约能源时，可复习前几课学过的词语，使语言更丰富些。如，尽可能(第十二课)，浪费(第十一课)

Sequencing and Suggestions for Key Grammar and Vocabulary
重要语法和词汇的顺序与教学建议

> 1. 保护；2. 节约；3. 能源；4. 石油；5. 太阳能；6. 地球；7. 利用；8. 有益(于)；
> 9. 瓶装水；10. 餐具；11. 筷子；12. 一次性；13. 扔；14. 污染；15. 减少；16. 危机；
> 17. 造成；18. 闹；19. 后果；20. 不堪设想；21. 温度；22. 规定；23. 国家；24. 赞成；
> 25. 从…做起；26. 爬山；27. 推；28. 出汗；29. 加油；30. V1的V1，V2的V2；
> 31. …吧，…吧；32. V着V着；33. 亮；34. 表示"比"的意思的"于"；
> 35. 形容词按照动词重叠方式重叠；36. 想起来；37. 可不是吗

1. 保护

More examples:	我们要保护自己的眼睛,不要躺在床上看书。
	他最近两年没有好好保护自己的身体,所以常常生病。
Collocation:	环境保护
Other combinations:	保:保险
	护:护林

2. 节约

More examples:	张天明比较节约,每个月的生活费不超过八百美元。
	地球上的水并不是取之不尽的,所以我们每个人都应该节约用水。
	这种汽车虽然比较贵,但是非常节约能源。
Q&A Practice:	我们在每天的生活中应该怎么节约能源?
Other combinations:	节:节能、节电、节水

3. 能源

Character:	注意"源"字中的"原"声符和意符"氵"。
Q&A Practice:	你觉得什么能源比较便宜?
	你觉得什么能源对环境比较好?
	什么能源不是取之不尽的?
Other combinations:	能:太阳能、风能、电能、水能
	源:水源、来源

4. 石油

Q&A Practice:	世界上地方的石油很多?
Other combinations:	石:石头、石林
	油:菜油、鱼油、原油、汽油、煤油、机油

5. 太阳能

Q&A Practice:	可以用太阳能来做什么?
	在美国什么地方用太阳能用得比较多?

6. 地球

Other combinations:	地:地热、地形、地图
	球:月球、星球

7. 利用

More examples:	我们在学习中应该好好利用学校图书馆。
	老师利用网上的资料帮助我们学中文。
Usage:	注意与"用"相区别:用中文写信;用笔写字
	有时候有贬义,"你不要让他利用你"。

Q&A Practice:	我们应该多利用什么能源？
Other combinations:	利：有利

8. 有益(于)

	"于"是一个介词，在书面语中常用在动词后，现代书面语中常用。"于"的意思较多，"有益于"中的"于"是"对"的意思，"有益于"就是"对…有好处"。介词"于"还有其他用法，如"生于"的"于"是"在"的意思。
Usage:	书面语，口语是"对…有好处"。 ①有人认为吃素不见得有益于身体健康。 ②少上网有益于孩子学习。 ③节约用纸有益于环境保护。 可以让学生把课本192页四个"有益于"的例句，改为"对…有好处"。

9. 瓶装水

Other combinations:	瓶：水瓶、油瓶 装：简装、装备、服装

10. 餐具

Q&A Practice:	餐具包括什么？ 中餐的餐具多还是西餐的餐具多？
Other combinations:	具：玩具、文具、工具、茶具、家具

11. 筷子

Character:	注意"筷"字中的"快"声符和意符"竹"。
Q&A Practice:	你平常用筷子吃饭吗？ 你用筷子用得怎么样？
Other combinations:	筷：竹筷

12. 一次性

Q&A Practice:	你赞不赞成用一次性的餐具？
Collocation:	一次性餐具、一次性水杯、一次性筷子

13. 扔

More examples:	把可乐瓶扔进回收垃圾筒里。 把衣服扔在床上。 不要随便乱扔垃圾。

14. 污染

More examples:	吸烟不但对自己的身体健康没有好处，而且污染空气，影响别人的健康。 这种塑料瓶要扔到回收垃圾筒里，否则会污染环境。
Collocation:	空气污染、环境污染、水污染、食品污染、精神 (jīngshén) 污染
Other combinations:	污：污水

15. 减少

More examples:	我们都应该随手关灯，节约用水，减少对能源的浪费。 如果我们多利用太阳能和风能，我们就能减少空气污染。
Q&A Practice:	我们怎么减少能源的浪费？
Other combinations:	减：减低、减法

16. 危机

Collocation:	经济危机、金融危机、信用危机、家庭危机、社会危机

17. 造成

Grammar:	动词，宾语一般是双音节抽象名词，往往表示不好的结果。学生学过的可搭配的宾语有：污染、负担、(不好的)影响、浪费、(不好的)结果、后果等。
Q&A Practice:	汽车太多会对什么造成污染？ 塑料袋有什么坏处？ 只吃青菜不吃肉会对健康造成不好的影响吗？
Completion:	我们点菜不要_____，否则吃不完，造成_____。

18. 闹

More examples:	你已经哭了两个小时了，别闹了。 公司已经三个月没给工资了，不少人要上街闹事。

19. 后果

More examples:	喝酒以后开车会有非常严重的后果。 生病了就得马上去看医生，不然的话后果可能很不好。
Other combinations:	果：结果

20. 不堪设想

Usage:	书面语。意为(负面)结果、影响等很不好，"没有办法想象"。一般作谓语，可搭配的词不多。
Preferred mode of practice:	可通过让学生互相问答或完成句子的形式练习，然后把答案告诉大家，否则不容易练习。

Lesson 16 • Environmental Protection and Energy Conservation 77

Q&A Practice:	如果我们不注意什么，后果会不堪设想？

21. 温度
Q&A Practice:	今天的最高温度是多少度？
Other combinations:	温：高温、低温、气温、温室、温水
	度：长度、高度、硬度、n度

22. 规定
Grammar:	可作动词或名词。
More examples:	学校规定学生晚上十一点半以前必须回到自己的宿舍。（动词）
	老师规定我们每个星期三要交功课。（动词）
	我们州规定开车的时候不能用手机。（动词）
	老师有规定，每个星期三要交功课。（名词）
	开车的时候不能用手机，这是州政府的规定。（名词）
Other combinations:	规：校规、厂规、常规、规范

23. 国家
Composition:	注意这个词里的"家"；一个国就像一个家。
More examples:	世界上一共有两百多个国家。
	大的国家和小的国家在世界上的地位都应该是平等的。
	中国有四、五千年的历史，是个古老的国家。

24. 赞成
More examples:	我完全赞成开车的时候不能用手机的规定。
	我非常赞成上餐馆吃饭自带餐具的做法。
Q&A Practice:	你赞成不赞成上课不能上网的规定？
	你赞成不赞成买东西自己带包，否则得花钱买塑料袋的做法？
Collocation:	举双手赞成

25. 从…做起
Q&A Practice:	节约能源可以从什么做起？
	减少白色污染可以从什么做起？
	锻炼身体可以从什么做起？
	提高中文水平可以从什么做起？

26. 爬山
Character:	注意"爬"字中的"巴"声符和意符"爪"。
More examples:	这孩子才半岁，还不会走路，可是会在床上爬了。
	周末爬山是锻炼身体的好办法。

27. 推
Character: 注意意符"扌"和"佳"声符（和"谁"字押韵）。
Collocation: 推门、推车、推动

28. 出汗
More examples: 今天天气真热，开着空调还出汗！
我刚刚打球回来，出了一身汗。
Other combinations: 汗：汗水、汗衫、流汗

29. 加油
Meaning: 注意字面意思和引申义的不同。
More examples: 美国队，加油！
今天的球赛很重要，走，我们一起去给我们学校的球队加油吧。
我的车两个星期加一次油。
Other combinations: 加油：加油站

30. V1的V1，V2的V2
Grammar: "上课的上课，找工作的找工作"中"上课的"是"的"字结构，相当于一个名词。"上课的上课，找工作的找工作"这种结构的意思是：在看见的人中，有一些人上课，有一些人找工作。含有都在做事，没有人闲着的意思。
More examples: ①A: 喂，我想去你家玩，你们现在忙吗？
B: 不好意思，今天我妈妈叫我们全家打扫房间，扫地的扫地，洗衣服的洗衣服，整理柜子的整理柜子，每个人都在忙。
②昨天我去朋友家，他有四个弟弟妹妹。我到他家的时候，看见他的弟弟妹妹在院子里，打篮球的打篮球，跳舞的跳舞，唱歌的唱歌，热闹极了。
Rewrite the sentences with V1的V1, V2的V2: ① 教室里，有一些学生写字，有一些学生听录音，有一些学生念课文。
② 星期六我的朋友们，有一些人看电影，有一些人去公园，有一些人去超市，都不在家。

31. …吧，…吧
Meaning: 说话人面临两种选择，常常难于决定。
Usage: 口语用法。
More examples: ①这件事跟不跟小张说呢？说吧，怕他难过，不说吧，觉得不够朋友。
②朋友给了我一张明天的电影票，这个电影非常好，可是，去看吧，后天有考试，不去看吧，怕那个朋友不高兴。
③暑假做什么好呢？去中国学中文吧，钱不够，打工吧，还没找到工作，真麻烦。

32. V着V着

Explanation: "V著V著… / V着V着…"：表示在一个动作进行当中，不知不觉第二个动作开始了。用在叙述性的句子中。

More examples: 我昨天睡得很晚，上课听老师讲课的时候，听着听着睡着了，很不好意思。

不知道妹妹在看什么书，她常常看着看着就笑起来了。

我的同屋去年开始玩网上的游戏，玩着玩着上瘾了，他父母很着急。

33. 亮

Grammar: 可作动词或形容词。

More examples: 早上五点钟，小王房间里的灯就亮了。我知道她很早就去公园锻炼身体。（动词）

这里冬天的夜晚很长，早上七点钟天还没亮呢。（动词）

王老师五岁的女儿很可爱，眼睛又大又亮。（形容词）

34. 表示"比"的意思的"于"

Explanation: 文言虚词"于"在形容词和数词等后也可以表示"比"的意思：

A大于B（A>B）——A比B大

A小于B（A<B）——A比B小

Grammar: 提醒学生，此处"于"的用法可用"比"表达，但"比"句中形容词后可加程度词语，"于"句则不行。

Usage: 注意，不是所有的形容词后都能用"于"表示"比"的意思，而且因为"于"是书面语，不宜在一般口语句子里用这个"于"。提醒学生在现阶段学了哪个"形容词+于"就用哪个，不忙扩大范围。

Preferred mode of practice: 建议先复习第十四课的"等于"（3+2=5, 7-1=6）。然后可以问学生：

6>5（六大于五），中文口语怎么说？

5<6（五小于六），中文口语怎么说？

再增加难度，用两个城市的气温练习"高于"、"低于"，用两个国家的人口练习"多于"，"少于"。

Completion:
A高于B　　　（温度）
B低于A　　　（温度）
A多于B　　　（人口）
A少于B　　　（人口）
今年好于去年　（考试成绩）

35. 形容词按照动词重叠方式重叠

Explanation: 双音节形容词的重叠方式AABB如：

轻松———>轻轻松松

高兴———>高高兴兴

漂亮———>漂漂亮亮

这样重叠的形容词作定语时，有"可爱"的意思：
　　漂漂亮亮的一个小女孩
单音节的形容词重叠也如此：
　　圆圆的小脸
　　大大的眼睛
作状语时，表示程度加强，含有"很xx"的意思：
　　这次他轻轻松松地就考完了三门课。
　　他在路上慢慢地走着，好像在想什么问题。

双音节动词的重叠方式是ABAB，如"享受享受"、"复习复习"、"研究研究"。有的形容词也可以按这一方式重叠，如书上的几个例句中的"轻松——轻松轻松"、"凉快——凉快凉快"、"热闹——热闹热闹"、"高兴——高兴高兴"。这种重叠方式有"使/让/叫…adj"的意思。再如：
教室里太热，你出来凉快凉快吧。
给妈妈买这件衣服吧，叫她也时髦时髦。
A: 你跟她说她的男朋友说要跟她分手了，叫她难受难受。
B: 我不去说，不能这样乱开玩笑。

Usage: 应该注意，很多形容词不能这样重叠使用，所以学过哪个形容词就用哪个，不要随意类推。

36. 想起来

Meaning: "想起来"的意思是 "to recall, remember"，和"想出来"（"to come up with an idea, solution, and so on"）不同。

Fill in blanks with "想起来" or "想出来"：
你_____你昨天午饭吃什么了吗？
王教授的手机号码你_____了吗？
王教授的手机号码很长不好记，怎么记容易些，你能_____一个好办法吗？

37. 可不是吗

Meaning: 同意确实是这样。

Preferred mode of practice: 只要求理解，不必特别练。

Exercises for the Main Text
主课文的练习

认读课文：可用幻灯片显示课文，让学生轮流扮演对话中的角色及其口译员。老师可用鼠标跟踪、凸显生词及难点。可借此机会纠正学生们的发音，并检查他们对所学内容的理解状况。

问答：课文认读完毕后，老师可就课文提问，以此方法来检查学生对课文的理解状况，同时可以帮助学生练习听力及口语。

Questions about the text:
- 张天明他们是怎么到山下的？
- 为什么他们这么去爬山？
- 什么垃圾是可以回收的？
- 中国政府对办公室和公共场所的温度有什么规定？
- 柯林说美国的教室怎么样？
- 我们应该怎么保护环境？
- 什么能源不是取之不尽的？
- 我们应该多利用什么能源？

Suggested Integrative Activities
综合练习活动

Speaking and Listening

1. Pair Activity: brainstorm the following:

- 骑自行车有什么好处？
- 开车有什么坏处？
- 哪些能源是传统能源？／哪些能源是绿色能源？
- 哪些能源是用不完的／取之不尽的？
- 怎么节约能源？
- 怎么保护环境？

2. Pair Activity: what more could our school do to protect the environment? Ask each other:

- 你觉得我们的宿舍环保吗？
- 冬天我们宿舍空调的温度怎么样，能不能调低一点？你觉得多少度比较合适？
- 夏天呢，空调的温度能不能调高一点？你觉得多少度比较合适？
- 学校里垃圾回收筒够不够多？
- 学校哪些地方可以用太阳能？
- 学校在环保方面还可以做什么？

3. Pair Activity: with a partner, reflect on your water use habits. Are there small things you could do to conserve water?

- 你每天洗几次澡？
- 你每次洗澡都花很长的时间吗？
- 你平常衣服只穿一次就洗吗？

- 你觉得用洗衣机洗衣服省水还是用手洗省水？
- 洗菜的水可以回收吗？
- 你家的马桶 (tǒng, "toilet") 是省水的吗？
- 你觉得多久洗一次车比较合适？
- 自己洗车省水还是付钱去外面洗车省水？

4. Take a look at the ad on page 187 of the textbook and tell your classmates if you think:

- 为什么有人买这些东西？
- 这些东西环保吗？
- 不用免洗餐具就一定环保吗？
- 洗筷子、洗碗会不会污染环境？

5. Who is the better environmentalist?

可让学生分组竞赛，说出自己如何从小地方做起来节约能源，保护环境。先限时让各小组讨论，讨论后，询问各组能说出几项。由可说出最多项(类似 dare or double dare)的小组上台报告，如果他们所说的内容符合预期，就获胜。如认为能说出10项，但只说出9项，内容或语言不符合要求，则让下一组上台报告，看看是否能完整说出。

Reading and Writing

1. Suppose you are the intended recipient of the email. Read the message and then write a response (Interpersonal):

老师：我是柯林，谢谢您帮我写介绍信，让我这个学期能在中国留学。给您发这封电子邮件，是为了说一件事情。我来中国后才知道，中国的办公室和公共场所，冬天暖气温度不能高于摄氏20度，夏天空调温度不能低于摄氏26度。这让我想到我们学校的教室大楼。在那儿，冬天穿衬衫还出汗，夏天穿毛衣还觉得冷。这要浪费多少能源啊。您能不能向学校建议，我们也像中国人那样，对教室大楼暖气和空调的温度作出规定？您觉得学校会考虑这样的建议吗？

柯林

2. Read the passage and answer the questions:

汽车使我们的生活变得方便了，可是现在汽车太多了。另外，开车的人也太多了，从十六岁到七、八十岁，差不多每个人都开车。这么多的人开车，不但要用很多能源，而且还造成了严重的空气污染。怎么解决这个问题呢？最近一位大学教授建议美国各州规定不到二十岁不能开车。他说这个新规定会使美国开车人减少一千多万。另外，他还建议各州政府规定每个家庭的汽车都不能多于两辆。我想很多美国人可能不会同意他的这些建议，可是我举双手赞成。

True/False:

( ) 1. The writer is concerned that the increasing number of cars has made life less convenient.
( ) 2. The writer thinks that Americans start to drive too early and stop driving too late.
( ) 3. The professor estimates that over ten million Americans start driving at the age of 16.
( ) 4. The professor proposes that each American family should have no more than two cars.
( ) 5. The writer enthusiastically agrees with the professor's proposals.

3. Take a look at the photograph on page 104 of the Workbook. Do you agree with the slogan "保护水环境人人有责"? Suppose you need to speak at a meeting to discuss this issue. Write a short paragraph to flesh out the importance of protecting clean water.

4. Reading signs: 老师可以带学生看 187、188、196、197、198 页上的照片。让学生简单说说照片上的语言大概是什么意思。

5. Poster/brochure making: 让学生制作环保文宣海报或小册子。鼓励学生用所学内容搭配图画或图片做出宣传环保的具体材料。亦可订出评分标准，当作本课评估测验学习成果的方式。

Grammar and Vocabulary

1. Fill in the blanks with vocabulary from this chapter.

- _____: 后果严重，不可想象。
- _____: 东西很多，拿不完。
- _____: 节省、不浪费。
- _____: 对什么有好处。

2. Draw a line connecting each verb with its proper object.

- 保护   能源
- 节约   太阳能
- 回收   规定
- 利用   环境
- 赞成   危机
- 造成   垃圾
- 减轻   树
- 爬   污染
- 闹   山
- 砍   环境
- 减少   别扭
- 浪费   压力/负担

3. Draw a line connecting each noun with its proper adjective.

- 污染　　　严重
- 空气　　　健康
- 身体　　　新鲜

4. Form combinations with the following key characters:

- ___能；
- 节___；
- 费___；
- 减___；
- ___于；
- ___处；

5. Complete the following sentences:

（一个办法、电话号码、时候、自己、很远、开车、否则）
- 你想起来他_____的____，请告诉我。
- 这个问题比较难解决，我们一起想想，看看能不能想出_____来。
- 骑自行车比_____健康。
- 电影三点开始，我们快走吧，电影院_____，我们还是坐出租车吧，_____就来不及了。
- 保护环境应该从_____做起。

Lesson 17 — Money Management and Investing 理财与投资

Chapter Structure

- Lesson Focus
- Priorities
- Focal Themes Teaching Suggestions
- Sequencing and Suggestions for Key Grammar and Vocabulary
- Exercises for the Main Text
- Suggested Integrative Activities
    - Speaking and Listening
    - Reading and Writing
    - Grammar and Vocabulary

Lesson Focus
本课重点

在本课中，不是所有的生词和语法点都一样重要。本课语言功能请参考第一页上的学习目标。若本课新内容超过学生负担老师应根据实际情况作适当的筛选。下面是我们的建议。

Function
1. 能说说自己一向乱花钱还是省吃俭用。
2. 能说说平常花钱花在什么上。
3. 能谈谈自己或家人把钱投资在什么上。
4. 会说股票涨了、跌了，或买的股票赚了还是赔了。

Priorities
取舍

由于不影响本课的学习目标，"劝""说服""中"等词语可不练习。

如果学生负担太重，可不练习"攒钱"与"挣钱"。

若时间有限，可不必介绍或练习如何存钱购买高消费的物品。

Teaching Suggestions for Main Themes
重点主题教学建议

1. 说说自己一向乱花钱还是省吃俭用。

    可先复习前几课，特别是第八课，学过的内容。如：(不)常去饭馆吃饭，(不)常叫外卖，(不)常上网购物，(不)乱买东西／衣服，(不)乱借钱，(不)乱刷卡…

    再进行问答练习：你觉得自己是个省吃俭用的人还是个随便乱花钱的人？

    可用 Language Practice F: "Are You a Spender or Saver?" 辅助。也可利用第八课的 Language Practice A: "Happy-Go-Lucky" 来复习 "…钱" 与 "…费"。

2. 说说平常花钱花在什么上？如用以下问答：

    A: 你平常把钱花在什么上？
    B: 我把钱花在生活上／教育上／衣、食、住、行上／旅游上。

    可利用本课 Language Practice G: "Be a Financial Consultant" 来复习 "收入与支出"。

3. 谈谈自己或家人把钱投资在什么上。

    可先从"银行"开始，复习以前学过的词语，然后带入本课的生词。

    a. 跟银行：借钱、换钱、贷款
    b. 去银行：存钱、存款＝(在银行存的钱)；解释"省钱"与"存钱"的不同。
    c. 把钱存在银行里的好处：安全、有利息
    d. 利息：利息多；利息少
    e. 赚钱：钱增加得慢，减少

    然后再进一步练习投资方面的语言。如用以下问答：

    A: 把钱投资在什么上？
    B: 把钱投资在买房上／房地产上／股票上／自己的教育上…

    如果学生年纪轻没有投资概念，或没有钱可以投资，可让学生想象假如有钱会把钱投资在什么上。

4. 说说股票涨了、跌了，或买的股票赚了还是赔了。

    先带出与股票有关的一些词语如：股票市场(股市)，炒股，再做问答：

    你炒股吗？
    炒股风险高不高？

今天纽约的股市涨了还是跌了？（涨了几点／跌了几点）
昨天上海的股市涨了还是跌了？

建议练习时打出(中文)网络上世界各大股市的日线图，让学生按图说出各国股市的涨跌。

Sequencing and Suggestions for Key Grammar and Vocabulary
重要的语法和词汇的顺序与教学建议

> 1.股市；2.投资；3.涨；4.增加；5.炒；6.存款；7.攒；8.剩余；9.方式；10.消费；
> 11.合同；12.享受；13.思考；14.想法；15.矛盾；16.郁闷；17.引起；18.劝；
> 19.说服；20.辛苦；21突然；22.接着；23.算是；24.一向／一直；25.合；26.终于；
> 27."把"字句小结；28.动词重叠

1. 股市
Composition:	股票市场
Other combinations:	股：股东

2. 投资
Character:	"资"字的意符为"贝"，声符为"次"。
More examples:	有人说，股市下跌的时候是投资股市的好机会。
	很多家长愿意在子女的教育上投资。
Q&A Practice:	你觉得买房子是一种很好的投资方式吗？
Other combinations:	资：资金、合资

3. 涨
Character:	"涨"字的意符为"氵"，声符为"张"。
More examples:	水果的价钱涨了不少，我听说还要涨。
	这种股票一定会涨，我觉得这时候买是一种很好的投资。
Q&A Practice:	今年什么东西的价钱涨了？
Other combinations:	涨：涨价、涨水、水涨船高

4. 增加
More examples:	这个国家在闹经济危机，很多公司好几年没增加工资了。
	政府今年增加了对教育的投资。
	最近经济情况不好，给大学毕业生找工作增加了困难。

5. 炒
Character: 注意"炒"字的意符为"火"；声符为"少"。原意为"炒菜"。
Collocations: 炒股票、炒股、炒新闻、炒房产、炒饭、炒面、炒作

6. 存款
Chinese gloss: 存在银行里的钱
More examples: 他工作十年了，可是银行里只有两百块钱的存款。
虽然她有不少银行存款，可是她不愿意用存款买房子。
Other combinations: 存：存钱、存包
款：收款、大款

7. 攒
Character: 意符为"扌"，声符为"赞"。
Usage: 口语，并由区域性。
Chinese gloss: 存钱，一般指把钱存在银行。攒钱，一般指把钱省下来。
More examples: 表哥真不会享受生活，他辛辛苦苦地攒钱，却从来不为自己花钱。
父母用攒了几十年的钱买了一套房子。
Other combinations: 攒：攒钱

8. 剩余
More examples: 我花了几百块钱买书，剩余的钱都给了我弟弟了。
上次搬家我只搬了一张床和一张桌子，剩余的家具我都送给朋友了。
懂了就可以了，不必练习。比较难。
Other combinations: 剩：剩菜、剩饭

9. 方式
Q&A Practice: 你用什么方式记生词？
Collocations: 投资方式、教学方式、研究方式

10. 消费
More examples: 他虽然工资不高，可是消费很低，所以每年都有一点存款。
要发展经济，就应该增加消费。
Other combinations: 费：费钱、费时、费力
Collocation: 最低消费、消费者

11. 合同
Collocation: 投资合同、付款合同、签合同

12. 享受

More examples: 别把钱都存到银行里，学会舒舒服服地享受生活吧。
真不想离开这里，想多享受一天这里的春天。
我觉得听音乐是一种享受，可是弟弟觉得是浪费时间，只爱玩电子游戏。

Other combinations: 享：分享、享福

13. 思考

Grammar: 可作名词或动词。
More examples: 他说最好的投资是享受生活，这种看法引起了我的思考。（名词）
我到底应该选文学还是化学作我的专业？这是我正在思考的问题。（动词）

Other combinations: 思：思想、思路、相思、思考

14. 想法

More examples: 姑妈突然有了买房子的想法。
你的想法很有意思，可是我劝你多听听朋友们的意见。

Q&A Practice: 毕业以后做什么好？你有什么想法，分享一下吧。
Other combinations: 法：说法、看法、做法、用法

15. 矛盾

Grammar: 可作名词和形容词。
More examples: 最近小张跟爸爸在闹矛盾。小张想打工挣钱，可是爸爸不同意。（名词）
他的女朋友两个星期没来电话了，他们俩是不是闹矛盾了？（名词）
你说你的专业是化学，可是你选的课都是文学课。我觉得这有点儿矛盾。（形容词）
暑假我本来找到一个公司去打工，可是今天收到一个大学的信，说给我奖学金去中国学中文。怎么办，我心里很矛盾。（形容词）

Collocation: 自相矛盾

16. 郁闷

Character: "闷"字的形旁为"心"，声旁为"门"。
More examples: 她昨天考试考得不好，所以她今天有些郁闷。
我前天决定投资股市，可是昨天股市就跌了，真让我郁闷。

Q&A Practice: 什么事情会让你郁闷？
郁闷的时候你怎么让心情好一点？跟朋友聊聊天，出去走走，还是听听音乐喝喝咖啡？

17. 引起

Grammar: 及物动词，宾语一般是双音节的抽象名词，如注意、思考、重视、反对、讨论、兴趣、危机等。

Q&A Practice:
穿红色的长裤去公司上班会不会引起别人的注意？
在饭馆抽烟会不会引起别人的反对？
我们学校有哪些问题？这些问题有没有引起学校的重视？
如果你是中文老师，你会怎么教来引起学生学习的兴趣？

Preferred mode of practice: 要求学生造句前，可先复习学过的可搭配的名词，用生词卡单独练一下，然后和"引起"组合，加深学生印象。

18. 劝

More examples:
我劝你别省钱了，好好享受生活吧。
我哥哥和嫂嫂这两天闹矛盾，两人都很郁闷，我真不知道怎么劝他们。
舅舅说股市风险太大，劝我不要投资股市。

19. 说服

Pronunciation: 在"说服"中"说"字又读 (shuì)。

More examples:
舅妈说买房子不是好的投资方式，可是她说服不了我。
张先生说最好的投资方式是舒舒服服享受生活，我被他说服了。
爸爸一开始不同意我一边上学一边打工，但是我后来说服他了。

Other combinations:
说 (shuì)：游说、说客
服：服从、口服、心服

20. 辛苦

Character: "辛"字不同于"幸"。

Grammar: 可作动词或形容词。

More examples:
父母辛苦了几十年，用省下的钱花为我交学费。（动词）
你每天工作十个小时，太辛苦了！（形容词）
他辛辛苦苦地工作了八年，才有了这么一点银行存款。（形容词作状语）

Other combinations: 千辛万苦

21. 突然

Grammar: 副词或形容词。

Meaning: 事情很快，"一下子"，没有思想准备，不难用。

More examples:
舅舅本来计划用存款买房子，可是上个星期突然决定投资股市了。
今天上午天气很好，可是中午突然下起雨来了。
上个星期他的女朋友说要来看他，可是昨天突然来电话，要跟他分手。

Lesson 17 · Money Management and Investing

Completion: 我和我大学的同屋有五年没有见面了，前天他突然_____。
去看他以前最好_____，否则太突然。
昨天我爸爸突然_____，我非常高兴。
本来以为今天是好天气，没想到网球比赛打到一半突然_____，只能明天接着比赛了。

22. 接着

Grammar: 副词，一件事情没有做完，继续做，或做完了一件事不停紧接着做第二件事。

Q&A Practice: 有人喜欢洗了热水澡以后接着洗冷水澡。你觉得好吗？
九点半了，我们继续讨论合同，还是明天再接着谈？

Completion: 明天出去旅游，行李还没有整理好，得接着_____，所以今天晚上没有时间_____。
小王跳舞已经跳了三个钟头了，还不休息，看来他想_____。

23. 算是

Meaning: 视为、看作、当作、"当"、"差不多是"。

Q&A Practice: 西瓜是水果，南瓜 (pumpkin) 算不算是水果？
小李算是我最好的朋友了。
你在你们学校算是好学生吗？

Completion: 奶奶马上就要八十了，我给她画了一张画，算是_____。
下个星期，我同屋要去中国留学，我们星期天一起去_____，算是给她送行 (sòng xíng, "see someone off")。
我中午吃了一个苹果，算是_____。

24. 一向/一直

Meaning: "一向"的意思是从过去一直到现在，没有时间的起点。而"一直"表示时间时，在过去的某一时间段里或从某一时间到现在，有时间的起点。

Fill in the blanks: 小张的哥哥_____不爱运动，又很喜欢吃东西，所以越来越胖。
昨天晚上他_____没回宿舍，不知道怎么了？
我_____不愿意跟不认识的人说话。
天明_____丢三落四，昨天把信用卡丢了。
上大学以后，我_____每天给妈妈打电话。
大学毕业以后，他_____在准备考研究生。
小张的哥哥性格_____开朗，大家都喜欢跟他交朋友。
王老太太_____自己理财，从不找别人帮忙。
这几年股票_____跌，房价也_____跌，真不知道该把钱投资在什么上？
那个国家_____赞成利用绿色能源，反对利用传统能源。

25. 合
Grammar: 用在单音节的动词前作副词。
Meaning: "共同"、"一起"。

Q&A Practice: 你愿意不愿意和别人合租一套公寓？
和别人合开一辆汽车对环境有好处，可是你觉得方便不方便？

Completion: 和别人合用＿＿＿＿，不卫生。
这部电影是中国和＿＿＿＿合＿＿的。

Collocation: 合用、合拍

26. 终于
Grammar: 副词。
Meaning: 表示经过一些时间和等待之后出现的情况，含有"好不容易"的意思。

Transformation: 用"终于"改写句子。
我昨天开了一个晚上夜车，今天早上5点才把历史课的功课做完。
我想选文学专业，跟我父母说了半年，他们好不容易才同意了。
我十年来省下这么多钱，现在好不容易可以买一辆车了。

27. "把"字句小结
Explanation: 在汉语语法中，动态助词"了"和"把"字句无论在语法研究上还是对外汉语教学上，都是难点。在 Level 1 中我们已经教了"把"字句。本课和第20课是对"把"字句做的小结。
句子的动词前用"把+宾语"的句子叫"把"字句，"把"是介词。"把"字句是汉语语法最难的语法结构之一。其所以难，第一，它和"主+动+宾"的句子包含同样意思。如：
　　我昨天买到了一本很有意思的书。
　　我昨天把那本很有意思的书买到了。
但是，在汉语里，有的时候必须用"把"字句，也就是说"把"字句不都是可以用"主+动+宾"的句子代替的；第二，"把"字句结构比较复杂，而且有一定的要求，学生掌握起来不那么容易。
"把"字句的结构是：
主语 + 把 + 名词 + 动词 + 其他成分(补语、了、动词重叠形式等)
在常见的"把"字句中，"把"后的名词是介词"把"的宾语，也是动词的宾语。
①外边很冷，你把这件衣服穿上吧。(把——衣服，穿——衣服)
②小李把我的车开走了。(把——车，开——车)
使用"把"字句要注意：
1) "把"的宾语必须是听话人已知的，至少是听话人可以辨识，知道指的是什么。如果你突然对一个人说：
你把那件衣服给我。那个人会不明白，会问：什么衣服/哪件衣服？

你要说：
　　你把我昨天买的那件衣服给我。那个人就明白了。
如果你说：
　　刚才我把一件衣服丢了。
听话人会明白你丢的是一件衣服，而不是裤子、鞋…，虽然不能确定你丢的是哪件衣服，但是不影响沟通。

2)"把"字句的动词后通常还有表示动作结果的补语、"了"等。这是因为某人对某物进行某个动作以后，通常会对某物产生影响，所以动词后会有表示影响结果的词语，主要是补语。如书上例(1)中的"上"，例(2)中的"走"。再如：

③考试的时候我把三个汉字写错了。（错）
④请把门关上。（上）
⑤请把这本书交给老王。（给）
⑥快把药吃了。（"了"在这里也表示结果—失去）。

动词也可以是重叠形式，出现于祈使句时，动作尚未发生，句中也没有表示结果的词语，但有缓和语气的作用。
⑦你看看我写得对不对？

如表示动作已经发生时，通常包含"把"的是一个分句，句子还没有结束：
⑧他把那本书看了看，又放下了。
结果在后面的句子中（放下）…

总之，使用"把"字句时，要注意动词后一般还有补语等成分。在第20课中我们还将继续总结"把"句。

28. 动词重叠

Explanation:
我们学过动词重叠形式，如：
①请你说说怎样才能学好中文？
②你听听，外边谁在吵架？
上面的句子是祈使句，动作尚未发生，有缓和语气的作用。
本课的动词重叠表示的动作是没有时间性的，即发生的时间不确定，表示一种经常性的动作：
③姑妈退休以后常跟过去在一起工作的老姐妹们打打麻将，聊聊天儿。
这样用的动词重叠形式通常连用几个，句子往往有"轻松"、"随便"的意味。再如：
④A: 你周末做什么？
　B: 看看电视，听听音乐，有的时候也去看电影。
⑤我妈妈已经退休了。她现在每天画画画儿，写写字，有的时候找朋友打打麻将，觉得生活很轻松。

Suggested mode of practice:

用本课故事，打出合适的图片，来引导学生练习：一般中国老人退休以后，怎么享受退休生活？
每天到公园散散步
打打太极拳
锻炼锻炼身体
跟老朋友见见面
喝喝茶/聊聊天
打打麻将

老师可带头提问，学生可个别按图片以单句/单项活动回答，接下来两两分组做问答练习。最后可检查一、两组学生，鼓励说出段落。可依样讨论美国老人退休以后，怎么享受退休生活。也可用 Language Practice A: "Happy-Go-Lucky" 做练习。

Exercises for the Main Text
主课文的练习

认读课文：可用幻灯片显示课文，让学生轮流扮演对话中的角色及其口译员。老师可用鼠标跟踪、凸显生词及难点。可借此机会纠正学生们的发音，并检查他们对所学内容的理解状况。

问答：课文认读完毕后，老师可就课文提问，以此方法来检查学生对课文的理解状况，同时可以帮助学生练习听力及口语。

Questions about the text:
- 中国改革开放以前一般人收入怎么样？
- 大家都开始用什么方法赚钱？
- 中国现在的房价怎么样？
- 炒股是什么？
- 天明和表哥在网上讨论什么话题？
- 表哥和姑妈怎么了？
- 姑妈要给表哥什么结婚礼物？
- 表哥想要什么结婚礼物？
- 表哥给姑妈讲了什么故事？
- 姑妈听了那个故事以后有什么变化？
- 姑妈突然有了什么想法？
- 跟李文父母一起打太极拳的一位老先生做了什么事？
- 买房子是不是就没有风险？
- 投资是一件简单的事吗？为什么？
- 钱存哪儿比较安全但利息太少？

Suggested Integrative Activities
综合练习活动

Speaking and Listening

1. Pair Activity: your friend is a spendthrift. He/she wants to manage his/her money better, so you sit down with him/her and try to help him/her do it. First, ask your friend some questions about his/her spending (see questions below). You may want to ask your friend to write down his/her answers.

- 你爸爸、妈妈每个月给你多少零用钱？
- 你每个月打工挣多少钱？
- 收入一共：_____ 元
- 你每个月吃饭(在学校、叫外卖)花多少钱？
- 你每个月买衣服花多少钱？
- 你每个月玩(看电影、看比赛等等)花多少钱？
- 你每个月买东西(书、碟、电脑游戏)花多少钱？
- 支出 (zhīchū, "expenses") 一共：_____ 元

Now go over the answers with your friend and see how he/she can make ends meet.

- 每个月吃饭不要超过 _____ 元。
- 每个月买衣服不要超过_____ 元。
- 每个月买东西不要超过_____ 元。
- 每个月玩不要超过_____ 元。

2. Pair Activity: how do you manage your money?

- 你一向省吃俭用还是偶尔会随便乱花钱？
- 你平常怎么省吃俭用？
- 你每个月存多少钱？
- 你把钱存在哪儿？／哪家银行？(利息多少？)
- 如果你有(剩余的)钱，你想存起来、还是想投资(股票、房地产、教育)？
- 你消费的时候，愿意把钱花在哪些方面？
- 你会找谁讨论投资理财的事？
- 如果你有一百万元，你会怎么投资？
- 如果你五年前花了三十万买了一套房子，今年卖了二十九万，你赚了还是赔了？
- 你认为什么是最好的投资？(可用 Language Practice E: "Best Ways to Invest" 辅助)

3. Brainstorm in groups.

- 昨天美国／日本／香港／上海股市涨了还是跌了？(上网查查？)
- 美国最近房价涨了还是跌了？
- 什么样的投资有风险？

- 什么样的投资风险比较高／比较低？
- 什么样的投资钱增加得比较快／比较慢？
- 你认为怎么理财没有风险？为什么？
- 你认为父母需要为子女将来的教育费担心吗？为什么？

Reading and Writing

1. Suppose you are the intended recipient of the email below. Read the message and then write a response (Interpersonal):

天明：你离开南京已经一个多月了，学习很顺利吧？有一件事想告诉你。你知道，我妈妈有一笔钱，我一直劝她买一套大一些的房子，舒舒服服地享受退休生活。她虽然考虑过投资股市，把钱留给孙子孙女，可是并没做出决定。上个星期股市一直在跌，她的一些老姐妹说现在是投资股市最好的机会，所以看来这次她真的要买股票了。我还是认为股市风险太大，可是我说服不了妈妈。我应该怎么办呢？请你说说你的看法，好吗？

表哥

2. Read the passage and answer the questions:

近几年中国的房价一直很高，而且一些城市的房价越来越高。高房价造成了一个严重的社会问题。一方面，不少人有几套房子，因为房价一直在涨，所以这些人变得越来越有钱了。另一方面，对没有房子的人来说，买房子也越来越难了。中国政府一直在想办法规定房价不能涨，希望让一般人买得起房子。可是政府也知道，如果房价跌得太快，不但那些有房子的人会抱怨，而且对中国的经济发展也没有好处。看来中国的房价真是一个很难解决的问题。

True/False:
( ) 1. Housing prices in some Chinese cities have been rising steadily in recent years.
( ) 2. According to the writer, housing prices are one of the reasons for the widening gap between the rich and the poor.
( ) 3. It is now difficult to buy a house because there are not many new houses on market.
( ) 4. The government has been trying to make housing more affordable.
( ) 5. Based on the passage, housing prices in China will drop considerably in the near future.
( ) 6. The writer offers some good suggestions for solving the problem of high housing prices in China.

Grammar and Vocabulary

1. Brainstorm related characters/words.

- Which characters in the vocabulary list have the 贝 radical?
- Which words have to do with stock and stock markets?
- Which words have to do with banking?

2. Q&A using the word 引起 with picture cues:

- 小孩一般怎么引起大人注意？　　　　　　　　（一张小孩哇哇大哭的图片）
- 日本的什么危机引起大家的重视？　　　　　　（一张日本核能电厂出事的照片）
- 中文老师怎么引起学生学中文的兴趣？　　　　（一张带学生唱歌或教学生做菜的图片）
- 最近美国经济上的什么问题引起许多人的讨论？（一张失业或房屋跌价的剪报）
- 很多石油公司想在美国找石油，会不会引起美国人的反对？（一张钻油井的照片）

3. Provide the antonyms:

- 涨←→
- 增加←→
- 赚←→

4. Fill in the blanks with the right choice.

- 我昨天一天给你打电话，可是你＿＿＿不在家。（一直、一向）
- 他＿＿＿不喜欢给人打电话，喜欢发电邮。（一直、一向）
- 今年＿＿＿涨了一百点。（股票、股市）
- 这家公司的东西没人买，昨天＿＿＿跌了50%。（股票、股市）
- 为了省钱，我想找人＿＿＿一套公寓。（合用、合买、合租）

5. You will graduate next week. Decide how you are going to dispose of your possessions using 把.

e.g. 我打算把车开回父母家。
- 我打算把电视机＿＿＿＿＿＿＿＿＿＿。
- 我想把书＿＿＿＿＿＿＿＿＿＿。
- 我想把家具＿＿＿＿＿＿＿＿＿＿。
- 我打算把自行车＿＿＿＿＿＿＿＿＿＿。
- 我想把毯子、被子＿＿＿＿＿＿＿＿＿＿。

LESSON 18

Chinese History 中国历史

Chapter Structure

- Lesson Focus
- Priorities
- Focal Themes Teaching Suggestions
- Sequencing and Suggestions for Key Grammar and Vocabulary
- Exercises for the Main Text
- Suggested Integrative Activities
  - Speaking and Listening
  - Reading and Writing
  - Grammar and Vocabulary

Lesson Focus
本课重点

本课语言功能请参考本课第一页上的学习目标。若新内容超过学生负担，应进行筛选。下面是我们的建议。

Function
1. 能说出几个中国历史上比较重要的朝代，并简单解释那些朝代为什么重要。
2. 能说出几个重要的中国历史人物，并简单说明他们为什么重要。

Priorities
取舍

如果学生对中国历史或中国历史人物无兴趣或陌生，可由美国历史、美国历史人物做类似的语言练习。

Focal Themes Teaching Suggestions
重要主题教学建议

1. 能说出几个中国历史上比较重要的朝代，并简单解释那些朝代为什么重要。

   这是语言与文化知识结合得较紧密的一课。必须两者并重。考试时，建议考虑语言与文化知识都给予计分，才能真正反映学生的学习成果。

首先可用中国历史年代简图，或课本文化点最后提供的历史年代表介绍中国几个最重要的朝代：秦、汉、唐、宋、清。让学生熟悉发音与朝代顺序。如果必要，可先复习一下第十课的中国地理，再介绍本课中国历史的内容。

接下来让学生练习简单地说一说那些朝代在历史上为什么重要。可利用 Language Practice E: "Chinese History 101" 来练习或检查。

2. 说一说中国历史上有哪些重要人物，他们为什么重要。

可让学生按文化点中提供的信息，加上 Language Practice G (b): "Be a Biographer" 的模式来介绍、说明这些历史人物。

由于语言功能的需要，学生可能会用到"…对…有(很大的)影响"、"…对…的印象很深"、"…对…有(很大的)贡献"等句式，应加强练习。

Language Practice F: "Know Your Own Country" 与学生练习本中的一些题目，都应鼓励学生上网查资料后再作答。网上也有一些跟本课所介绍的朝代与历史人物有关的短片，可播放给学生观看。有英文字幕的无妨。

Sequencing and Suggestions for Key Grammar and Vocabulary
重要语法和词汇的顺序与教学建议

> 1. 文明；2. 记载；3. 发展；4. 发明；5. 发达；6. 部分；7. 之一；8. 其中；9. 伟大；
> 10. 思想；11. 基础、在…基础上；12. 建立；13. 修；14. 统一；15. 贡献；16. 曾经；
> 17. 革命；18. 先进；19. 领导；20. 关系；21. 进行；22. 参观 vs. 游览；23. 千千万万；
> 24. 在…方面；25. 再也没/不

1. 文明
Collocation: 东方文明、西方文明、世界文明、文明小区、文明习惯

2. 记载
Character: "载"字里有"车"字，可用来帮助记忆。不同于"装载"的"载"（四声）
Grammar: 可作名词和动词。不常用，可以不练习。
More examples: 老师说，中国古代有三个好皇帝，但是他们的事情没有文字记载。（名词）
秦始皇杀读书人这件事历史书上有记载。（名词）
史书上记载了不少这样的事情。（动词）

3. **发展**
Other combinations: 发：发财

4. **发明**
Grammar: 可作名词或动词。
More examples: 电话是一个伟大的发明。(名词)
有人说 Alexander Graham Bell 发明了电话。(动词)

Q&A Practice: 你知道飞机是谁发明的吗？
你觉得二十一世纪以来最伟大的科技发明是什么？

5. **发达**
Character: 注意简体字"达"字里有"大"的声符。
More examples: 云南风景很美，所以旅游业很发达。
虽然中国的经济发展很快，但是农村经济还不很发达。
Other combinations: 发：发电、发热、发烧、出发

6. **部分**
More examples: 纽约市是纽约州的一部分。
中国是第三世界的一部分。
Other combinations: 部：北部、南部、东部、西部、中部、上部、下部

7. **之一：**
Meaning: "之一"就是"…当中的一个"。
Grammar: "之一"前面一定要有表示范围的词语，如下面的句子中的"我最喜欢的老师"、"四门课"、"最常去的国家"。
More examples: 王老师是我最喜欢的老师之一。
我这个学期选了四门课，经济是其中之一。
我爸爸常常去国外旅行，日本是他最常去的国家之一。
Usage: "之"在文言文中与结构助词"的"意思一样，书面语。
Fill in blanks: 唐朝是中国历史上最有名的＿＿＿之一。
指南针是中国历史上最有名的＿＿＿之一。
长城是中国历史上最有名的＿＿＿之一。
孔子是中国历史上最有名的＿＿＿之一。

8. **其中：**
Grammar: "其"是代词。用"其中"时，前面一定要有表示"其"的词语，如下面例句中的"很多好朋友"、"中国很多地方"、"三个大学"。
Meaning: 意思是"他/她(的)"、"那、那些"。"其中"的意思是"在那些当中"。

More examples:	我在高中有很多好朋友，其中经常给我写电子邮件的有三个人。 我去过中国很多地方旅游，其中给我印象最深的是北京和云南丽江。 高中毕业后我妹妹选了三个大学，其中她最想去的是离家最近的那个大学。

9. 伟大

Q&A Practice:	谁是美国篮球运动史上最伟大的运动员？ 谁是西方文明史上最伟大的哲学家？
Collocation:	伟大的国家、伟大的文化、伟大的领导人、伟大的贡献
Other combinations:	伟：伟人、伟绩

10. 思想

More examples:	孔子的思想在中国历史上有很大的影响。 不少人还有重男轻女的思想。
Collocation:	思想家、革命思想

11. 基础

Character:	简体字"础"字的声符为"出"。
More examples:	他在小学就开始学中文了，所以她的中文基础非常好。 这家有名的大医院是在一家很小的医院的基础上建立起来的。
Q&A Practice:	你觉得学好中文的基础是什么？
Other combinations:	基：基地、地基、基本 在…基础上
Explanation:	用在动词后或句首作状语。意思不难理解，难处在于语体和词汇都比较正式。
Q&A Practice:	有人认为应该在保护环境的基础上发展经济。你同意这个看法吗？ 有人认为夫妻之间的感情应建立在互相了解、相信的基础上，你认为呢？

12. 建立

More examples:	最近几年这个城市建立了好几个公共图书馆。 政府决定明年在这里建立一家大医院。 国家与国家之间建立良好的关系是很重要的。 很多夫妻之间的感情是慢慢建立起来的。
Q&A Practice:	中华人民共和国是哪年建立的？ 美国是哪年建立的？
Other combinations:	建：建国、建军、建设

13. 修
- Meaning: 除了建造的意思外，还有修理的意思。
- Collocation: 修鞋、修车、修路、修房子

14. 统一
- Grammar: 可作动词和形容词。
- More examples: 在中国，各个城市都统一使用北京时间。
  有的东西有好几个说法，外国人学太麻烦，我觉得应该统一起来。
- Q&A Practice: 有人说世界上应该有一种统一的语言，你同意这种意见吗？
- Collocation: 统一思想、统一文字、统一中国、国家的统一

15. 贡献
- Character: "贡"字里有"贝"的意符和"工"的声符，可用来帮助记忆。
- More examples: 中国是文明古国，应该对世界文明做出更大的贡献。
  这家公司这几年对美国经济的贡献非常大。

16. 曾经
- More examples: 我曾经去过中国两次，但是这两年没去。
  过去我曾经对南京很熟悉，可是我对现在的南京感到很陌生。
  这家公司的电脑技术曾经发展到了很高的水平，但是现在被别的公司超过了。

17. 革命
- Collocation: 法国革命、美国革命、文化大革命
- Other combinations: 革：改革、革新
  命：生命、人命

18. 先进
- More examples: 这家公司的电脑技术是很先进的，所以很多公司都学他们的技术。
  这是世界上最先进的汽车，非常节约能源。
- Q&A Practice: 你觉得哪个国家的工业最先进？
- Collocation: 先进国家、先进技术、先进工作者
- Other combinations: 进：后进

19. 领导
- Grammar: 可作动词或名词。
  George Washington 领导人民 (people) 建立了美国。
  如果没有孙中山的领导，就不会有中华民国。
  我希望以后工作的时候，有一个好领导。
- Other combinations: 领：领子、领带、白领、蓝领
  导：导游、导航、导师

20. 跟…有关系

Collocation:	师生关系➔老师和学生的关系；父子关系➔父亲与儿子的关系
More examples:	科学家认为天气变暖跟环境污染有关系。
	她昨天考试没考好跟她上个星期生病有关系。
Meaning:	练习"…跟…有关系"时，除了注意句式外，也必须注意语意，否则学生可能会说出"汉朝跟丝绸之路有关系"这样的句子。
Q&A Practice:	一个人身体健康不健康跟生活或工作压力有没有关系？
	睡眠好不好跟心情有没有关系？
Fill in blanks:	健康跟____有很大的关系。
	大城市的空气污染跟_____有关系。

21. 进行

Usage:	书面语，动词。
More examples:	中国和美国对贸易问题进行了多次讨论。
	张教授对这个哲学问题进行了二十年的研究。
Transformation:	按上面例句模式，用"进行"改写下面的句子：
	美国政府多次讨论了移民问题。 ➔
	马教授研究过人口问题。 ➔

22. 参观 vs. 游览

Explanation:	"参观"一般带有学习的目的，而"游览"的对象更多的是名胜古迹。
Q&A Practice:	你的老家可以游览的地方多不多？
	你参观过什么博物馆？
Fill in blanks with the right word:	我想____中国的大学，看看他们的太阳能研究。
	去年夏天，我们____了长城和云南石林。

23. 千千万万

Grammar:	形容词，多作定语。
Related:	成千上万 (tens of thousands)

24. 在…方面

Q&A Practice:	你这个学期在哪方面取得了成绩？
	你的老家在饮食方面有什么特色？（你老家在哪方面--建筑、音乐、风景--很有特色？）
	你认为学校在保护环境方面还可以做哪些事情？

25. 再也没/不

Grammar:	用于否定句。

Completion: 那家饭馆的菜＿＿＿＿，我以后再也不去了。
我觉得我网球比我的同屋打得好多了，没想到昨天比赛我竟然＿＿＿＿＿＿。我以后再也不那么骄傲了。
我小时候去过一次＿＿＿＿＿＿＿＿，以后再也没去过。
有一年她爸爸的生日，她忘了＿＿＿＿＿＿＿＿＿，后来再也没＿＿＿＿＿＿＿＿＿＿。

Exercises for the Main Text
主课文的练习

认读课文：可用幻灯片显示课文，让学生轮流扮演对话中的角色及其口译员。老师可用鼠标跟踪、凸显生词及难点。可借此机会纠正学生们的发音，并检查他们对所学内容的理解状况。

问答：课文认读完毕后，老师可就课文提问，以此方法来检查学生对课文的理解状况，同时可以帮助学生练习听力及口语。

Questions about the text:
- 李文在哪儿工作？
- 中国国家博物馆在哪儿？
- 李文给大家介绍了哪几个朝代？其中你认为哪一个朝代最重要？为什么重要？
- 李文给大家介绍了哪几个有名、重要的历史人物？其中你认为哪一位最重要？他为什么重要？
- 中国有文字记载的历史有多长？
- 孔子是什么人？
- 世界上有多少孔子学院？
- 中国第一个统一的朝代是哪一个朝代？
- 请问，秦朝是从什么时候到什么时候，有多少年历史？
- 中国的第一个皇帝是谁？
- 秦始皇做了什么好事？什么坏事？
- 秦始皇有什么贡献？
- 什么跟汉朝有关系？
- 唐朝为什么重要？
- 宋朝有什么发明？
- 中国有哪四大发明？
- 中国最后一个朝代是哪一个朝代？
- 中国没有朝代，没有皇帝了以后，建立了什么？

Suggested Integrative Activities
综合练习活动

Speaking and Listening

1. Pair work: Jeopardy. Given the key word, try to come up with the right questions:

Key word   Example of possible questions
- 李白   唐朝最有名的诗人是谁？
- 孙中山   领导革命，建立中华民国的是谁？
- 秦始皇   杀读书人，烧古书，修长城的皇帝是谁？
- 孔子   中国最伟大的教育家／思想家是谁？
- 汉朝   由丝绸之路开始跟西方进行贸易的是哪一个朝代？
- 唐朝   历史上文化经济很发达，有很多外国留学生的朝代是哪一个朝代？
- 清朝   中国最后一个朝代是哪一个朝代？
- 宋朝   活字印刷是哪一个朝代发明的？

2. Presentation: "My most memorable visit to a historical site." Describe the details of the visit and tell everybody why it was so memorable. You can use pictures to accompany your presentation.

3. Group discussion: which Chinese dynasty would you have enjoyed living in the most? Why? Designate one person to present the group's preference.

Reading and Writing

1. Suppose you are the intended recipient of the email below. Read the message and then write a response (Interpersonal):

爸爸，您好。上个周末我们去了西安，看到了有名的兵马俑。我记得您说过，秦始皇让千千万万的老百姓修长城，死了很多人。他还杀了不少读书人，烧了很多古书。可能是因为他做了太多的坏事，所以他才会觉得需要那么多兵马俑保护他的坟墓。您说是不是这样？可是我们的老师说，秦始皇对统一中国有很大的贡献，中国文字的统一也跟他有很大的关系。您说他到底算是好皇帝还是坏皇帝？

天明

2. Read the passage and answer the questions:

很多中国人一说到中国的历史，就会提到四大发明。可是四大发明是好几百年前的事了。中国的科学技术确实曾经发展到一个很高的水平，可是几百年来中国在科学技术上的进步并不大。我们现在生活中一些最重要的东西，电话、火车、汽车、飞机、电脑什么的，都不是中国人发明的。中国是一个有五千年历史的文明古国，应该对世界做出更大的贡献。今天的中国人不应该还在为四大发明感到骄傲了。

True/False:
( ) 1. According to the writer, Chinese people often bring up the Four Great Inventions when talking about Chinese history.
( ) 2. According to the writer, China has made remarkable progress in science and technology since the era of the Four Great Inventions.
( ) 3. The writer does not think that the Four Great Inventions have a big impact on modern life.
( ) 4. The writer believes that China, as a nation with a long history, has made great contributions to the world in terms of science and technology.
( ) 5. Significant as the Four Great Inventions were, they are no longer inventions that modern Chinese people should feel proud of.

3. Put the following dynasties in the right chronological order:

元、汉、清、秦、宋、唐、明

4. Use the following template to begin writing a short bio of a historical figure:

- 他的名字是_____。
- 他是_____国人。
- 他是_____年在_____出生的。
- 他是一个有名的_____家。
- 他对_____做出了很大的贡献。
- ....
- ....
- ....

Grammar and Vocabulary

1. Match the verb with the right object.

- 选   古书
- 杀   历史
- 修   人
- 烧   课
- 记载   博物馆 / 工厂 / 学校 / 公司
- 参观   长城/宫殿/坟墓/车
- 游览   景点/名胜古迹
- 统一   文字/国家
- 发展   国家 / 学院 / 学校
- 领导   经济
- 发明   火药 / 活字印刷 / 指南针 / 造纸的技术
- 建立   革命
- 进行   贸易

2. Come up with a positive attribute (adj.) for the following nouns (高、发达、先进、悠久, etc.):

   - 水平 _____
   - 技术 _____
   - 经济 _____
   - 贸易 _____
   - 文化 _____
   - 历史 _____

3. Come up with at least two compound words for each of the following dynasties:

   秦、汉、唐、宋、明

4. Come up with at least two compound words for each of the following word elements:

   - ___朝
   - ___代
   - ___子 (famous historical figures)
   - ___家 (person with a special expertise)
   - 发___
   - 古___

5. Completion:

   - _____国的历史有_____长。
   - 中国历史上最有名的教育家是_____。
   - 中国历史上最有名的哲学家是_____。
   - _____是一个伟大的发明。
   - _____是_____之一。

LESSON 19

Interviewing for a Job   面试

Chapter Structure

- **Lesson Focus**
- **Priorities**
- **Focal Themes Teaching Suggestions**
- **Sequencing and Suggestions for Key Grammar and Vocabulary**
- **Exercises for the Main Text**
- **Suggested Integrative Activities**
  - Speaking and Listening
  - Reading and Writing
  - Grammar and Vocabulary

Lesson Focus
本课重点

本课语言功能请参考第一页上的学习目标。若本课新内容超过学生负担，应进行筛选。下面是我们的建议。

Function
1. 面试的经验和注意事项。
2. 能简单地解释为什么中国能吸引大家到中国去工作、投资。
3. 能谈谈自己紧张时会怎么样？会不会安排时间？个人的一些优点、缺点。
4. 能恭喜别人毕业、找到工作。

Priorities
取舍

如果学生负担太重，在不影响达成语言功能的前提下，可不练习"学有所成"等词语。

Focal Themes Teaching Suggestions
重要主题教学建议

1. 当学到本课时，大多学校学年都将结束，应届毕业生可能因为申请学校或找工作而需要面试。让学生练习说说自己是否面试过，面试时是否紧张，紧张的时候会怎么样。接下来扩展到面试时应该注意什么。

a. 你曾经面试过吗？面试的时候，紧张不紧张？/面试的时候会不会紧张？
b. 你紧张的时候会怎么样？（出汗；脸红；说话越说越快，越说越不清楚…）（如果简单句掌握了，可增加难度用补语练习：我紧张得会出汗/脸红／说话越说越快…。亦可用 Language Practice F: "Nerve Racking Interview" 做扩展。
c. 面试的时候应该注意什么？

面试以前，准备一下面试可能会问的问题；
上网查该/那个公司的资料，了解其历史与产品；
面试的时候，应该注意服装，穿西装／套装／正式的服装，别穿T恤衫、牛仔裤；
应该注意说话清楚、客气，态度好，别太严肃，别乱开玩笑，别随便笑；
别忘了问一、两个跟工作有关的问题；
面试结束的时候，别忘了跟面试你的人握手，谢谢他/她。

2. 简单地说说为什么中国吸引了那么多海外人材和跨国公司。

   可先引导学生说出：最近几年以来中国经济高速发展［动词］/有很大的发展［名词］。

   可用幻灯打出一些跨国公司名，练习说 "XX 公司是一家跨国公司，已经进入中国市场。"

   可由个人切入，作以下问答：

   XX 公司在美国有没有分公司？会吸引你去工作吗？

   什么样的公司可能会吸引你去工作？（工资高，不累，机会多，假期多，环境好，分股票，有退休计划/健康保险…）跟此话题有关的问题：

   a. 你希望将来在什么样的公司工作？（小公司、大公司、跨国公司）
   b. 你觉得哪一方面的工作(比较)适合你？（管理、金融、贸易、销售、电脑、科学技术、翻译、教育…方面）
   c. 什么样的工作环境才会让你满意？

3. 可复习第九课来简单地说说自己怎么安排时间。然后扩展到让学生谈谈自己的优、缺点。

   a. 你有什么优点？（我的优点是：性格开朗，对人态度好，愿意帮助别人，很会安排时间，听父母的话…）
   b. 你有什么缺点？（我的缺点是：懒，丢三拉四，忘这忘那，不会安排时间…）

4. 从复习第十一课过年过节的祝贺，过渡到怎么恭喜别人毕业了，找到工作了…。可利用 Language Practice H: "I'm So Happy for You" 辅助。

Sequencing and Suggestions for Key Grammar and Vocabulary
重要语法和词汇的顺序与教学建议

> 1. 干吗；2. 严肃；3. 可怕；4. 吓人；5. 解释；6. 通知；7. 回答；8. 短期；9. 满意；
> 10. 吸引；11. 优秀；12. 优点；13. 缺点；14. 能力；15. 善于；16. 好在；17. 零食；
> 18. 叫做；19. 进入；20. 因此；21. 既然；22. 纷纷；23. 往往 vs. 常常；24. 又；
> 25. 越⋯越⋯

1. 干吗
Chinese gloss:	为什么。另有一意思是"做什么"。
Usage:	口语，有地域性。
More examples:	你家不在纽约，干吗一放假就去纽约？
	你在美国已经找到工作了，干吗还要申请那家中国公司？
	你周末都干吗？不是待在家里上网吧？

2. 严肃
More examples:	那位总经理看起来很严肃，其实是个很幽默的人。
	别开玩笑了，这是个严肃的问题，我们要好好讨论讨论。

3. 可怕
More examples:	只要你不紧张，面试其实并不可怕。
	如果你只看到自己的优点，看不到自己的缺点，后果是很可怕的。
Other combinations:	可：可爱、可口、可笑、可气

4. 吓人
Character:	注意简体字声符"下"。
More examples:	我觉得面试很吓人，一想到明天的面试我就紧张得出汗。
	A: 听说今年百分之五十的大学毕业生都还没找到工作。
	B: 别说得那么吓人，我认识的大学毕业生都找到工作了。

5. 解释
Grammar:	可作动词或名词。
More examples:	无论我怎么解释，她还是不理解我为什么要回中国工作。（动词）
	我说了半天，可是他对我的解释一点儿也不满意。（名词）
Q&A Practice:	你觉得老师解释语法解释得清楚吗？
Other combinations:	解：解题、解答

6. 通知
   Grammar: 可作名词和动词。
   More examples: 我昨天接到公司的通知,让我去当销售部经理。(名词)
   我上个星期去一家跨国公司面试,可是昨天他们通知我,公司已经录用了别人。(动词)
   Other combinations: 通：通告

7. 回答
   More examples: 请你回答这个问题。
   我回答了她的两个问题,可是她对我的回答不太满意。
   Other combinations: 答：答题、答话、答谢、答复

8. 短期
   Collocation: 短期工作、短期计划、短期发展
   期：长期、星期、学期、期中、期间

9. 满意
   More examples: 老师说我最近的学习进步很快,可是我自己不满意。
   小李最近在一家跨国公司找到了工作,可是她对那儿的工作环境不太满意。
   你连这么好的车都不喜欢,什么样的车才会让你满意?
   Q&A Practice: 你对你的中文学习成绩满意吗?
   你对你这个学期的成绩满意吗?
   Other combinations: 满：不满、自满、满月

10. 吸引
    More examples: 这座美丽的城市每年都吸引很多游客。
    这个大学不太有名,可是因为学费便宜,吸引了很多外国留学生。
    这家跨国公司吸引了很多大学毕业生来工作。
    Q&A Practice: 哪方面的工作最能吸引你?教育方面、金融方面还是科技方面?
    Other combinations: 吸：吸气、吸管、吸收
    引：引导、引领、引入

11. 优秀
    More examples: 五年以后,雪梅一定会成为一位优秀的销售经理。
    同事们都认为王老师是一位优秀的经济学教授。
    Collocation: 优秀学生、优秀教师、优秀职工
    Other combinations: 优：优良、全优、优等生

12. 优点
More examples: 他的缺点是经验不够，优点是善于科学地安排自己的时间。
他最大的优点就是能看到自己的缺点。

Q&A Practice: 你最大的优点是什么？

13. 缺点
More examples: 每个人都有缺点，没有缺点的人世界上是找不到的。
她觉得自己长得太美了，没有缺点，所以骄傲得不得了。

Q&A Practice: 你最大的缺点是什么？

14. 能力
More examples: 我觉得公司没有录用他，不是因为他没有能力，而是因为他面试的时候表现不太好。
他虽然很有能力，可是有点儿骄傲，所以总经理对他不太满意。

Other combinations: 能：风能、电能、水能、太阳能
力：用力、给力

15. 善于
Meaning: "善"是好的意思，"于"是"在"；意思为：good at, to excel in。
Usage: 书面语。
Grammar: 后接动词。

Q&A Practice: 你善于投资理财吗？
你善于和别人打交道吗？
你善于适应新的环境吗？

16. 好在
Meaning: Fortunately, luckily；不是 good at。见"善于"。
Grammar: 后接分句。
Completion: 那台电脑很贵，好在_____，他不在乎。
他的车坏了，好在明天_____。
我的现金不够，好在_____。

17. 零食
More examples: 他爱吃零食，所以饭吃得不多。
每次离开家，妈妈都给我准备一些零食。

Q&A Practice: 什么东西是零食？
常常吃零食对身体健康有没有好处？

Other combinations: 零：零钱、零花钱、零用钱

18. 叫做

Explanation: 课本 290 页列了三种句型：
什么被叫做 (something or somebody is called)，
把什么叫做 (call something or somebody something)，
什么叫做 (something is called)。
"什么叫做"和"什么被叫做"用法不完全相同。第三个例句：Peanut 在中国南方的有的地方叫/叫做"土豆"，北方叫/叫做"花生"，这个句子用"叫做"和"叫"都可以，一般不大说"被叫做…"。但如果是一种比喻的说法，而不是名称/名字，则一般要用"被"，如下面翻译练习的第二个句子，"海南被叫做中国的夏威夷"。本课要练习的也正是这种句子。
"什么叫做"的意思就是"什么叫"，只不过更正式。这种句子比较简单，练习几个名称就可以了。

Q&A Practice: 人们把从海外归来的留学生叫做什么？
你知道为什么很多中国孩子被叫做"小皇帝"吗？

Translate: The Chinese call Hainan "China's Hawaii (夏威夷)".
Hainan is called "China's Hawaii."

19. 进入

Character: 注意"入"跟"人"的区别。
Composition: "进"和"入"意思相同，后者为文言。
More examples: 进入新世纪以来，中国经济发展很快。
雪梅收到那家公司的录用通知，进入了国际销售部工作。
Other combinations: 入：入学、入口、入门、入手

20. 因此

Chinese gloss: 因为这样，连词。
More examples: 雪梅的父母都在中国，因此她对中国的工作特别感兴趣。
小王以前从来没有面试过，因此今天面试的时候有点儿紧张。
雪梅申请的是经理的工作，因此面试的时间特别长。
Completion: _____，因此他不申请那个工作了。
妈妈来电话说爸爸突然得了很重的病，因此_____。
Other combinations: 此：此人、此时、此地

21. 既然

Explanation: 连词，用于第一个分句，提出已经知道的前提(情况、原因等)，后一分句是由此得出的结论。
①A: 我爸爸一定叫我上医学院，可是我不喜欢跟病人打交道。
　B: 既然这样，你就应该跟你爸爸解释清楚，他应该尊重你的选择。
②A: 你知道吗？明天面试的老师不能来，我们不用去学校了。
　B: 既然明天不面试了，咱们去海边玩吧。

More examples:	既然你是班上最好的学生，干吗考试那么紧张？
	既然那家公司没有录用我，我只好申请别的工作。
Completion:	既然你们没有时间，＿＿＿＿＿＿。
	既然＿＿＿＿＿＿，那我们就不去了吧。
	既然 vs. 因为
	"因为"也有表示原因的意思，但当原因是前面已经提起过的，是已知的时候，不宜用"因为"，上面两个句子中的"既然"就不宜换成"因为"。
	③因为你不是我们学校的学生，所以不能参加我们的表演。
	这个句子里的"因为"也不能用"既然"替换。

22. 纷纷

Character:	注意声符"分"。
More examples:	开学了，大学生纷纷回到了学校。
	今天是中国新年，大家纷纷给朋友打电话拜年。

23. 往往 vs. 常常

Explanation:	前者指概率或倾向，后者指频率。有时能互换，有时不能，见课本292–293页。
Q&A Practice:	常常运动的人，身体往往比较健康。你同意吗？
	善于投资理财的人，往往对世界各国经济的发展有兴趣，你也常常注意世界经济发展吗？
Fill in blanks:	请你＿＿＿跟我联系。
	中国北方人＿＿＿比南方人高。

24. 又

Explanation:	加强否定的语气，往往针对某种想法或说法。
More examples:	别等他了，他又没说一定来。（针对听话人以为"他会来"）
	别买这么不好的家具，你又不是没有钱。
	A: 你看，为了给你们攒学费，你爸爸投资的钱又减了不少。
	B: 这不是我们的错，又不是我们叫他买那个股票。

25. 越…越…

Explanation:	表示程度上后一个情况随前一个情况变化。
More examples:	那些女孩们在一起聊天，越说越高兴，一直到吃饭还不想走。
	姐姐决定下个星期结婚，妈妈越想越怕，怕姐夫以后对姐姐不好。
	考试的时候，我老担心时间不够，可是越着急越想不起来该怎么回答。

Translate into English then back into Chinese
1. 水果越甜越好吃。
2. 雨越下越大。
3. 诗他越写越好。
4. 零食越吃越想吃。
5. 她这身套装自己越看越满意。
6. "了"这个语法点老师越解释学生越不懂。
7. 股票跌得越多，炒股的人越紧张。

Exercises for the Main Text
主课文的练习

认读课文：可用幻灯片显示课文，让学生轮流扮演对话中的角色及其口译员。老师可用鼠标跟踪、凸显生词及难点。可借此机会纠正学生们的发音，并检查他们对所学内容的理解状况。

问答：课文认读完毕后，老师可就课文提问，以此方法来检查学生对课文的理解状况，同时可以帮助学生练习听力及口语。

Questions about the text:
- 为什么中国吸引了那么多世界各地的人材？
- "海归"是什么人？
- 林雪梅为什么也是海龟？
- 林雪梅为什么回中国工作？
- 雪梅怎么找工作？
- 她申请了哪个公司的工作？
- 她申请了什么职位？
- 她穿什么衣服去面试？为什么？
- 是谁面试她的？
- 为什么雪梅面试的时候她的套装上衣都湿了？
- 那两张纸是什么？
- 雪梅说她为什么想回中国工作？
- 丽莎开玩笑地说雪梅的缺点是什么？
- 雪梅认为自己的缺点是什么？
- 为什么丽莎对雪梅说"恭喜你，林经理！"？
- 一个优秀的管理人才应该能怎么样？
- 雪梅得到那个职位了吗？

Suggested Integrative Activities
综合练习活动

Speaking and Listening

1. Pair work: brainstorm job interview questions.

2. Pair work: brainstorm the best answers to each job interview question from above.

3. Mock job interview: form two groups. One student from each group takes turns conducting the mock interview. Others observe and rate the performance.

将全班分成两组：一组为面试官，一组为应试者。每组成员贡献自己认为进行面试所应注意事项。讨论到一段落，各组派出一名组员进行面试模拟。如此轮流换人模拟进行四、五次。进行过程中，其他学生可评估各个面试官、应试者的表现如何，最后可从发音、词汇、语法与表演各个方面评分投票选出最佳面试官与应试者。

4. My most memorable interview: tell the class a story about your most memorable interview. Be sure to include the following information:

   a. Location, time;
   b. Who the interviewer was;
   c. Job interviewed for;
   d. What you wore;
   e. How you felt;
   f. What the hardest questions were to answer;
   g. Which questions you answered the best;
   h. The results

Reading and Writing

1. Suppose you are the intended recipient of the email below. Read the message and then write a response (Interpersonal):

雪梅：我先恭喜你面试成功，找到了自己喜欢的工作。我昨天也收到了通知，要我下个星期三去面试。这虽然不是我第一次面试，可是以前两次都是小公司，而这次是一家有名的跨国公司，所以我特别紧张。您已经很有经验了，能不能告诉我应该怎样准备这次面试？我特别担心他们会问我为什么要回中国工作，我觉得这个问题很难回答。另外，如果他们让我问几个问题，我应该问些什么问题呢？你能帮帮我吗？

小红

2. Read the passage and answer the questions:

一般来说，找工作的时候都会有一次面试，面试时的表现往往能决定自己能不能拿到录用通知。面试的时候应该注意哪些事情呢？我认为最重要的是做好准备，上网查资料，多了解那家公司的情况，特别是总经理的情况。另外就是在面试时尽可能地介绍自己，特别是多让他们了解自己的优点和能力。你去参加面试就好比去销售一个产品，那个产品就是你自己。没有人会在完全了解这个产品以前花钱买它的。

True/False:

( ) 1. The writer thinks that a person's job interview performance is often the decisive factor in getting a job offer.
( ) 2. The writer believes that the interviewee should get to know the potential employer as much as possible before the interview.
( ) 3. The writer suggests that the general manager usually plays a crucial role in the employment decision.
( ) 4. The writer thinks that the interviewee should not brag about her strengths and abilities.
( ) 5. The writer suggests that the interviewee should demonstrate how to sell the employing company's products.
( ) 6. According to the writer, if the interviewee wishes to know a product thoroughly then she should buy it first.

3. Go online and find some job ads by searching the keywords 诚聘 (chéngpìn, "earnestly hire=help wanted")、待优 (dàiyōu, "compensation")、etc. Answer the following questions after reading the ads:

- Who is hiring?
- What is the job being advertised?
- What is the compensation?
- What are the qualifications?

4. "Nail that interview!": In small groups, collectively write a 'how to' pamphlet for job interviews.

将学生分组，每小组讨论面试前应该做的准备以及面试时应该注意的事情。讨论到一阶段，让各小组列出一份面试"教战手册"，呈现给全班。也可鼓励学生画插画使手册更加增色。此活动可分多次渐进式进行，每小组也可有机会修改或借由小组的启发，学生回家各自做出自己的成品，再交由老师检查。

Grammar and Vocabulary

1. Review measure words. The teacher/a student says the noun out loud to elicit the right measure word.

- 一只海龟/狗/猫/熊猫
- 一只鞋
- 一双鞋/筷子
- 一片海洋

- 一片树林
- 一件衣服/毛衣/衬衫/旗袍
- 一套西装
- 一身套装
- 一份工作
- 一辆(自行)车
- 一笔钱
- 一瓶水
- 三顿饭
- 一条河
- 一段路
- 一段时间

2. Fill in the blanks with the right word (既然、因为、因此、往往、常常、纷纷).

- 西方人＿＿＿不会用筷子。
- 他找到了工作，朋友们＿＿＿给他打电话恭喜他。
- 他很幽默，＿＿＿开玩笑。
- ＿＿＿你不喜欢这个工作，就再找一个别的工作吧。
- ＿＿＿他常常熬夜，所以它觉睡得不够。
- 他想了解那个公司的情况，＿＿＿就上网去查。

3. Explain in Chinese.

- 海归：
- 优点：
- 缺点：
- 套装：
- 优秀：

4. Paraphrase in Chinese (clues: 阴、多云、晴).

- 从严肃变高兴，可以说脸上"＿＿＿＿＿"了。
- 从高兴变严肃，可以说脸上"＿＿＿＿＿"了。

LESSON 20

Foreigners in China 外国人在中国

Chapter Structure

- Lesson Focus
- Priorities
- Focal Themes Teaching Suggestions
- Sequencing and Suggestions for Key Grammar and Vocabulary
- Exercises for the Main Text
- Suggested Integrative Activities
  - Speaking and Listening
  - Reading and Writing
  - Grammar and Vocabulary

Lesson Focus
本课重点

本课语言功能请参考本课第一页上的学习目标。若新内容超过学生负担，应进行筛选。下面是我们的建议。

Function
1. 能简单叙述适应新生活时所经历的困难。
2. 能在新来乍到的情况下，客气地向有经验的友人或前辈寻求帮助与照顾。
3. 能筹划各种聚会。
4. 能在接风或饯行的聚会场合说出适当的欢迎或送行语言。

Priorities
取舍

本课语言功能着重于学生能否在不同的聚会场合，说出适宜的语言。课文内容许多为复习。如果学生负担太重，可不练习"面熟、流、而已、不仅、众人"等词语。

Focal Themes Teaching Suggestions
重要主题教学建议

1. 简单叙述适应新生活时所经历的困难：

a. 你在中国生活习惯吗？你觉得你很快就适应了中国的生活吗？
（对在美国的外国留学生以及中国来的老师：已经适应美国的生活了吗？融入美国社会了吗？）
如果学生没有出国的经验，则可多练习学生可能比较熟悉的情况。如，你已经适应大学／学校宿舍／这个城市的生活了吗？

b. 很多留学生在中国，一边学习，一边打工，他们大多做什么工作？（翻译、家教）

可用 Language Practice F: "Foreigners in China" 做扩展。并可联系学生在美国半工半读的经历。

2. 如何在新来乍到的情况下，客气地向有经验的友人或前辈寻求帮助与照顾（请多关照；麻烦多照顾）。如以下这些场合：

刚到一个新地方／公司
刚搬到一个新城市，交了新朋友
刚到新公司上班，看到新同事
第一天到公司上班，看到总经理

可用 Language Practice D: "Being a Newcomer" 做辅助。

3. 能筹划各种聚会。由复习学过的带出本课生词：

跟谁聚会？（家人、朋友、同学、同事…）

为什么聚会？（周末，过生日，过年/过节；庆祝X毕业／找到工作／考上研究生／拿到学位／面试成功／退休；给人接风/饯行…）

在哪儿聚会（比较合适）？（家、宿舍、学生活动中心、小区活动中心、公园、餐馆、火锅店、快餐店、咖啡馆儿…）

聚会的时候做什么？／怎么庆祝？（聚餐、吃火锅、唱卡拉OK、跳舞、爬山、喝茶、聊天、打麻将…；先…再…）

在家聚会的时候准备点儿什么？（饮料、零食、水果、火锅、音乐、游戏、［叫］外卖…）（也可复习一年级第14课内容）

聚会的时候说什么？以茶代酒，举起杯来，为x干杯／祝x／恭喜x；太棒了，真为你高兴。

可用 Language Practice C: "It's Party Time!" 做阶段练习。

4. 在一些聚会场合说出适宜得体的话，包括以下这些场合：

给人过生日
庆祝别人毕业
庆祝别人找到工作
给人接风/饯行

可用 Language Practice E: "What to Say?" 做辅助。

Sequencing and Suggestions for Key Grammar and Vocabulary
重要语法和词汇的顺序与教学建议

> 1. 聚会；2. 庆祝；3. 接风；4. 接受；5. 饯行；6. 客人；7. 面熟；8. 关照；9. 搞；
> 10. 出差；11. 流；12. 值得；13. 年轻；14. 不仅；15. 放心；16. 友谊；17. 永远；
> 18. 稳定；19. 联系；20. 而已；21. 在…一下；22. 你说呢？；23. 汉语的语序

1. 聚会

Character:	注意"聚"字的声符为"取"。
More examples:	下个月我跟我以前的同事有个聚会。
	昨天晚上十几位中国留学生在这家中国餐馆聚会。
Other combinations:	聚：聚餐

2. 庆祝

More examples:	你找到工作了，我们应该好好庆祝庆祝。
	雪梅去欧洲出差，推销了很多太阳能热水器，我们今天晚上要聚会，庆祝她的成功。
Q&A Practice:	中国人庆祝哪些传统节日？
Other combinations:	庆：国庆、庆功、欢庆

3. 接风

More examples:	雪梅昨天刚从欧洲回来，王太太今天要开晚会，给雪梅接风。
	今天又来了五位中国留学生，这个周末中国同学会要给他们接风。
	送行的饺子、接风的面。
Other combinations:	接：接球、接机、接电话、接手

4. 接受

Character:	注意"受"字不同"爱"。
Q&A Practice:	你是在哪儿接受的中学教育？
	老师应该不应该接受学生的礼物？

	如果天气很好，老师会不会接受我们的建议到外面去上课？
	你会不会接受很有意思但不太稳定的工作？
Collocation:	接受建议、接受教育、接受意见、接受他/她。
Other combinations:	受：受教育、受礼、受苦、受累、受气

5. 饯行

Character:	注意"饯"字跟"钱"字的区别。两字的声符相同，但"饯"中的形符为"饣"。
More examples:	李哲下个星期要去中国实习了，李哲的哥哥和嫂子请他吃饭，为他饯行。
	今天的晚饭我请客。你要出差了，这顿饭就算是给你饯行吧。
Other combinations:	行：行人、出行、送行、衣食住行、行走

6. 客人

Character:	注意"客"字的声符为"各"。
More examples:	王太太为今天的聚会准备了很多吃的东西，可是来的客人并不多。
	你是我们的客人，怎么能让你洗碗呢？
Other combinations:	客：旅客、贵客、客气、客套

7. 面熟

Pronunciation:	注意"熟"字读 shóu 或 shú。
More examples:	我觉得你很面熟，可是想不起来在哪儿见过你。
	难怪我见到她就觉得面熟，原来我们十年前上的是同一个中学。
Other combinations:	面：面生、见面、面具、面子
	熟：熟悉、熟人、熟食、熟路

8. 关照

Chinese gloss:	关心照顾
More examples:	李哲的哥哥是总经理的朋友，所以李哲得到了总经理的特别关照。
	我工作经验不多，请您多关照。
Other combinations:	关：关心、关注、关爱
	照：照顾、照管

9. 搞

Character:	注意"搞"字中的声符"高"。
Usage:	相当口语化，而且大陆用得比较多。
More examples:	他来我们公司二十年了，一直搞销售工作。
	对不起，我是搞电影的，不懂经济学。
	我们不但要把自己的工作搞好，而且要帮助别人的工作。

10. 出差
- **Pronunciation:** 注意在"出差"这个词里"差"字读 chāi。
- **More examples:**
  - 李哲差不多每个星期都要出差,所以常常不在家。
  - 因为他常常为公司出差,所以到过很多地方。
- **Q&A Practice:**
  - 做哪一方面的工作必须经常出差?
  - 你觉得出差跟出门旅游的感觉一样吗?
- **Other combinations:** 差:差事、美差

11. 流
- **More examples:**
  - 弟弟在高中的学习成绩非常好,有希望考上一流的大学。
  - 姑妈的病很严重,怎么能送她去二流的医院呢?我们要送她去最好的医院。
- **Other combinations:** 流:上流、下流、三教九流、不入流

12. 值得
- **Character:** 注意"值"字中的声符"直"。
- **More examples:**
  - 云南是个美丽的地方,值得去看看。
  - 那个问题太简单了,不值得我们花时间讨论。
- **Other combinations:** 值:价值、物有所值、物超所值、面值

13. 年轻
- **Character:** 注意"轻"字中的声符同"经"字。
- **More examples:**
  - 舅妈每天都练习瑜伽,所以显得很年轻。
  - 美国的历史只有两百多年,是个年轻的国家。
- **Other combinations:**
  - 年:年青、年老、年长 (zhǎng)、年事已高
  - 轻:轻重、轻音乐、轻视

14. 不仅
- **Chinese gloss:** 不但。"不但"比"不仅"更口语化。
- **More examples:**
  - 他来中国两年了,不仅习惯了中国的生活,而且已经融入了中国的社会。
  - 丽莎在李文家住了三个月,不仅跟李文学会了做不少中国菜,也跟李文的父母学会了太极拳。

15. 放心
- **Character:** 注意"放"字中的声符"方"。
- **More examples:**
  - 我本来有些担心自己推销热水器没经验,既然李经理跟我一起出差,我就放心了。
  - 雪梅成为销售部经理,总经理因此对公司的销售工作很放心。
  - 小王高中毕业后出国去上大学,爸爸妈妈有一点儿不放心。
- **Other combinations:** 心:用心、小心、担心、上心

16. 友谊
More examples: 我虽然明天就要回国了，但是我永远不会忘记我们的友谊。
他在中国留学两年，跟一些中国朋友建立了很深的友谊，回到美国后还常常跟他们联系。

Other combinations: 友：友人、友情、友好、友爱、好友、老友

17. 永远
More examples: 这里的人对我太好了，我永远不会忘记。
很多女孩子希望自己永远年轻、美丽。

Other combinations: 永：永生、永别

18. 稳定
More examples: 表姐的工资不高，但工作很稳定。
钱先生和钱太太结婚好几年了，可是感情还是不太稳定。
这几年我们这个城市的经济发展不太快，不过很稳定。

19. 联系
More examples: 高中毕业快十年了，可是同学之间的关系还很近，联系很多。
大学毕业以后，他就很少跟同学们联系了。

Q&A Practice: 你平常怎么跟朋友联系？打电话、发短信、还是写电邮？
你还跟中学同学联系吗？

Collocation: 联系电话、联系人

20. 而已
Usage: 书面语，"no more than"。口语中用得较多。
Completion: 开车到那里不远，只要____而已。
做凉拌菜很快，只需要____而已。
我们只是_____而已，不是男朋友女朋友。
我只是说说而已，你不必接受我的_____。

21. 在…下：表示条件
在…的帮助下，
在…的领导下，
在…的指导下，
在…安排下，
在…劝说下（quànshuō 意思同"劝"）
需要连同后边的动词一起记。

22. 你说呢?

Chinese gloss: "你觉得呢？""你怎么看？"

Q&A Practice: 我建议今年夏天我们去墨西哥旅游。你说呢？
他觉得做销售太累。你说呢？
我觉得炒股风险太大，不如把钱存在银行。你说呢？
明天是她的生日，我觉得请她吃饭比送她花好。你说呢？

23. 汉语的词序(小结):

在没有任何语境和上文的情况下，汉语的基本词序是：
主语(动作者)+状语+动词+补语+宾语(动作所涉及的事物)
①我星期日晚上才做完上周的功课。
②我回家的时候，看见家里有两个我不认识的人。

当有某种语境或上文时，汉语的基本词序会变化：

a. 话题——说明句

如果动作所涉及的事物是已知信息，谓语对其进行说明描写时，表示已知信息的词语应该放在句首：
①你买的那种股票我也买了，不知道今天会不会涨？
②A: 我们暑假去哈尔滨旅游好吗？
 B: 哈尔滨我去过了，我想去云南。

b. "把"字句：

如果句子里有主语(常常表示动作者)，动作所涉及的事物是已知信息或者是听话人能辨识(知道说的是什么)的，一般用"把"字句：
①A: 小李的车呢？
 B: 他弟弟把他的车开走了。
②屋子里太热了，把窗户打开吧。

虽然下面的说法也不算错：
①'A: 小李的车呢？
 B: 他弟弟开走了他的车。
②'屋子里太热了，打开窗户吧。

但句子连接得不好。用"把"的句子更有表现力。

3)汉语的词序还受认知的影响。
 a. 范围大的在前，小的在后：
 年——月——日——时——分——秒
 国家——省/州——市——街——号

b. 按照动作发生时间的顺序安排句子
①你坐公共汽车去医院看医生吗？（先坐公共汽车，再去医院，然后看医生）
②他们早上很早就出发了。骑了很长的一段路以后，有点热，也有点累，就下了车，一边推着车，一边聊了起来。

2. "把"字句小结(II)
当一个句子有表示动作者的主语，又有表示动作所涉及的事物的名词，有下列情况时，一定要用"把"字句：

a. 句子中还有一个表示动作后动作所涉及的事物所在的处所的词语：
①你把新买的衣服挂在**柜子里**吧。
  不能说：　　　　*你挂新买的衣服在柜子里吧。
b. 句子中还间接宾语时：
②哥哥把他的车送给**妹妹**了。
  不能说：　　　　*哥哥送他的车给妹妹了。
c. 动词后有补语"成"时：
③考试的时候，我把"人"字写**成**了"入"字。
  不能说：　　　　*考试的时候，我写"人"字成了"入"字。
④他把宿舍变**成**了一个垃圾场。
  不能说：　　　　*他变宿舍成了一个垃圾场。

"把"字句的句首一定有一个主语，主语表示动作者或责任者，见前面各例。在一定的语境中主语很清楚时，也可以不出现：
①(你)把窗户打开。
②我洗了很多杯子，(洗杯子)把手都洗疼了。

下面的句子句首没有主语，所以可以不用"把"：
①杯子洗干净了。("话题—说明句")
②这件衣服我穿，那件衣服你穿。("话题—说明句")

3) 在"把"字句中，否定副词要放在"把"字前：
明天就要去云南了，我还没把箱子整理好。
不能说：　　　　*明天就要去云南了，我还把箱子没整理好。
还要注意，可能补语不能用于"把"字句：
①*我把车钥匙找不到了。
②*他把我的电话号码想不起来了。

"把"字句是汉语中一个比较复杂的句子结构，"把"字句的使用，还跟语言环境、上文以及其他条件有关系。在以后的学习中我们还有机会讲解。可用 Language Practice A 辅助练习。

Exercises for the Main Text
主课文的练习

认读课文：可用幻灯片显示课文，让学生轮流扮演对话中的角色及其口译员。老师可用鼠标跟踪、凸显生词及难点。可借此机会纠正学生们的发音，并检查他们对所学内容的理解状况。

问答：课文认读完毕后，老师可就课文提问，以此方法来检查学生对课文的理解状况，同时可以帮助学生练习听力及口语。

Questions about the text:
A. 可就各人在中国的工作和生活情况提问。
- 雪梅下个星期做什么？（开始上班）
- 她第一个工作是做什么？（出国推销公司的太阳能热水器）
- 听马克说，最近什么样的产品在市场上卖得很火？（跟环保、节能有关的绿色产品）
- 马克在中国的发展怎么样？（他做过很多不同的工作。当过英文家教，搞过翻译，演过电视剧，拍过广告。不过有时候忙，有时候没事做，工作不稳定。）
- 马克在中国生活得怎么样？（他生活得很快乐，交了很多中国朋友，已经融入中国社会了。）
- 丽莎习惯/适应中国的生活了没有？（她在衣食住行各个方面都习惯/适应中国的生活了。）

B. 或以雪梅的"聚会"为主题做引导，先复习练习聚会时必须准备什么，再谈谈聚会分哪些。
- 大家为什么到雪梅家聚会？（庆祝雪梅顺利找到工作；给李哲接风；给丽莎、天明饯行）
- 雪梅准备了些什么？（准备了饮料、零食、水果、火锅、还叫了外卖）
- 雪梅说了些什么话来欢迎大家？（不要客气，好好吃，好好玩儿）
- 大家恭喜雪梅找到工作时，说了些什么？（恭喜你找到了好工作。）
- 大家给李哲接风的时候说了些什么？（欢迎来北京）
- 大家给丽莎、天明饯行的时候，说了些什么？（为我们的友谊干杯；祝你们一路平安；祝事业成功；以后多联系…）

Suggested Integrative Activities
综合练习活动

Speaking and Listening

1. Party! Party! Party! Brainstorm party ideas. 以学生为中心，分组讨论以下主题：

- 聚会/晚会有哪几种？
- 你常常跟谁聚会？

- 你怎么过生日？自己一个人过，跟家人一起过，还是跟朋友聚会开个生日晚会/舞会？
- 如果你明天毕业，你会怎么庆祝？/希望别人怎么给你庆祝？
- 如果你找到工作，你会怎么庆祝？
- 如果你父母或爷爷奶奶要退休了，你会怎么给他们庆祝？
- 如果你的哥哥/姐姐/好朋友要结婚了，你会怎么给他/她庆祝？
- 在家聚会/开晚会得准备什么吃的、喝的、玩儿的？

2. Party Time! Plan a real end of school year party.

学到此课时，应是一学年的最后，可让学生筹办一次期末聚会，庆祝学期结束，恭喜某些学生毕业。聚会中让学生说几句彼此勉励／祝贺的话语。先在小组中讨论，然后派代表向全班报告，以下为讨论的话题。

Who: 跟谁聚会？
            （同学、朋友…）
When: 什么时候聚会？
            （周末、学期最后一天、最后一节中文课）
Where: 在哪儿聚会比较合适？
            （宿舍里、学生活动中心、公园里、餐馆、火锅店、快餐店、咖啡馆儿…）
How: 聚会的时候做什么／怎么庆祝？
            （吃饭／聚餐、吃火锅、唱卡拉OK、跳舞、爬山、喝茶、聊天、打麻将…）
            （先…再…）
What: 在家聚会的时候准备什么？
            （饮料、零食、水果、火锅、音乐、游戏、［叫］外卖…）
What to say: 我们以茶代酒，举起杯来，为x干杯／祝x yyy／恭喜x yyy；太棒了，我真为你高兴。

Reading and Writing

1. Suppose you are the intended recipient of the email below. Read the message and then write a response (Interpersonal):

雪梅，你好。谢谢你请我和天明下个周末参加你们的聚会。你找到了很好的工作，我们在聚会上一定要好好庆祝庆祝。我跟天明很快就要回美国了，所以这次聚会上我们可以向各位朋友说再见。另外，你知道我一直住在李文家，她和她的父母给了我很多照顾。我每天跟李文练习中文，跟她爸爸打太极拳，觉得自己差不多已经融入他们的家庭了。这次聚会，我想请李文跟我一起来，可以吗？我想你们都会喜欢她的。

丽莎

2. Read the passage and answer the questions:

刚来中国发展的时候，马克有些担心，怕自己适应不了中国的生活。可是他很快就知道了自己完全不必担心。中国每天都在变化，对外国人来说机会很多。马克本来在一家翻译公司当翻译，公司的总经理有个朋友两年前拍电影，要找一位西方人演电影里的法国律师，总经理介绍了马克，结果马克的表现让大家很满意。因此后来马克又演了几个电影。现在他虽然算不上一流演员，可是也比较有名了。

True/False:
- (　) 1. For a long time, Mark was concerned about his ability to adapt to life in China.
- (　) 2. The writer suggests that China offers plenty of opportunities to foreigners because of the rapid changes occurring in the country.
- (　) 3. Before he became an actor, Mark was a lawyer in France.
- (　) 4. The way that Mark started his acting career was accidental.
- (　) 5. Everyone was quite satisfied with Mark's performance in his first film.
- (　) 6. Having improved his acting over the years, Mark has now become one of the best actors in China.

3. You are invited!: design an invitation for a party.

可让每个学生设计制作一个简单的期末聚会邀请卡，卡上列出聚会的原因、时间、地点、方式。

- Why: 为什么聚会？（庆祝学期结束；X毕业／找到工作／考上研究生／拿到学位）
- Who: 跟谁聚会？（同学）
- When: 什么时候聚会？（周末、学期最后一天、最后一节中文课）
- Where: 在哪儿聚会？（家里、宿舍里、学生活动中心、餐馆、火锅店、快餐店、咖啡馆儿…）
- How: 聚会的时候做什么／怎么庆祝？（吃饭、喝茶、聊天、唱卡拉OK、跳舞；先…再…）

Grammar and Vocabulary

1. Fill in blanks:

- 他___过很多不同的工作。___过英文家教，___过翻译，___过电视剧，___过广告。
- 我们___茶代酒，举起杯来，___我们的友谊干杯！
- 太棒了，我真___你高兴。
- 我们开个晚会，___她饯行。

2. Explain the following words in Chinese:

- 饯行：
- 接风：
- 干杯：
- 聚会：
- 衣食住行：
- 卖得很火：
- 搞教育：
- 期末：

3. Write out the following abbreviations:

- 环保：
- 节能：
- 家教：
- 影视：

4. Complete the following congratulatory sentences:

- 恭喜你_____！
- 祝你_____！
- 明天我们开晚会，庆祝_____。
- 你就要出国了，明天我们开个晚会，给你_____。
- 欢迎你来，明天我们在餐馆聚餐，给你_____。
- 为_____干杯！
- 欢迎你来_____！

Workbook Answer Key

A Note to Teachers: At this level of study, many of the exercises in the workbook are designed to be open-ended. We have provided sample answers where possible, but please keep in mind that a broad range of responses may be acceptable.

LESSON 11

中国的节日

I. Listening Comprehension

A.
1. It is a clean and beautifully furnished apartment in a nice residential area.
2. She tried to order the dinner at a restaurant, but all the restaurants were booked.
3. A fish dish, because it symbolizes surplus for the year.
4. The Dragon Boat Festival, the Mid-Autumn Festival, and the Lantern Festival.
5. Red envelopes with cash in them.
6. Her parents, Zhang Tianming, and Lisa.

B. ［男：这是我们搬到这个小区以后的第一个年夜饭。我们这儿不但房子好，而且环境又干净又漂亮，住起来很舒服。

女：看得出来，你很喜欢我们的新家。

男：可是你不觉得我们家还少点儿什么吗？

女：每个房间都是新家具，什么也不少啊。

男：孩子！我们现在还没孩子呢！难道我们就一直生活在二人世界里吗？

女：你说得对，我也想要孩子。

男：来，我们以可乐代酒，为我们将来的孩子干杯！］

1. (T)
2. (T)
3. (T)
4. (F)
5. (F)
6. (F)

C. 1. ［男：喂，小林，我是小江。打电话给你拜年，没想到你不在。你过年过得好吗？我是在我南京的舅舅家过的春节。第一次在中国过年，觉得真热闹。电视里的春节晚会太棒了，我舅舅做的红烧鱼也非常好吃！下次你给我发电子邮件，一定得告诉我你年夜饭吃了什么。祝你在新的一年里学习进步。］

a. To give New Year's greetings to a friend.
b. No, because he just spent his first Chinese New Year in China.
c. The TV program and the fish his uncle prepared.
d. He expects to hear about Little Lin's New Year's Eve dinner.

2. ［女：老王家今年过年人不少，儿子从四川回来了，女儿也从北京回来了。老王家房子不大，所以他跟太太想到餐馆订餐，可是没想到比较好的餐馆家家都没有位子了。没办法，王太太只好在家里准备年夜饭。老王买了很多鞭炮，可是都没放，因为儿

子说，今年的春节晚会特别好，放鞭炮太吵，会影响别人看电视。］
   a. Elsewhere. He does not live in Sichuan or Beijing, because his son and daughter came back home from Sichuan and Beijing respectively.
   b. They tried, because they felt their apartment did not have enough room for their son and daughter.
   c. They had their New Year's Eve dinner at home, because all the better restaurants were booked.
   d. Because firecrackers are noisy and he did not want to disturb others watching TV.

D. ［男：今天太累不想做饭。我给餐馆打电话订餐，但家家都说没位子了。
   女：
   a. 家里的电话坏了。
   b. **那只好我做饭了。**
   c. 那些餐馆都不好，没人去。
   d. 在餐馆找位子很累。］

II. Speaking Exercises

A. (Answers may vary.)

B. (Answers may vary.)

III. Reading Comprehension

A.

New Word	Pinyin	English
社区	shèqū	community
福气	fúqi/fúqì	good fortune
怪物	guàiwu/guàiwù	monster
饼干	bǐnggān	cookie/cracker
年糕	niángāo	New Year's cake, made of glutinous rice flour

B. A: 您的新家环境真不错，<u>住起来很舒服</u>吧？
   B: 还行，挺安静的。请喝咖啡。
   A: 谢谢！…您这咖啡喝起来特别香。您在咖啡里放了什么？
   B: 咖啡里什么都没放，<u>做起来很简单</u>，有空我教你。来，吃点儿月饼。
   A: 您的月饼<u>吃起来</u>真香，肯定很贵吧？
   B: 我也不清楚，是朋友送的。我今天穿的这件衣服，也是同一个朋友送的。
   A: 您的朋友真会买东西。这件衣服，您<u>穿起来</u>特别好看。

C. 1. 1. (T)
      2. (F)
      3. (F)
      4. (T)
      5. (c)
      6. (b)

   2. 1. (T)
      2. (T)
      3. (F)
      4. (T)
      5. (T)
      6. (F)

D. (Answers may vary.)

IV. Writing and Grammar Exercises

A. (Answers may vary for the word/phrase/sentence.)
   1. 是<u>福倒了</u>/<u>贴倒了</u>的倒。
   2. 是<u>气氛</u>的氛。
   3. 是<u>成功</u>/<u>用功</u>/<u>功课</u>的功。
   4. 是<u>浪费</u>的浪。
   5. 是<u>传统</u>的传。
   6. 是<u>团圆</u>/<u>脸圆圆的</u>的圆。
   7. 是<u>恭喜发财</u>的财。
   8. 是<u>感恩节</u>的恩。

B. (Answers may vary.)
   1. A: 丽莎呢？她忙什么呢？
      B: 她忙着打电脑呢。/她忙着上网呢。
   2. A: 雪梅呢？她忙什么呢？
      B: 她忙着买菜呢。/她忙着买东西呢。

3. A: 柯林呢？他忙什么呢？
   B: 他忙着做菜呢。/他忙着做年夜饭呢。

C. (Answers may vary.)
1. 他能吃得出来菜是什么地方的菜和地道不地道/他能吃得出菜是什么地方的菜和地道不地道。
2. 他能看得出来谁能唱歌，谁能跳舞/他能看得出谁能唱歌，谁能跳舞。
3. 他能听得出来谁的发音好/他能听得出谁的发音好。

D. (Answers may vary.)
1. 家家餐馆都没位子/家家都没位子。
2. 他的同学个个都是球迷/个个都是球迷。
3. 她天天都有中文课。

E. (Answers may vary.)
1. 雪梅一般(都)先做功课再吃晚饭。
2. 丽莎一般(都)先整理客厅再整理卧室。
3. 柯林一般(都)先上网查资料再去图书馆查资料。

F. (Answers may vary.)
一个卧室出租----
离北京语言大学很近；离地铁走路只要十分钟。(带家具，)有电视、冰箱、洗衣机、空调、微波炉、床、书桌、桌子、沙发、茶几等等。一天二十四小时可上网，有热水。(有兴趣请给 Joe (打)电话：158016xxxx。)

G. (Answers may vary.)
1. A: 你决定学期结束后做什么？
   B: 去纽约实习和找工作。
2. A: 你们那儿过年能不能放鞭炮？
   B: 不能，也买不到鞭炮。
3. A: 你们家过感恩节有什么传统？
   B: 我们家感恩节全家一起吃午饭，吃完饭下午看美式足球。感恩节那天我们家非常热闹。
4. A: 你的小区环境怎么样？
   B: 环境很好，很安静，而且离学校很近，很方便。

5. A: 你春节去哪儿了？
   B: 去杭州看我舅舅和舅妈了。他们有一套三房两厅两卫的公寓，住起来很舒服。
   A: 你是什么时候到的杭州？
   B: 我是除夕到的杭州。我舅舅在一家饭馆订餐，所以年夜饭我们没有在家里吃。
   A: 你舅舅舅妈做饭吗？
   B: 他们很喜欢做饭，可是他们把时间都放在自己的事业上，所以很忙，常常没有时间做饭。
   A: 你舅舅舅妈做什么工作？
   B: 我舅舅是大学教授，舅妈是律师。
   A: 他们有孩子吗？
   B: 他们没有孩子。他们是二人世界，感情很好。

6. A: 我的中国同学请我去她家吃春节年夜饭，不知道中国人年夜饭吃什么。
   B: 如果你的同学家里是北方人的话，一定会吃饺子。
   A: 太好了，我喜欢吃饺子。还有呢？
   B: 还有，中国人年夜饭一定要有鱼，而且不能都吃了，要剩下一些。
   A: 为什么？那不是浪费吗？
   B: 因为"鱼"跟"余"发音一样，"余"有"剩下"的意思。
   A: 真有意思！谢谢你告诉我，要不然，我可能把鱼都吃了。

H. (Answers may vary.)
中国有很多的传统节日。除了春节以外，还有元宵节、端午节、中秋节和清明节等。每年农历正月十五是元宵节，那天中国人吃元宵。农历五月初五是端午节，家家都吃粽子。农历八月十五是中秋节，是一家人团圆的节日。中秋节有点像美国的感恩节。过中秋节，大家一定得吃月饼。四月五日是清明节。清明节也是一个重要的传统节日。

I. (Answers may vary.)

J. (Answers may vary.)

K. (Answers may vary.)

L. (Answers may vary.)
1. 今天是中国的除夕。张家四口人坐在一起,准备吃年夜饭。桌上有很多好吃的菜。外边有人在放鞭炮。很热闹。
2. 张先生做的清蒸鱼太棒了,又香又嫩,大家都说是年夜饭中最好的菜。张先生五岁的儿子最喜欢吃爸爸做的鱼,所以张太太就把那盘鱼放在他前边。张先生的女儿说爸爸做的鱼比有名的餐馆里的鱼更好吃。张先生听了很高兴。
3. 大家说着说着,没想到儿子很快就把盘子里的鱼吃完了。女儿看了就说:"你不应该把鱼都吃完啊!年年有鱼,年年有余嘛!"儿子知道自己错了,很难过。张太太对儿子说:"孩子,没关系,别难过。"张先生没说话,他离开饭桌,到厨房去了。
4. 现在张先生回到了饭桌边。他又做了一盘鱼。儿子和女儿都高兴极了。张太太笑着说:"我们有很多鱼。年年有鱼,年年有余嘛!"

LESSON 12

中国的变化

I. Listening Comprehension

A.
1. No, because their applications for studying in China have been accepted and they can now stay in China for a few months.
2. Tianming's father wanted Tianming to take a few pictures of the middle school/high school that he attended, but Tianming is not able to find it.
3. He thinks that it is a busy city, full of high-rises and cars.
4. There are more cars, more high-rises, more foreigners, and more foreign businesses.
5. The Temple of Confucius.

B. 〔女：这个地方以前很安静，没想到现在这么热闹。
男：是啊，这几年我们这儿的变化的确很大。你看，马路对面的餐馆，以前是两层楼，现在变成四层楼了。
女：我记得以前餐馆门前来来去去的都是自行车，现在来来去去的都是汽车，完全不是以前那个样子了。
男：可是有些东西没有变。
女：什么东西没有变？
男：这家餐馆的菜单没变，还是那些传统的菜，所以来吃饭的人特别多。看来，不管中国怎么变，中国人的口味还是没变。〕

1. (F)
2. (F)
3. (T)
4. (F)
5. (T)
6. (T)

C. (Answers may vary.)

1. 〔男：钱先生是杭州人，大学毕业以后就去北京工作，好几年没回杭州了。上个星期公司让他到杭州开会，他觉得杭州对他来说完全是一个陌生的城市了。除了他上大学时常去的那家电影院以外，很多熟悉的地方都没有了。钱先生有点儿难过。〕

a. No, because he went to Beijing only after he graduated from college.
b. Yes, he found the movie theater that he often visited as a college student.
c. He was sad, because most of the places that he had been familiar with were nowhere to be found.

2. 〔女：南京原来是个很有特色的城市，楼房不太高，马路两边都是树。可是现在呢？到处都是新盖的高楼，大街上挤满了汽车，马路上的树都没有了。我上个月去南京，要不是街上的人都说南京话，我还以为是在上海呢。我很担心，这样下去，南京的特色会越来越少了。〕

a. It had its own characteristics, with relatively low buildings and many trees.
b. High-rises are everywhere and the trees have disappeared.
c. She would have mistaken it for Shanghai if not for the pedestrians' Nanjing accent.
d. She is concerned about the loss of the city's special characteristics.

D. 〔男：旅游不能老购物，老拍照片，时间到了也得吃饭呀！
女：
a. 没错，我可不喜欢拍照。
b. 同意，购物中心太挤了。
c. **是啊！民以食为天啊！**
d. 是吗？我没尝过这里的小吃。〕

II. Speaking Exercises

A. (Answers may vary.)

B. (Answers may vary.)

III. Reading Comprehension

A.

New Word	*Pinyin*	English
绿化	lǜhuà	to make (a place) green
班车	bānchē	regular bus (service)/shuttle bus (service)
座位	zuòwèi	seat
回声	huíshēng	echo
农民	nóngmín	farmer/peasant

B. A: 元宵节快到了，咱们做点元宵吃，怎么样？
B: 做元宵？我<u>可</u>不行，<u>从来没</u>做<u>过</u>。
A: 你在中国出生、长大的，<u>竟</u>没做过元宵？
B: 我最不喜欢进厨房，<u>能</u>不做菜就<u>尽可能</u>不做菜。别说做元宵了，我连一般的菜都不太会做。
A: <u>看来</u>这次做元宵得<u>完全</u>靠我了。
B: 没错，<u>的确</u>得靠你。

C. 1. (c)
2. (a)
3. (b)
4. (d)

D. 1. 1. (F)
2. (T)
3. (F)
4. (F)
5. (T)
6. (b)
7. (c)

2. 1. (T)
2. (F)
3. (F)
4. (F)
5. (a)
6. (c)
7. (b)

E. (Answers may vary.)
1. 我去过。/我(也)从来没去过。
2. (饺子：dumplings; 面条：noodles; 米线：rice noodles…)

F. (Answers may vary.)
With regard to food, (food) safety is the top priority.

IV. Writing and Grammar Exercises

A. (Answers may vary.)
1. 是<u>环境</u>的<u>境</u>。
2. 是<u>街上</u>的<u>街</u>。
3. 是<u>骑自行车/骑马</u>的<u>骑</u>。
4. 是<u>老百姓</u>的<u>姓</u>。
5. 是<u>一座</u>/一座传统建筑的<u>座</u>。

B. (Answers may vary.)
1. 天气预报说今天天气会很好，可是下午<u>竟然下大雨</u>。
2. 今天是张天明母亲的生日，没想到他<u>竟然忘了</u>。
3. 张天明以为他能找到父亲的中学，但是中学<u>竟然已经变成购物中心了/竟已经变成购物中心了</u>。
4. 丽莎以为南京是个安静的小城，没想到南京<u>竟然已经变成一个热闹的大城市了/竟已经变成一个热闹的大城市了</u>。

C. 1. A: 咱们一起去吃早饭吧！
B: 早饭，我吃<u>过了</u>。
2. A: 你去<u>过</u>天津吗？
B: 去<u>过</u>，我是两年前去的。
3. A: 粽子好吃吗？
B: 我不知道，我没吃<u>过</u>。
4. A: "民以食为天"这句话你听说<u>过</u>吗？
B: 听说<u>过</u>，但不懂什么意思。
5. A: 这本书可以借给我看看吗？
B: 可以，我看<u>过了</u>，你拿去看吧。

D. (Answers may vary.)
1. 舅妈做的清蒸鱼味道的确不错。
2. 除夕的春节晚会的确很有意思。

Workbook Answer Key • Lesson 12   139

3. 张天明的父亲熟悉的南京的确已经变得完全不一样了。
4. 夫子庙的确是个很有特色的地方。
5. 张天明的确觉得中国已经融入国际社会了。

E. (Answers may vary.)
1. 要不是雪梅给柯林打电话，柯林上课肯定迟到。
2. 要不是到处都是中文，丽莎还以为她在纽约呢。
3. 要不是雪梅告诉柯林"年年有余（鱼）"的意思，柯林吃年夜饭的时候就会把鱼都吃了。

F. (Answers may vary.)
1. （已经十一点了，）看来他今天晚上不会来了。
2. （他吃得那么高兴，）看来他很喜欢吃月饼。
3. 看来她不太会滑冰。
4. 看来他们两个人感情很好。

G. (Answers may vary.)
1. A: 表哥，我们到火车站了。你在哪儿？
   B: 我也快到了。对不起，路上车很多。你们对这个城市不熟悉。别乱跑。
   A: 那我们在哪儿等你？
   B: 从火车站出来，旁边有一家购物中心。你们在购物中心门口等我。
   A: 好。
2. A: 这是什么声音？
   B: 对不起，这是我肚子咕噜咕噜叫的声音，我饿了。
   A: 你想吃什么？马路对面有很多小吃店。
   B: 你想吃粽子吗？
   A: 今天是元宵节，咱们吃元宵吧。

H. (Answers may vary.)
1. 丽莎的日记
今天天明的表哥当我们的导游，带我们在街上走了走，看了看南京。天明的爸爸常常说南京是个安静的城市，我没想到竟这么热闹！到处都有外国游客，还有美国快餐店，日本银行，和法国服装店。天明说南京融入世界了，这是件好事。可是我担心，这样下去，有中国特色的东西会不会越来越少呢？天明的表哥说南京还是保留了很多有中国特色的东西，比如说夫子庙。我们去看了以后，觉得那儿非常有意思。看来，南京人真的是想尽可能保留老南京的传统。

2. 张天明的日记
我们昨天从上海坐高速火车，两个小时就到南京了。火车很干净也很舒服。表哥开车来火车站接我们。今天早上一吃过早饭我们就去找爸爸以前的中学。没想到那个中学没有了，变成一个购物中心了。爸爸熟悉的南京已经不在了。南京现在到处都是新盖的高楼，大街上挤满了汽车。如果爸爸看到南京的变化，他会怎么想呢？

3. 好，我们到了夫子庙了。我介绍一下夫子庙的历史：它最早是1034年盖的，所以南京夫子庙的历史快一千年了。我们现在看到的建筑虽然没有那么老，可是很有老南京的特色。大家可以看到这里有很多中国和外国的游客。谁是孔夫子呢？他是一位很有名的哲学家。以前，中国很多地方都有夫子庙。很多人去夫子庙拜孔子，希望考试能考得很好。

I. (Answers may vary.)

L. 1. 张天明和丽莎今天坐飞机去南京。天明的爸爸到机场送他们。天明的爸爸是在南京出生的。他告诉天明，到了南京以后，千万别忘了去看看他以前的中学，南京XX中学。天明说："爸爸，您放心吧，我不会忘的，一定会找到那个中学。"
2. 天明和丽莎到了南京以后，就开始找天明爸爸的中学。可是那儿已经完全不一样了。爸爸的中学是一座两层的房子，可是那儿已经变成了一栋高楼。天明正在问一位老先生："请问，您知道这儿以前的那个中学搬到哪儿去了吗？"

3. 那位老先生告诉天明和丽莎："我来帮你们找那个中学。"他把天明和丽莎带到了图书馆。在图书馆里，那位老先生找到了一本书，他让天明和丽莎好好看看那本书。

4. 这是什么书呢？天明一看，才知道原来这是一本介绍南京历史的书。在书里，天明看到了爸爸以前的中学的照片。天明想，今天晚上就打电话给爸爸，告诉他那个中学找到了，可是是在南京的历史书里找到的。不知道爸爸听了会高兴还是会难过。

LESSON 13

旅游

I. Listening Comprehension

A. (Answers may vary.)

1. He chose to buy a hard-berth ticket, because he thought it would be easier to practice speaking Chinese with other travelers in a hard-berth sleeper car.
2. He didn't like it. He thought it was expensive and didn't taste good.
3. The tour guide was waiting for them outside the train station, holding a sign with their names on it.
4. It features dark-colored rock formations that are all kinds of shapes. Viewed from a distance, they look like a forest of trees, which is why it is called the Stone Forest.
5. Lin Xuemei and Lisa did, while Zhang Tianming and Ke Lin did not.
6. They drank tea at a teahouse, watching the river outside and the red lanterns by the doors.

B. ［男：这次你们去云南丽江玩儿，住在什么旅馆？
女：我们住在一家有名的大旅馆，旅馆里边有餐厅，还有几个卖纪念品的商店，又舒服又方便。
男：我还以为你们会住家庭旅馆呢。
女：我知道家庭旅馆比较便宜，可是听说不太舒服，不如住大旅馆。
男：丽江的少数民族很多，住在家庭旅馆，你可以亲眼看看不同民族的生活，了解不同民族的风俗习惯。再说，家庭旅馆虽然房间小一点，可是也很干净，听说还能上网呢。
女：是吗？你怎么不早点告诉我？
男：你没问我呀。］

1. (F)
2. (T)
3. (F)
4. (F)
5. (T)
6. (F)
7. (T)

C. (Answers may vary.)

1. ［(男声)三天前我坐火车从杭州去广州。我买的是软卧票。软卧票虽然比较贵，可是软卧车厢很干净，枕头毯子都是新的。另外，我想软卧车厢只有四个人，一定比较安静，晚上可以睡个好觉。没想到睡在上铺的一位先生晚上竟不停地打呼噜，所以我一个晚上都没睡好。］

   a. He departed from Hangzhou and traveled to Guangzhou.
   b. He thought that a soft-berth sleeper car would be cleaner and that he would be able to sleep well in it.
   c. He did not, because the man in the upper bunk snored constantly.

2. ［(女声)怎么，你也想去哈尔滨旅游？我跟小钱上个月刚去过。小钱在网上找到一个旅游团，团费包括机票、旅馆、三餐和景点门票。我们觉得很合适，就报名了。我们玩得还不错，只是好几个中午导游让我们吃盒饭，饭菜味道很不好。你找旅游团，最好找团费不包括三餐的，这样你吃饭就比较自由了。］

   a. Harbin, with Little Qian.
   b. Plane tickets, hotel, meals, and admission fees for tourist spots.
   c. No, because she did not like the lunches that the tour guide arranged for them.
   d. It would be better to join a group tour that does not include meals, so you can have more freedom to arrange meals.

D. ［男：我们的导游介绍景点介绍得很不错，人又幽默，就是老叫我们买纪念品！
女：
  a. 对，千万别听他讲故事。
  b. 不，我不爱买纪念品。
  c. 别抱怨了，你们的导游比我们的好多了。
  d. 难怪你什么纪念品都没买。］

II. Speaking Exercises

A. (Answers may vary.)

B. (Answers may vary.)

III. Reading Comprehension

A.

New Word	Pinyin	English
享受	xiǎngshòu	to enjoy
硬件	yìngjiàn	hardware
床铺	chuángpù	bed
包厢	bāoxiāng	box seat (at a theater or stadium)
麵條/面条	miàntiáo	noodles

B. Form a complete sentence by matching each construction on the left with an appropriate phrase on the right.
1. (d)
2. (e)
3. (b)
4. (a)
5. (c)

C.
1. 没有去过中国就不能<u>亲身</u>感觉到中国节日的气氛。
2. 这次天明和丽莎<u>亲眼</u>看到了云南美丽的风景。
3. 你是<u>亲耳</u>听见她说她和她的男朋友吹了吗?
4. 丽莎很喜欢这件衬衫,因为是她<u>亲手</u>做的。
5. 对不起,别人不能帮你申请去中国留学,你得<u>亲自</u>申请。

D.
1.
  1. (T)
  2. (F)
  3. (F)
  4. (T)
  5. (c)
  6. (b)

2.
  1. (F)
  2. (F)
  3. (T)
  4. (T)
  5. (F)
  6. (b)
  7. (a)

E. (Answers may vary.)
1. (这个广告是)旅行社贴的。
2. Five-day tour of Yunnan (Lijiang, Dali, and Kunming), including roundtrip flights, for 2610 yuan.

F. (Answers may vary.)
(学生考试之前来这个办公室)报名和准备考试。

G. (Answers may vary.)
You can choose your own hotel (3 to 5 stars).
You can decide on your departure date and the duration of your tour.
You can select your city of departure from more than twenty options.
You can choose a group tour or a DIY tour.
You can make advance reservations for airport pick-up and drop-off, scenic tours, and admission tickets to scenic spots.

IV. Writing and Grammar Exercises

A. (Answers may vary.)
1. 是硬卧的<u>硬</u>。
2. 是软卧/软件的<u>软</u>。
3. 是(打)呼噜的<u>呼</u>。
4. 是拥抱的<u>抱</u>。
5. 是灯笼的<u>笼</u>。

B. (Answers may vary.)
1. 王老师的学生和柯老师的学生分别住在一个大旅馆和一个家庭旅馆里。
2. 明天我的旅行团和她的旅行团分别出发到昆明和丽江。
3. 老田和小田分别买了软卧票和硬卧票。
4. 哥哥和弟弟分别睡上、下铺。

5. 午饭(的时候)，姐姐和妹妹分别吃了盒饭和方便面。

C. (Answers may vary.)
1. 柯林给雪梅的舅舅留下了很好的印象。
2. 那家纪念品商店给天明留下了不太好的印象。
3. 南京城市的变化给天明留下了很深的印象。
4. 舅舅住的小区给雪梅留下了很不错的印象。

D. (Answers may vary.)
1. 柯林觉得在电话里聊天没有在网上聊天省钱。
   柯林觉得在电话里聊天不如在网上聊天(省钱)。
   柯林觉得在网上聊天比在电话里聊天省钱。
2. 丽莎觉得一个人长大以后事业成功没有小时候有个快乐童年重要。
   丽莎觉得一个人长大以后事业成功不如小时候有个快乐童年(重要)。
   丽莎觉得一个人小时候有个快乐童年比长大以后事业成功重要。
3. 雪梅觉得在美国过新年没有在中国过春节热闹。
   雪梅觉得在美国过新年不如在中国过春节(热闹)。
   雪梅觉得在中国过春节比在美国过新年热闹。

E. (Answers may vary.)
1. 只好在家里吃(年夜饭)。
2. 只好(在旁边)等。
3. 只好跟表哥一起去吃饭。

F. (Answers may vary.)
1. 睡觉以前，千万别喝咖啡
2. 出门的时候/以前，千万别忘了带钥匙。
3. 下出租车的时候，千万别把包拉在出租车上。
4. 过春节的时候，千万别把鱼都吃了。

G. (Answers may vary.)
1. 这家商店的衣服很便宜，一条牛仔裤<u>不过二十块(钱)</u>。/<u>不过二十元</u>。
2. 还早，你再坐一会儿吧。现在<u>不过(晚上)七点半</u>。/<u>不过七点三十(分)</u>。
3. 这栋楼不高，<u>不过四层楼(高)</u>。
4. 他的老家不大，人口<u>不过一千</u>。

H. (Answers may vary.)
1. A: 需要盒饭吗？
   B: 有素的盒饭吗？
   A: 对不起，素的盒饭卖完了。
   B: 你们还有什么？
   A: 我们还有方便面。
   B: 那我买方便面吧。
2. A: 爸，你想睡上铺还是下铺？上铺安静一点，可以睡个好觉。下铺比较方便。
   B: 那我睡下铺吧。我从家里多带了一条毯子和一个枕头。你需要吗？
   A: 我一条毯子和一个枕头够了，你喜欢用两个枕头，家里的枕头你用吧。
3. A: 喂，妈，我们从云南回北京了。
   B: 是吗？你们是怎么去的云南？
   A: 我们在网上报名参加了一个旅行团，然后坐火车去昆明等雪梅和柯林。
   B: 你们坐的是什么火车？
   A: 我们想和别的旅客练习说中文，所以我和丽莎买了两张硬卧票。
   B: 你们去了哪几个地方？
   A: 我们去了石林、大理和丽江，还游览了大雪山。
   B: 你对云南的印象怎么样？
   A: 云南太有意思了！各个地方的风景不一样，还有很多好玩的地方，可是我们来不及去了。
   B: 那下次去吧。

I. (Answers may vary.)
1. 丽莎：
   我在网上查了查，云南有很多地方风景都很漂亮，我们可以自助游：

第一天：石林，住三星级旅馆

第二天：大理，游览大理三塔，住四星级旅馆

第三天：丽江古城，住家庭旅馆

你觉得怎么样？我们先坐火车去昆明。柯林和雪梅也想去云南玩，我们可以在昆明见面。

天明

2. （天明：

我也喜欢自助游，因为比较自由。可是我们刚到了中国，我觉得我们还是参加一个旅行团比较方便。这样，我们不用自己订旅馆、买门票。如果我们每天去不同的地方，自助游的话，会很累。旅行团有导游给我们介绍云南的建筑、服装、饮食，帮助我们了解/学习各个民族的风俗习惯。你说呢？

丽莎）

3. （我们去年去英国，住在一个家庭旅馆。旅馆的后面有一条小河。旅馆不大，很安静，也很干净。房东给我们做家常菜，味道很不错。房东说他给我们做的鱼是旅馆后面的河里的，所以非常新鲜。）

J. (Answers may vary.)

K. (Answers may vary.)

1. 在一个旅游城市有一家很大很新的旅馆，那家旅馆对面有一个很小的家庭旅馆。因为那家大旅馆很有名，所以去那儿住的客人很多，而去那个家庭旅馆住的客人很少。

2. 我们看到，住在那家大旅馆的客人都走了。他们为什么看起来不太高兴呢？可能是因为那家旅馆的房间不太干净，或者菜不好吃。为什么住在家庭旅馆的客人看起来非常高兴呢？一定是因为家庭旅馆的服务很好，房间特别干净，还可以上网。

3. 现在，那家大旅馆没有以前那么有名了，看起来也旧了，去那儿住的客人比以前少多了。而那家家庭旅馆却越来越有名了，去那儿住的客人越来越多了。

4. 很多人都知道了这两家旅馆的变化。有一个人去那家大旅馆住了一晚上，又去那家家庭旅馆住了一晚上。他明白了为什么会有这样的变化。于是他写了一篇文章，他把那篇文章叫做"两家旅馆的故事。"

生活与健康

I. Listening Comprehension

A. (Answers may vary.)
1. No, because she is Li Wen's English tutor.
2. She sees many people exercising.
3. Because she wants to learn tai chi from Li Wen's parents.
4. She thinks that weight is not very important as long as one is healthy.
5. One should eat more for breakfast and lunch and less for dinner.
6. She finds it hard not to stay up late, because she often has to burn the midnight oil to prepare for the graduate admission exam.

B. 〔男：孩子，你今天晚饭怎么吃得这么少？

女：爸，从现在开始我要好好注意饮食习惯了。您没听到过那句话吗？"早饭要吃好，午饭要吃饱，晚饭要吃少。"

男：我知道那句话，可是你今天晚上不是要工作吗？

女：对，夜里两点才下班呢。可是工作晚也不能随便乱吃啊。

男：晚上要工作七个小时，晚饭一定要吃饱吃好。否则，晚上十点钟就饿了，还得买东西吃。这是我的经验。

女：您放心吧，我晚饭虽然吃得不多，可是营养已经够了。

男：你这孩子…〕

1. (F)
2. (F)
3. (F)
4. (F)
5. (T)
6. (T)

C. (Answers may vary.)
1. 〔男：李文的父母去年退休以来，很注意身体健康，差不多每天早晨都去小区附近的公园打太极拳。前两天一直下雨，他们就在家里客厅里打。今天早上又下雨了，可是他们的女儿李文昨天晚上熬夜学习，今天早上要补充睡眠。李文的父母怕影响女儿睡觉，今天早上只好给他们自己放假了。〕

   a. In the park near their residential area.
   b. In their living room, because it was raining.
   c. She stayed up late studying.
   d. No, because they did not want to affect their daughter's sleep.

2. 〔女：在中国的很多城市里，每天早晨到处可以看到打太极拳的老年人。可是很少有二、三十岁的人跟他们一起锻炼身体。难道这些人不注意身体健康吗？不是。他们觉得太极拳的动作虽然很美，但是太慢。所以他们更喜欢游泳，打球。最近几年，去健身房锻炼的人也越来越多了。〕

   a. No, because they think the movements of tai chi are too slow.
   b. Yes, they do.
   c. Swimming, playing ball, and working out at the gym.

D. 〔女：你常常熬夜，必须补充睡眠，否则会生病。

男：

a. 是啊，你的眼睛快变成熊猫眼了。
b. 即使天天吃饱，睡好，也会老。
c. 随便，只要你高兴就好。
d. 我的身体好得很，不用担心。〕

II. Speaking Exercises

A. (Answers may vary.)

B. (Answers may vary.)

III. Reading Comprehension

A.

New Word	*Pinyin*	English
散心	sàn xīn	to drive away one's cares/to relieve boredom
圆圈	yuánquān	circle
队伍	duìwǔ	procession/battalion
呼吸	hūxī	to breathe
补习	bǔxí	to go to cram school/to take additional classes/tutorials after school

B. 1. 1. (F)
    2. (F)
    3. (T)
    4. (F)
    5. (a)
    6. (c)

   2. 1. (F)
    2. (F)
    3. (T)
    4. (b)
    5. (c)

C. (Answers may vary.)
   1. 觉得很有活力。
   2. 茶、咖啡

D. 1. (太极拳有)两个(班)。
   2. (每次上课)五十分钟。
   3. 6月29日(开始上课)/6月29号(开始上课)。
   4. (在)足球场(上课)。
   5. 留学生/外国学生。
   6. (报名时间是)(从)6月25日到7月20日。/(报名时间是)(从)6月25号到7月20号。

IV. Writing and Grammar Exercises

A. (Answers may vary.)
   1. 是锻炼的锻。
   2. 是排(成)/排(成)队的排。
   3. 是瑜伽的伽。
   4. 是吃饱的饱。
   5. 是吸烟的吸。
   6. 是睡眠的眠。
   7. 是否则的否。

B. (Answers may vary.)
   1. 早晨锻炼的人们使丽莎觉得北京看起来很有活力。
   2. 云南美丽的风景使天明对云南的印象非常好。
   3. 天明担心父亲的中学已经变成了购物中心会使父亲难过。
   4. 丽莎认为多运动、注意饮食能使人身体健康。

C. (Answers may vary.)
   1. 只要多运动、注意饮食，身体就会好。
   2. 只要多练习，动作就不会忘了。
   3. 只要多复习，多跟家教练习，英文就会进步了。

D. (Answers may vary.)
   1. 衣柜里的衣服你随便试。/衣柜里的衣服你随便拿。/衣柜里的衣服你随便穿。
   2. 书架上的书你随便看。/书架上的书你随便拿。
   3. 我的椅子(请)(你)别随便坐。
   4. 我的手机(请)(你)别随便用。/我的电话(请)(你)别随便用。

E. (Answers may vary.)
   1. 哈尔滨即使冬天很冷，我也要去。
   2. 坐船游览长江即使很花时间，我也要坐。
   3. 春节夫子庙那儿即使人山人海，我也要去。
   4. 这套运动服即使得花我一个月的工资，我也非买不可。
   5. 这门金融课即使难学，我也要选。

F. (Answers may vary.)
1. 丽莎常吃青菜、水果，可见她非常注意饮食。
2. 李文的眼睛成熊猫眼了，可见她常常熬夜，睡眠不够。/李文的眼睛成熊猫眼了，可见她常常开夜车，睡眠不够。
3. 天明的导游说话常逗的大家哈哈大笑，可见他很幽默。
4. 雪梅的舅妈忙着做年夜饭，舅舅在旁边帮忙，可见两个人的感情很好。

G. (Answers may vary.)
1. 丽莎告诉李文(千万)别熬夜，否则眼睛会变成熊猫眼/丽莎告诉李文(千万)别开夜车，否则身体健康会受影响。
2. 天明告诉丽莎(千万)别买软卧(车厢的票)，否则晚上(可能)睡不着觉。
3. 柯林告诉朋友(千万)别参加有"购物"的旅行团，否则实在是浪费时间。

H. (Answers may vary.)
1. A: 老李，你应该多注意身体健康，多运动。
   B: 医生，我家离健身房很远，去健身房太不方便了。
   A: 只要你运动，哪儿都行，不必非去健身房不可。比如，你可以在家里做瑜伽。
   B: 我是一个老人，做瑜伽有点奇怪。
   A: 老李，你的看法有问题。好吧，如果你不想做瑜伽，你可以去楼下打太极拳。
   B: 太极拳的动作太慢了，再说我学不会。
   A: 那跑步怎么样，不用学。
   B: 街上挤满了车，不安全。我们小区也太小，没有地方跑步。
   A: 散步也是很好的运动。
   B: 散步可以考虑。
2. A: 老李，我看你身体好多了。
   B: 医生，我听了你的话，每天早上都散步。
   A: 我看你也没有以前那么胖了。
   B: 我以前很喜欢吃肉，很少吃青菜和水果，不吃早饭，中午随便乱吃，晚饭吃得很多。现在除了每天散步，我也开始注意饮食了。
   A: 很好，你现在有了良好的生活习惯，这对身体很有好处。
3. A: 你看没看见每天早上在街边、在公园有很多老年的中国人在锻炼身体？
   B: 没有。来中国后，我常常熬夜，看我的熊猫眼。
   A: 我喜欢早睡早起，早上吃完早饭后就出去散步。
   B: 我应该像你一样有良好的生活习惯。可是我看到晚上也有老人在街边跳舞，非常有意思。
   A: 对。在我们国家，大家一般付钱一个人去健身房锻炼，又贵又没意思。
   B: 我同意，在我们国家也一样。中国老人和朋友在街上锻炼多好！又不用花钱又可以跟老朋友见面！

I. (Answers may vary.)
1. 林雪梅的舅舅和舅妈很重视锻炼身体。虽然他们都快五十岁了，但是身材都很好，显得很有活力。柯林看见林雪梅的舅舅每天早上都去小区里的小公园打太极拳，就让舅舅教他。舅舅说他打太极拳已经打了十年了。至于舅妈，她喜欢晚上做瑜伽，林雪梅就跟舅妈一起做。柯林和雪梅都说他们在舅舅家不但吃得好，而且学会注意身体。
2. 医生，这是我的狗，肥肥。你看它很胖，需要减肥。它每天吃得很多，不喜欢喝水，饮食习惯很不好，很懒，也不喜欢运动，所以有很多健康问题。我姐姐说这是因为我的生活习惯也很不好。她说我一点儿活力都没有，应该多锻炼，注意饮食。她让我每天带肥肥跑步。有人说狗会越来越像主人，可是我姐姐说我必须注意，否则我会越来越像肥肥。

J. (Answers may vary.)

K. (Answers may vary.)
1. 丽莎在北京留学。她住在朋友李文家。她每天早上都去公园散步，每次散步都看到一群中国退休老人在一条小河边打太极拳。丽莎想：中国老人真是注意身体健康，重视锻炼身体啊。
2. 丽莎觉得太极拳不但对身体有好处，而且动作很美，象表演一样。这天，她又看到那些老人在打太极拳，她就走到他们的后边，一边看他们打，一边学了起来。
3. 丽莎学太极拳学得很快。两个星期后，丽莎在学校里告诉张天明和别的留学生她学太极拳的事。天明请她打太极拳给他们看看。丽莎就开始打了。
4. 天明和同学们都觉得太极拳不但对身体有好处，而且动作很美，象表演一样。他们一个个走到丽莎后边，一边看丽莎打，一边学了起来。

男女平等

I. Listening Comprehension

A. (Answers may vary.)

1. Women's status was much lower than men's.
2. After the 1950s, women's status improved, but in recent years the phenomemon of gender inequality has resurfaced in some places.
3. He is a big soccer fan. Whenever there is a soccer game on TV he does not do any housework.
4. When there is no soccer game on TV, the uncle often helps with cooking and does the dishes.
5. No, because she thinks that the players on the men's soccer team are arrogant and do not play well.
6. The men's soccer team managed to win a soccer game against Chinese women ping-pong players with a score of 1:0.

B. 〔男：咱们小区昨天搬来一对夫妻，你知道吗？

女：我当然知道。那位女的姓钱，是我们学校的教授，我研究生一年级的时候还选过她的课呢。她非常有名，写过好几本书。

男：是吗？她看起来才三十多岁，就有这么棒的成绩了。

女：可是钱教授常常说，她的成绩有一半是她先生的。

男：为什么？

女：她先生对她非常照顾体贴，知道她工作忙，在家里连洗碗这样的小事都不让她做。

男：听起来他们的家庭生活十分幸福美满啊。〕

1. (F)
2. (T)
3. (T)
4. (F)
5. (T)

C. (Answers may vary.)

1. 〔(女声)什么，今天晚上电视里又有男足比赛？我一看他们的比赛就生气，从去年到现在没赢过一次比赛。我觉得他们应该请女足队员当他们的老师，用他们的工资付学费。〕

   a. Her attitude is very critical.
   b. No, because watching the game would make her angry.
   c. They should hire players on the women's soccer team to be their teachers.

2. 〔男声：妹妹，你真的要跟李小阳结婚吗？李小阳上高中的时候是我的同学。他平常骄傲得不得了，很少跟女同学说话，我们都觉得他有点儿大男子主义。我不知道他现在变了没有。结婚是一件大事，希望你好好考虑考虑再决定。〕

   a. Li was the speaker's schoolmate in high school and is now the fiance of the speaker's younger sister.
   b. The speaker wants to urge his sister to reconsider the marriage.
   c. The speaker thought Li Xiaoyang was arrogant and somewhat chauvinistic, because he rarely spoke to girls.
   d. No, because he has no idea whether Li Xiaoyang has now changed.

D. 〔男：奇怪，我跟他做同样的事，他的薪水怎么比我高？

女：

a. 你们单位做到同工同酬了。

b. **毕竟他比你早来公司好几年，学位也比你高。**

c. 他这个人奇怪得不得了，大家都讨厌他。

d. 只要做同样的事，你的薪水就会比他高。〕

II. Speaking Exercises

A. (Answers may vary.)

B. (Answers may vary.)

III. Reading Comprehension

A. (English translations may vary.)

New Word	*Pinyin*	English
困境	kùnjìng	difficult position/predicament
厂房	chǎngfáng	factory building
事务	shìwù	work/general affairs
厌食	yànshí	to be anorexic
傲慢	àomàn	arrogant/snobby

B.
1. c
2. d
3. b
4. a

C. 1.
   1. (T)
   2. (T)
   3. (T)
   4. (F)
   5. (c)
   6. (b)

2.
   1. (T)
   2. (F)
   3. (T)
   4. (T)
   5. (a)
   6. (c)

D. (Answers may vary.)
1. 不到三十岁的人都可以申请。
2. 我对这份工作没有兴趣。因为我没有工作经验。

IV. Writing and Grammar Exercises

A. (Answers may vary.)
1. 是<u>男</u>人/<u>男</u>子/<u>男</u>女平等/大<u>男</u>子主义的<u>男</u>。
2. 是同工同<u>酬</u>的<u>酬</u>。
3. 是气管<u>炎</u>的<u>炎</u>。
4. 是<u>休息</u>/<u>消息</u>的<u>息</u>。
5. 是<u>相信</u>/<u>短信</u>/<u>信用卡</u>/<u>写信</u>的<u>信</u>。

B. (Answers may vary.)
1. 这件衣服毕竟是名牌。
2. 毕竟你高中毕业以后他就没再看到过你。/他毕竟很长时间没看到你了。
3. 他毕竟踢足球踢了十年了。
4. 毕竟她从公司一开始，就在那儿工作。

C. (Answers may vary.)
1. （我同意，）我（也）认为工厂的困难是能解决的。
2. （我同意，）我（也）觉得他们夫妻二人的感情是会越来越好的。
3. （没错，）这种汤是很有营养的。
4. （对，）世界各种职业比赛都是很公平的。

D. (Answers may vary.)
1. 很多在美国长大的中国学生也学中文。拿(张)天明来说吧，他就学中文。
2. 很多人觉得网上有很多垃圾。拿雪梅来说吧，她就说过网上有很多垃圾。
3. 很多人喜欢在旅游景点买纪念品。拿丽莎来说吧，她就常常在旅游景点买纪念品。
4. 很多中国夫妻不想要孩子。拿雪梅的舅舅舅妈来说吧，他们(两人)就不要孩子。

E.
1. 那家饭馆的菜咸得不得了。
2. 中国除夕夜热闹得不得了。
3. 这个古城保留中国特色的建筑多得不得了。
4. 雪梅的舅舅对舅妈体贴得不得了。
5. 放假的时候，中国各大旅游景点都挤得不得了。

F.
1. 二分之一
2. 三分之二
3. 八分之七
4. 百分之百

G. (Answers may vary.)

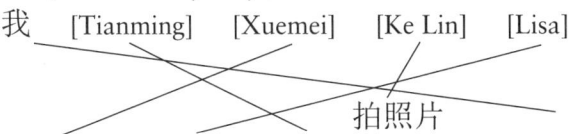

买火车票　订旅馆　安排活动　计划旅游路线

(Answers may vary. Sample answers in this section are based on the matching above.)

1. 火车票由雪梅买。
2. 活动由天明安排。
3. 旅馆由丽莎订。
4. 照片由柯林拍。

H. (Answers may vary.)

1. A: 我听说某公司买了一个女子足球队。看来，女足逐渐受欢迎了。
   B: 是啊，毕竟踢足球、看足球的女性越来越多了。

2. 售货员： 请问，您想买什么？
   李哲： 下个月是我侄女的生日，我想给她买个礼物。
   售货员： 她多大了？
   李哲： 她下个月九岁。
   售货员： 你看这个熊猫怎么样？打六折。
   李哲： 上小学以来，我侄女就爱踢足球，我给她买个足球吧。
   售货员： 但她毕竟是个女孩儿啊！
   李哲： 你说这句话有点不公平。难道女孩儿就不能踢足球？这是一个男女平等的社会。
   售货员： 先生，对不起，我不是这个意思。你在二层/二楼可以买到足球。

3. A: 今天的足球比赛，谁会赢？巴西队还是意大利队？
   B: 这两队以前都是世界冠军，我看比分会零比零。
   A: 可是最近巴西队表现得不好，老输，我觉得可能意大利队会赢。

4. A: 昨天我在你哥哥家跟你哥哥一起看足球冠军赛，家务事都是你嫂子在做。你哥哥是不是有点大男子主义？
   B: 不，我哥哥是个模范丈夫，他只有电视里有足球比赛的时候，才有点大男子主义。你知道吗？我嫂子是律师，她和我哥哥只有一个女儿。我哥哥在家里照顾女儿、做饭、洗碗、整理屋子，我嫂子工作。

I. (Answers may vary.)

1. 历史上，中国社会重男轻女。很多家长都要男孩儿。女孩儿没有受教育的机会。妇女的家庭和社会地位也比男人低。一九四九年以后，情况有了变化。特别是在城市，妇女都开始工作了。今天中国有很多女医生和女教师。但是，中国还有男女不平等的现象。比如，在农村，女孩儿受教育的机会比男孩儿少。一般来说，妇女的收入也比男人低。

2. 高明的嫂子叫王文音，是香港移民。结婚以后，她成了高王文音。高明问雪梅，中国大陆妇女结婚以后也用先生的姓吗？雪梅说不用。如果她结婚，她也不会用，还会叫林雪梅。雪梅问，高明的哥哥是不是有点大男子主义？高明说没有。他说女人结婚以后用丈夫的姓，是香港的社会习惯。哥哥其实是一个模范丈夫。除了偶尔为孩子的教育意见不同以外，哥哥和嫂子感情很好，互相体贴、互相照顾。两个人在家里的地位很平等。

J. (Answers may vary.)

K. (Answers may vary.)

1. 李平对网球很有兴趣。她最喜欢的网球运动员叫高明。高明常常拿冠军。李平希望长大以后能跟高明比赛。
2. 李平每天练习打网球，网球越打越好。
3. 这一天终于来到了。李平在网球场看到了高明，她跟高明比赛。高明很骄傲。他看到李平只是一个女孩，觉得很好笑。
4. 比赛结束了，李平赢了高明，成了冠军，她非常高兴。高明再也不是冠军了。他没想到自己竟输给一个女孩，非常不好意思。

Let's Review (Lessons 11–15)

I. How Good Is Your Pronunciation?

(Answers may vary: space between pinyin syllables may vary, some neutral tones may vary, and English translations may vary.)

1. Xuéqī jiéshù le, dàjiā juédìng jìxù liú zài xuéxiào.
   The semester has ended; everyone has decided to stay on campus.
2. Chī niányèfàn bié wàng le "nián nián yǒu yú" zhè jù huà.
   When you have Chinese New Year's Eve dinner, don't forget to say "surplus every year."
3. Zhōngqiūjié shì yì jiā tuányuán de jiérì.
   Mid-Autumn Festival is the holiday for family reunions.
4. Wǒ de xiǎoxué biànhuà díquè hěn dà, ràng wǒ gǎnjué yǒu xiē mòshēng.
   My elementary school has indeed changed greatly, and it makes me feel a bit like a stranger.
5. Bú shì zhōumò, lǚyóu jǐngdiǎn jìng jǐ mǎn le chē, jǐ mǎn le yóukè.
   It is not the weekend, but the tourist spots are unexpectedly congested with buses and sightseers.
6. Shǎoshù mínzú de jiànzhù hé fúzhuāng dōu bǎoliú le hěn duō chuántǒng tèsè.
   The architecture and costumes of minority groups all retain their traditional characteristics.
7. Wúlùn shì zài yìngwò háishi ruǎnwò chēxiāng, wǒ dōu shuì de zháo.
   Whether in a hard-berth sleeper or a soft-berth sleeper, I can sleep well.
8. Wǒ cónglái bù xǐhuan zìzhùyóu, dōu shì cānjiā lǚxíngtuán.
   I have never liked do-it-yourself tours; I have always joined group tours.
9. Gāo qiáng shàng guà zhe hóng dēnglong, qìfēn tèbié hǎo.
   Red lanterns are hanging on the high walls; the atmosphere is extremely nice.
10. Pái duì mǎi ménpiào kàn xióngmāo de yóukè fēicháng duō.
    There are so many tourists in line for admission tickets to see the pandas.
11. Nà duì tuìxiū fūqī zǎochen cháng zài gōngyuán sàn bù, ǒu'ěr yě dǎ tàijíquán.
    That retired couple often strolls in the park in the early morning; occasionally they also do tai chi.
12. Áo yè de rén bìxū bǔchōng shuìmián, zhùyì yǐnshí, fǒuzé róngyì shēng bìng.
    People who stay up late at night should get more sleep and pay more attention to their diet, otherwise they could easily get sick.
13. Dàjiā dōu xiāngxìn shìjiè jīngjì huì zhújiàn biàn hǎo.
    Everyone believes that the global economy will gradually improve.
14. Qǐng zhùyì fāyīn: shì "qì guǎn yán", ér bú shì "qìguǎnyán".
    Please pay attention to the pronunciation: it is "qī guǎn yán," not "qìguǎnyán".
15. Wǎng shàng yǒu xiāoxi shuō Zhōngguó nǚ zú yíng le shìjiè guànjūn.
    There is news on the Internet that says that the Chinese women's soccer team has won the world championship.

II. Put Your Chinese to Good Use!

(Answers may vary.)

III. Getting to Know China Better!

(Answers may vary.)

IV. Express Yourself!

(Answers may vary.)

LESSON 16

环境保护与节约能源

I. Listening Comprehension

A. (Answers may vary.)

1. They wanted to get close to nature and relax a little bit.
2. They rode bicycles, because taking a cab is too expensive and public transportation is too crowded.
3. Offices and other public sites should set the heating no higher than 20 degrees Celsius in winter and the air conditioning no lower than 26 degrees Celsius in summer.
4. People bring their own chopsticks instead of using disposable ones.
5. Supermarkets no longer provide plastic shopping bags for free.
6. People should start with small things such as turning off the lights and conserving water.

B. [女：喂，我在超市买菜，你赶快开车给我送个包来。
男：为什么？
女：我来了以后才知道，从今天起，超市不给塑料袋了，买东西都得自己带包了。
男：好啊，这有益于环保，可以减少白色污染啊。
女：别说那么多了，快点开车把包送来。
男：为了一个包，需要开车吗？你等着，我马上骑自行车过去，又能锻炼身体，又不会污染环境。]

1. (F)
2. (T)
3. (T)
4. (F)
5. (F)

C. (Answers may vary.)

1. [(男声)小林，给你打了两次电话，你都不在。我有个问题，想听听你的意见。你知道我在找夏天的工作。有个公司想让我到山里砍树，工资不错，可是我还没决定去不去。去吧，我知道这个工作对环保没有好处；不去吧，我怎么挣钱付下个学期的学费呢？我不知道应该怎么办。晚上给我打电话，好吗？]

    a. The job is cutting trees in the mountains.
    b. He knows that the job is not environmentally friendly, but he needs money to pay for his tuition fees.
    c. To seek advice.
    d. Answers may vary.

2. [(女声)小明，我知道你急着要出去玩儿，先看看你房间的灯关了没有？我说过很多次了，要随手关灯，可是你老忘。别以为这是小事，环境保护就是得从这些小事做起。要是我们现在不节约能源，不保护环境，等你长大了，地球不知道会变成什么样了！]

    a. Mother and son.
    b. Xiaoming did not turn off the light when he left the room.
    c. To protect the environment, one must start with small things in daily life.

D. [女：这次的能源危机非常严重。
男：
a. 否则后果不堪设想。
b. 毕竟太阳能是取之不尽的。
c. **可不是吗，政府老百姓都应该节能。**
d. 即使规定大家环保，也没人重视。]

II. Speaking Exercises

A. (Answers may vary.)

B. (Answers may vary.)

III. Reading Comprehension

A. (English translations may vary.)

New Word	Pinyin	English
资源	zīyuán	resources
益处	yìchu/yìchù	benefit
亮丽	liànglì	beautiful
阳历	yánglì	solar calendar
体温	tǐwēn	(body) temperature

B.
1. (e)
2. (d)
3. (f)
4. (a)
5. (c)
6. (b)

C.
1.
    1. (T)
    2. (T)
    3. (F)
    4. (F)
    5. (b)
2.
    1. (T)
    2. (T)
    3. (F)
    4. (F)
    5. (b)
    6. (a)
    7. (c)

D. (Answers may vary.)
1. Happiness Superstore.
2. Please close the door behind you.
3. No, because 厨房垃圾筒 is not translated accurately. "Food rubish" is incorrectly spelled and awkwardly translated as well.
4. To protect the water's environment.

E. (Answers may vary.)
1. Any four of the following: non-staple foods, seasoning, staple foods, daily necessities, cigarettes, alcohol, beverages, fruits, vegetables, frozen food, water, etc.)
2. Free delivery.

IV. Writing and Grammar Exercises

A. (Answers may vary.)
1. 是<u>能源</u>的<u>源</u>。
2. 是<u>推(自行)车</u>的<u>推</u>。
3. 是<u>取之不尽</u>的<u>取</u>。
4. 是<u>规定</u>的<u>规</u>。
5. 是<u>砍树</u>的<u>砍</u>。

B. (Answers may vary.)
1. 夫子庙前，人们拍照的拍照，吃小吃的吃小吃，买纪念品的买纪念品，很热闹。
2. 公园里，人们跳舞的跳舞，跑步的跑步，很有活力。
3. 足球场上，人们笑的笑，跳的跳，很高兴。

C. (Answers may vary.)
1. 买梨吧，太贵，卖西瓜吧，太重，我还是买苹果吧。
2. 打篮球吧，太热，看电影吧，太贵，我还是在家看碟吧。
3. 送花吧，她对花过敏，送电脑吧，太贵，我还是送蛋糕吧。

D.
1. 你<u>想起来</u>了吗？
2. 大家还不知道怎么给爷爷过八十岁生日，希望能赶快<u>想出</u>一个好主意。
3. 她的手机号码你<u>想起来</u>以后，请告诉我。
4. 柯林<u>想出(来)</u>一个去长城的好办法，又省钱又好玩儿。
5. 叔叔在哪个企业单位工作我到现在还没<u>想起来</u>。

E.
1. (c)
2. (d)
3. (a)
4. (b)

1. 运动有益于身体健康。
2. 利用太阳能或风能有益于节约传统能源。

3. 不随便乱扔垃圾有益于环境保护。
4. 不用塑料袋有益于减少白色污染。

F.
1. 八小于九。
2. 一百零一大于一百。
3. 三分之二大于二分之一。
4. 七十九加二十四等于一百零三。
5. 一千减四百三十八等于五百六十二。

(Answers may vary: time expressions may also be placed at the beginning of the sentences.)

6. 深圳今天晚上的温度高于天津。／今天晚上深圳的温度高于天津。
7. 上海明天的温度低于杭州。／明天上海的温度低于杭州。
8. 纽约昨天的温度高于哈尔滨。／昨天纽约的温度高于哈尔滨。

G. (Answers may vary.)
1. 马克爬山，<u>爬着爬着爬到了山上</u>。
2. 柯林吃鱼，<u>吃着吃着（就）把鱼都吃了</u>。
3. 丽莎听故事，<u>听着听着（就）笑了起来</u>。

H. (Answers may vary.)
A: 你的衬衫真漂亮！在哪儿买的？
B: 这是我妈妈的旧衣服。我的家具也是在旧家具店买的。
A: 你真节约。
B: 我还在付学生贷款，没有很多钱，而且我觉得旧的东西如果还可以用，为什么要买新的呢？我现在尽可能少买、少浪费东西。
A: 难怪你用纸也很节约。
B: 如果我们不节约、不注意回收的话，地球上的垃圾就会越来越多。
A: 我同意。

I. (Answers may vary.)
1. "保护地球，保护我们的家。"我们星期四晚上七点在5号楼305室开会，讨论环保怎么样从小地方做起，从我做起。欢迎大家都来参加。
2. "爱绿色，不爱白色。"让我们一起保护绿色的地球，减少白色污染。请大家节约用纸，不要用一次性筷子，不要喝瓶装水。周末，我们去城外种树、回收塑料袋和塑料瓶，欢迎大家参加。
3. 我表哥天亮以前骑自行车上班，现在开起车来了。可是他的女朋友小音觉得骑自行车又能锻炼身体，又省钱，而且有益于环境保护，所以她不想买汽车。她说天亮有了车以后，很少锻炼，人也胖了。再说，大街上挤满了汽车，开车不如骑自行车方便。天亮觉得小音说的有道理，就打算把车卖了，买自行车和小音一起骑自行车上班。
4. 爸爸：
昨天我和朋友一起骑自行车去城外爬山。我们看见很多房子都利用太阳能发电，觉得很酷。晚上回到宿舍后，我上网查了查，原来中国很多地方都利用太阳能和风能发电。现在世界上很多国家都跟中国一样在闹能源危机，如果继续用煤和石油的话，后果不堪设想。而太阳能和风能可是取之不尽的，而且能帮助世界解决能源危机。

天明

J. (Answers may vary.)

K. (Answers may vary.)
1. 以前很多中国人不注意环保。他们到餐馆吃饭，喜欢用餐馆给的一次性筷子。为什么呢？因为一次性筷子很干净／卫生，而且不要钱。
2. 这些人不知道，中国一共有多少餐馆啊？这些餐馆都让客人用一次性筷子，每年要砍多少树啊？因为很多树被砍了，自然环境变坏了，河里的水也不干净了。
3. 现在不一样了。越来越多的中国人开始重视环保了。很多人到餐馆吃饭，不用一次性筷子，而用自己带的筷子了。
4. 因为大家都开始保护环境，而且都从小事做起，我们的环境开始好起来了。新的树长得越来越高了，小鸟在树上跳舞呢。河里的水也变得干净了。

LESSON 17

理财与投资

I. Listening Comprehension

A. (Answers may vary.)

1. Because they think savings accounts do not give a good return.
2. Different people like different investment methods, and some people prefer spending over investing.
3. She was going to use her personal savings for her granddaughter's college education.
4. They said that they wouldn't need another car, and they tried to persuade her to spend the money on a larger apartment.
5. No, because she changed her mind and wanted to invest in the stock market.
6. Answers may vary.

B. [男：我看别人炒股赚钱很容易，可是我自己一买股票，股市就跌！
女：别生气，慢慢说。
男：我一向省吃俭用，存了一点钱，上个月我把钱放进股市里，没想到已经赔了一半。
女：炒股是有风险的。
男：我想明天就把股票卖了。
女：别急着卖。现在股市不太好，可是说不定过几天就涨上来了。]

1. (F)
2. (T)
3. (F)
4. (T)
5. (F)
6. (T)

C. (Answers may vary.)
[(女声)我一直说，咱们都已经快六十岁了，还是把钱存在银行安全，可是你就是不听。看到别人炒股赚了钱，你就非把钱放进股市里不可。现在怎么样？不到三个月，赔了三分之一！我们几年以后就要退休了，退休以后怎么生活？]

a. Husband and wife.
b. She prefers to put the money in the bank, because she thinks it is safer.
c. He invested in the stock market, and lost one third of the investment.
d. She is worried, because they are planning to retire in just a few years.

2. [(男声) 喂，大亮，我是你爸，怎么手机又没开？我跟你妈已经看中了一套两室两卫的房子，离你现在住的地方不远。我们昨天已经把银行存款都拿出来，下个星期就要签购房合同了，可是你还没告诉我们，贷款的问题解决了没有。要是银行不给贷款，我们可以用老房子抵押。你今天下午一定再给银行打个电话，别忘了。]

a. Because Daliang's cellphone is not on.
b. They plan to use their savings to apply for a mortgage.
c. No, because he is not sure yet whether they will get the loan or have to mortgage their current apartment.
d. He wants Daliang to call the bank one more time.

D. [男：赚钱就是为了享受，走，咱们去餐馆好好儿吃一顿。
女：

a. 现在赚钱不容易，还是省吃俭用比较好。
b. 剩余的钱应该存在银行里，别乱买东西。
c. 随便，你去哪家餐馆，我就去哪家餐馆。
d. 这种生活方式引起你的思考。]

II. Speaking Exercises

A. (Answers may vary.)

B. (Answers may vary.)

Workbook Answer Key • Lesson 17

III. Reading Comprehension

A.

New Word	*Pinyin*	English
炒面	chǎomiàn	stir-fried noodles
闷气	mènqì	sulking
苦功	kǔgōng	hard work/painstaking effort
签字	qiān zì	to sign one's name
突变	tūbiàn	sudden change/spontaneous mutation

B.
1. 旁边的几个朋友正在分享自己投资理财的经验，这引起小王的兴趣。
2. 导游的建议，有些人赞成，但也引起某些人的反对。
3. 在安静的病房里，突然有人的脚步声，引起了医生的注意。
4. 煤和石油越来越少，如果再不节能，恐怕会引起全世界的能源危机。
5. 张教授希望用报上的文章来引起大家对环保问题的讨论。

C. 1. Questions (True/False):
   1. (F)
   2. (T)
   3. (F)
   4. (T)
   5. (a)
   6. (c)
   7. (b)

   2. 1. (F)
   2. (F)
   3. (T)
   4. (F)
   5. (T)
   6. (F)
   7. (c)
   8. (b)

D. (Answers may vary.)

E. (Answers will vary.)

户　名	[Name]		
账户/卡号	012345		
种　类			
币　别	RMB	钞(汇)	
存　期		起息日	
存款金额：	1000		元
手续费：	10		元
流水号：			
	银行签章		

客户回单

IV. Writing and Grammar Exercises

A. (Answers may vary.)
1. 是房价涨/股票涨/涨价/涨跌/的涨。
2. 是炒股的炒。
3. 是的郁闷的闷。
4. 是攒钱的攒。
5. 是想法的想。

B.
1. 小王上大学以来，一直在理财公司实习。
2. 知道自己这个学期的成绩后，小王一直很郁闷。
3. 小王一向怎么说就怎么做，所以大家都很相信他。
4. 小王昨天晚上手机一直关机，害得同学找不到他。
5. 小王一向十分注意自己的生活习惯与饮食健康。

C. (Answers may vary.)
1. 她们(姐妹)合用一个卫生间/她们(姐妹)合用一个洗澡间/她们(姐妹)合用一个洗手间/她们(姐妹)合用一个厕所。
2. 她们(姐妹)合用一个电脑。
3. 她们(姐妹)合开一辆车。
4. 她们(姐妹)合养一只狗。

D. (Answers may vary.)
1. (林)雪梅找工作找了很长时间，终于找到一份合适的工作。

2. 李文准备考研究生准备了很长时间，终于准备好了。
3. (张)天明找钥匙找了很长时间，终于找到了。
4. 柯林爬山爬了很长时间，终于爬到了山上。

E. (Answers may vary.)
1. 不能，接着听，再听半个钟头。
2. 不行，接着做，再做五次。
3. 不够，接着拍，再拍二十张。
4. 不能，接着扔，再多扔几件。

F. Word Association (Answers may vary.)
1. <u>我们可以上网聊天、购物、查资料等等。</u>
2. <u>我们可以去银行存钱、取钱、换钱、借钱等等。</u>

G. (Answers may vary.)
1. (请)把窗户打开。/(请)把窗户开开。
2. (请)把灯关上。/(请)把灯关了。
3. (请)把茶喝了。
4. (请)把(你的)杯子洗干净。
5. (请)把(你的)房间整理好。
6. (请)把晚饭做好。

H. (Answers may vary.)
1. A: 最近哪些股票涨了？
   B: 现在大家都重视环保，如果你不想短期炒股，而是想长期投资的话，我觉得买太阳能和风能方面的股票可能是不错的主意。
2. A: 你知道不知道有一位经济学家开了一个银行，把钱借给没有钱的妇女，因为他觉得妇女会理财，知道怎么用钱。
   B: 我从来没听说过有这样的银行。
   A: 他把钱借给没有钱的妇女，还因为他想提高妇女的社会地位。他今天晚上来学校介绍他的想法，我们可以一起去听听。
3. A: 我想问一些理财的问题，可以吗？
   B: 没问题。请问你今年多大？
   A: 二十五岁。
   B: 我觉得你可以买一些股票。虽然股市有时候跌，买股票有风险，可是你不是短期炒股，问题不大。如果你已经退休了，最好把钱存在银行里。
   A: 那买房子呢？有人说买房子也是很好的投资。
   B: 如果房子是自己住的话，不算是投资。如果你买房子租出去，就的确是好投资。
   A: 谢谢。我回家想想。

I. (Answers may vary.)
1. 我的表哥把车卖了，他炒股也赚了一点钱，所以想买一套房子。他看中了一套三室一厅两卫的房子，但是在城外，上班不太方便。他的未婚妻说，"城里的房子太贵，我们贷款很困难。星期一到星期五，我们可以和我父母或你父母一起住。周末，我们骑自行车去城外住。再说，将来一定有地铁，如果我们现在不买，以后房价涨了，我们就更没机会了。
2. 李文的父母工作了三十多年，终于退休了。他们一向省吃俭用，所以在银行里有些存款。他们觉得虽然钱存在银行增加得很慢，但是最安全。他们不喜欢炒股。李文认为有钱就应该消费享受。虽然她的存款很少，但是她常常炒股。她说现在房子太贵了，如果她不炒股赚点钱，她的钱就不够买一套房子。她的父母看她有的时候赚钱有的时候赔钱，很担心。他们偶尔还为李文炒股的事闹矛盾。

J. (Answers may vary.)

K. (Answers may vary.)
1. 张先生打算拿钱去买股票。为什么呢？因为现在股票正在涨，以前买股票的人现在都赚了不少钱。张先生也想把钱放到股市里，觉得明年肯定会赚钱。
2. 张先生想错了。他开始炒股以后，股市一直跌。张先生越来越担心，怕自己的钱会越来越少，所以就把他的股票都卖了。他炒股炒了一年，赔了一半钱。张先生非常难过。

3. 到了第三年，房价涨起来了。张先生很高兴，他觉得这是个投资的好机会。他用炒股剩下的钱买了一栋房子。他想，房价涨得这么快，明年一定能赚不少钱。

4. 可是张先生又想错了。他买房子以后，很多房子就开始减价了。张先生很担心自己的房子会越来越便宜，所以第二年就把房子卖了。才一年时间，他又赔了一半钱。张先生看起来难过极了。

LESSON 18

中国历史

I. Listening Comprehension

A. (Answers may vary.)

1. Because Lisa is taking a course in Chinese history, and her friends are also interested in Chinese history.
2. She considers Confucius to be the most important educator in Chinese history.
3. He helped unify China and the Chinese script, but he was ruthless in killing scholars and forcing people to build the Great Wall, his palace, and his mausoleum.
4. Because during these two dynasties China enjoyed steady development in politics, economy, and culture.
5. Paper, gunpowder, the compass, and movable-type printing.
6. There was a revolution led by Sun Yat-sen.

B. ［(男：你说谁是中国历史上最有名的皇帝？
女：有好几个皇帝都很有名，我觉得秦始皇是最有名的皇帝之一。
男：为什么？因为他做了很多好事吗？
女：他在有的方面做了一些好事，在另外一些方面也做了不少坏事。
男：听说他杀了很多读书人。
女：是啊，其中有些读书人是很有贡献的。
男：可是你怎么还说他是有名的皇帝呢？
女：有名的皇帝不见得就是好皇帝啊。)］

1. (T)
2. (F)
3. (T)
4. (F)
5. (T)
6. (T)

C. (Answers may vary.)

1. ［(女声)李文，你好。我是丽莎。本来我打算明天下午请你带我去参观中国国家博物馆的，可是我的几个同学知道了，他们都对中国历史很有兴趣，也想跟我一起去。其中有一个同学明天下午有课，我们可不可以后天下午去？请你给我回个电话。谢谢。］

   a. No, because some other people would like to go with her and tomorrow afternoon will not work for everyone.
   b. Lisa wants to confirm with Li Wen whether they can go to the museum the day after tomorrow.

2. ［(女声)丽莎，后天来参观没问题。可是我想告诉你，中国国家博物馆是世界上最大的博物馆之一。如果什么都看，非要一个星期不可。所以我们只能看看中国的几个朝代，别的东西以后再参观。另外，这个星期参观的人非常多，可能跟最近天气特别好有关系。所以你们最好早点儿来。］

   a. Li Wen. She wants to confirm with Lisa that it is fine to go to the museum the day after tomorrow.
   b. It is one of the largest.
   c. She suggests that they only visit the exhibits on some of the Chinese dynasties, leaving the rest for a later visit.
   d. The number of visitors has increased this week, probably because of the nice weather.

D. ［男：他是我最讨厌的诗人之一，你怎么会喜欢他？
女：
   a. 历史上有很多诗人，我都讨厌。
   b. 我跟你一样，也不喜欢诗人。
   c. 你喜欢哪一个诗人跟我没关系。
   d. 你怎么会讨厌他？他的诗很有感情。］

II. Speaking Exercises

A. (Answers may vary.)

B. (Answers may vary.)

Workbook Answer Key • Lesson 18 161

III. Reading Comprehension

A. (English translations may vary.)

New Word	*Pinyin*	English
伟业	wěiyè	great exploit
建国	jiànguó	to found a state/nation
展览	zhǎnlǎn	to exhibit; to put on display
皇宫	huánggōng	(imperial) palace
修理	xiūlǐ	to repair/to fix

B. 1. 明天有一个外国人要来参观我们的工厂，请大家做好准备。
2. 石林的石头千奇百怪，我们一边游览，一边听导游给我们讲跟石头有关的故事。
3. 参观博物馆的时候，千万别随便乱拍照。
4. 坐船从东往西游览长江，感觉非常特别。
5. 我们想参观一下你们建筑公司在城东盖的那栋大楼，不知道方便不方便？
6. 听说有个老外坐飞机到北京参观各个有名的烤鸭店。

C. 1. 1. (F)
   2. (T)
   3. (F)
   4. (T)
   5. (c)
   6. (c)

   2. 1. (F)
   2. (T)
   3. (F)
   4. (T)
   5. (c)
   6. (b)

D. (Answers may vary.)

E. (Answers may vary.)
自行车(坏了，可以来这儿修)。

F. (Answers may vary.)
游客在参观博物馆的时候会问这些问题。

IV. Writing and Grammar Exercises

A. (Answers may vary.)
1. 是<u>皇</u>帝的<u>皇</u>。
2. 是<u>秦始皇/ 开始</u>的<u>始</u>。
3. 是<u>塑料袋</u>的<u>袋</u>。
4. 是<u>贡献</u>的<u>贡</u>。
5. 是<u>基础</u>的<u>基</u>。

B. 1. (c)
2. (a)
3. (e)
4. (f)
5. (d)
6. (b)

1. Aristotle 是世界上最伟大的哲学家之一。
2. Thomas Edison 是世界上最伟大的发明家之一。
3. Marie Curie 是世界上最伟大的科学家之一。
4. Shakespeare 是世界上最伟大的文学家之一。
5. Frida Kahlo 是世界上最伟大的画家之一。

C. (Answers may vary.)
1. 北京、上海、东京、纽约都是世界上的大城市，<u>其中北京的面积最大</u>。
2. 北京、上海、东京、纽约都是世界上的大城市，<u>其中东京的生活费最贵</u>。
3. 北京、上海、东京、纽约都是世界上的大城市，<u>其中纽约的房价最高</u>。
4. 北京、上海、东京、纽约都是世界上的大城市，<u>其中北京的空气污染最严重/其中北京的空气污染最糟糕</u>。

D. 1. (c)
2. (d)
3. (e)
4. (b)
5. (a)

1. 在电脑网络方面，(张)天明比其它人都懂得多/在电脑网络方面，(张)天明懂得比其它人多。
2. 在健身与饮食方面，丽莎比其它人都懂得多/在健身与饮食方面，丽莎懂得比其它人多。
3. 在环保与节能方面，(林)雪梅比其它人都懂得多/在环保与节能方面，(林)雪梅懂得比其它人多。
4. 在中国历史方面，李文比其它人都懂得多/在中国历史方面，李文懂得比其它人多。

E. (Answers may vary.)
1. 我常常上网查跟＿＿＿有关的资料。
2. 我比较注意跟＿＿＿有关的新闻。
3. 跟＿＿＿有关的事情更会引起我的重视。

F. (Answers may vary.)
1. 丽莎说从明年开始她再也不喝咖啡了。
2. (张)天明的表哥说从明年开始他再也不吃快餐了。
3. 李文说从明年开始她再也不熬夜了/李文说从明年开始她再也不开夜车了。

G. (Answers may vary.)
1. A: 我们明天考中国历史，请大家今天晚上复习一下清朝的皇帝。
   B: 什么，老师，明天要考中国历史？我们不喜欢考试，也不喜欢复习。
   A: 大家都知道孔子给我们留下很多话，其中"有朋自远方来，不亦乐乎！"是最有名的。另外还有一句话同样有名，那就是"学而时习之不亦乐乎！"/"学而时习之不亦说乎！"（"说"同"悦"，意思是"愉快、快乐"。）祝大家今天晚上复习快乐。
2. A: 你参观过兵马俑博物馆吗？
   B: 没有，可是我想去，我对秦始皇很有兴趣。

A: 秦始皇在中国历史上很重要，可是也有很多人不喜欢他，因为他杀了很多读书人，还让很多人给他修宫殿、坟墓。
B: 不管你喜欢不喜欢秦始皇，我觉得他对中国文化发展的影响都很大，比如他统一了中国的文字。
A: 这我同意。汉朝就是在秦朝的基础上，使中国的政治和经济都有了很大的发展。

3. A: 我们明天去爬长城，怎么样？
   B: 好啊，我早就想去了，可是一直没有机会去。听说长城的历史差不多有两、三千年，秦代以前就开始修了。
   A: 对，可是我们的历史老师说，现在我们看到的长城大部分是明朝修的。
   B: 我们怎么去？
   A: 我们可以坐公共汽车去。
   B: 坐公共汽车没意思。我们骑自行车去怎么样？
   A: 好，一言为定。骑自行车又省钱又能锻炼身体。

H. 孔子说："有朋自远方来，不亦乐乎。"欢迎大家来山东。孔子是中国历史上最重要的教育家和思想家，对中国有很大的影响。现在世界各国都有孔子学院。山东是孔子的家乡，中国最有名的孔庙就在山东。山东还有很多的旅游景点，比如泰山。希望大家在山东，除了有很多机会练习中文以外，还能爬泰山。最后，我把这些印了孔子的话的T恤衫送给大家。

I. (Answers may vary.)

J. (Answers may vary.)
1. 小李和小张都对中国历史很感兴趣。这天上午他们一起去参观这家跟中国历史有关的博物馆。九点钟，他们来到汉朝展厅。汉朝是从公元前206年到公元220年。汉朝时，中国是统一的国家，经济很稳定，从那时候就开始和西方进行贸易了,有了丝绸之路。

2. 上午九点半,他们来到了唐朝。唐朝是从公元618年到公元907年。唐朝时,中国的经济很发达,在唐朝的首都有很多外国留学生。唐朝的文化也很先进,特别有名的是唐诗。

3. 上午十点钟,他们来到了清朝。清朝是从1644年到1911年。清朝时,中国的科学技术不够发达,政治经济也不太稳定。1911年的革命以后,中国就再也没有皇帝了。

4. 上午十点半,他们来到了今天的中国展厅。1978年以来,中国进行了改革开放,经济发展得很快,人民生活水平有了很大的提高。现在中国是世界经济大国之一了。小李和小张花了一个多小时,看了一遍中国两千多年的历史。

LESSON 19

面试

I. Listening Comprehension

A. (Answers may vary.)

1. Because the Chinese expression for "person who returned from overseas" sounds like a pun on the word for "sea turtle."
2. Because the general manager who interviewed her looked very serious.
3. She showed him the letters from the American companies that had offered her jobs.
4. No, because she did not want to create a wrong impression that she only planned to work in China for the short term.
5. Not knowing how to rest well.
6. She sounds optimistic, because the general manager asked her to wait for good news from them.

B. ［女：中国现在有二十几家汽车公司，你为什么希望来我们公司工作？

男：我找工作的标准是，一定要找有益于环保的工作。中国的汽车公司虽然很多，可是你们生产的汽车污染最小。所以我希望能到你们公司来工作。

女：我不太同意你的解释。如果你真的重视环保，为什么不去大地汽车公司呢？他们的汽车污染比较大，更需要你这样的人材。

男：其实他们录用我了，可是他们公司的薪水…

女：我知道了，你找工作的标准不是环保，而是薪水。］

1. (F)
2. (F)
3. (T)
4. (T)
5. (F)
6. (F)

Question: (Answers may vary.)

C. (Answers may vary.)

1. ［(女声)去年五月我毕业以后申请了四个工作，三家公司让我去面试，其中一家公司的总经理觉得我的工作经验不够，另外两家公司都录用了我。可是我对那两家公司的产品和管理都不太满意，所以最后还是没有接受他们的工作。］
   a. She was a student.
   b. Because the general manager considered her work experience inadequate.
   c. She did not accept either of the job offers, because she did not like either company's products or management.

2. ［(男声)张小姐在学校的学习成绩非常好，毕业以后在日本一家公司工作了两年多，最近才回到中国。因为我们公司和那家日本公司打过很多次交道，所以她对我们的产品和销售都很熟悉。另外，张小姐也特别善于安排时间。所以我认为我们应该录用她。］
   a. The speaker is a leader of the company, and Miss Zhang is a job candidate.
   b. He wants to convince his colleagues that their company should hire Miss Zhang.
   c. She was a good student and worked in a Japanese company for two years.
   d. Because the speaker's company has had a business relationship with the Japanese company that Miss Zhang worked for.

D. ［女：我们经理非常严肃，跟他工作压力太大，害我每天都紧张得不得了。

男：
   a. 我也觉得他工作的时候不严肃，得给他一些压力。
   b. **既然你觉得有些受不了，就换工作吧！**
   c. 你又不严肃，别紧张。
   d. 我的工作压力也大，但我不严肃。］

II. Speaking Exercises

A. (Answers may vary.)

B. (Answers may vary.)

Workbook Answer Key • Lesson 19

III. Reading Comprehension

A. (English translations may vary.)

New Word	*Pinyin*	English
西装	xīzhuāng	Western-style clothes/suit
湿度	shīdù	humidity
肃静	sùjìng	solemn silence
阴阳	yīnyáng	*yin* and *yang*/yin-yang
解答	jiědá	answer; explain

B.
1. 经理告诉雪梅开始上班以后<u>常常</u>需要出国开会。
2. 太极拳要打得好必须<u>常常</u>练习。
3. 我很喜欢参观博物馆，无论去哪个博物馆，<u>常常/往往</u>都得花好几个小时的时间。
4. 刚从大学毕业的人，没有实习经验，<u>常常/往往</u>找不到工作。
5. 面试人的人<u>常常/往往</u>很严肃，一点都不幽默，甚至有点儿吓人。

C. 1.
1. (T)
2. (F)
3. (T)
4. (b)
5. (a)
6. (c)

2.
1. (F)
2. (T)
3. (F)
4. (F)
5. (a)
6. (c)
7. (a)

D. (Answers may vary.)
上早班薪水最高/从早上6点上到下午2点的薪水最高。

E. (Answers may vary.)
Today's weather: cloudy with some sun, 23-32 degrees Celsius

F. (Answers may vary.)
1. A restaurant owner/manager is conducting the survey. Restaurant patrons are being surveyed.
2. 是不是
3. (Answers may vary.)

IV. Writing and Grammar Exercises

A. (Answers may vary.)
1. 是<u>海外/上海/沿海</u>的海。
2. 是<u>旗袍</u>的袍。
3. 是<u>因此/因为</u>的因。
4. 是<u>销售/售货员</u>的售。
5. 是<u>握手</u>的握。

B.
1. (c)
2. (h)
3. (f)
4. (b)
5. (a)
6. (g)
7. (d)
8. (e)

(English translations may vary.)
1. "国际贸易"也叫做"国贸"，英文翻译成"international trade"。
2. "环境保护"也叫做"环保"，英文翻译成"environmental protection"。
3. "节约能源"也叫做"节能"，英文翻译成"energy conservation"。
4. "国营企业"也叫做"国企"，英文翻译成"state-run enterprise"。
5. "科学技术"也叫做"科技"，英文翻译成"scientific technology"。
6. "电子邮件"也叫做"电邮"，英文翻译成"email"。
7. "丝绸之路"也叫做"丝路"，英文翻译成"the Silk Road"。

C. (Answers may vary.)
1. 我<u>又没(有)</u>钱，怎么借钱给你？
2. 我<u>又不穿</u>旗袍，买了是浪费。
3. 我<u>又不是</u>服务员，要换自己换。

D. (Answers may vary.)
1. 四川菜越辣越好(吃)。
2. 薪水越多越好/薪水越高越好。
3. 工作压力越小越好。
4. 空气越新鲜越好。
5. 银行(存款)的利息越高越好。

E. (Answers may vary.)
1. 既然(你)没钱，干吗投资股市？
2. 既然城里空气污染(挺)严重(的)，就别搬了吧！
3. 既然你(对他的表现)很满意，就通知他下星期来上班。

F. (Answers may vary.)
1. 好在我们家的钱都(存)在银行(里)。
2. 好在我们(家的人)从来不熬夜/好在我们(家的人)从来不开夜车。
3. 好在我们(全)家(都)吃素。

G. 1. (c)
2. (d)
3. (e)
4. (a)
5. (b)

(Answers may vary.)
1. 雪梅善于销售，是销售方面的优秀人材。
2. 总经理善于管理，是管理方面的优秀人材。
3. 张天明善于网络设计，是网络设计方面的优秀人材。
4. 天明的表哥善于理财，是理财方面的优秀人材。

H. (Answers may vary.)
1. A: 你在网上查什么呢？
   B: 查资料找工作。
   A: 你想做哪方面的工作？
   B: 我想找跟环保有关的工作，我对这家太阳能发电公司很有兴趣。
   A: 这是不是一家跨国公司？你不但善于研究发展新技术，而且对中国和西方文化都很熟悉，他们一定会欢迎你这只"海龟"。

2. A: 你能不能告诉我你为什么要申请这份工作？
   B: 因为我大学学的是环保专业，再说太阳能取之不尽，而且不污染环境，有益于环保。
   A: 你有工作经验吗？
   B: 我在美国一家太阳能公司实习过半年。
   A: 你是打算在中国短期工作吗？
   B: 不，我是在中国出生，在中国长大的，我的父母都在中国，所以我打算在中国长期工作。
   A: 好，请你等我们的通知。

3. A: 你觉得今天来面试的人怎么样？
   B: 我觉得很好，有很多优点。中英文都好，又有在美国实习的经验。
   A: 但她也有一个缺点，没有国际销售的经验。
   B: 大学刚毕业，不可能有很多销售经验。从她回答问题的样子看，她好像很聪明。另外，她的大学专业是环保，我相信她有能力把我们的产品给客户介绍得很清楚。
   A: 有道理，那就录用她吧。

4. A: 明天你就要去公司上班了。你一定得科学地安排自己的时间。除了工作以外，也要注意休息，不要熬夜。多学习别人的优点。
   B: 妈，别担心，我知道。我又不是小孩子。
   A: 既然你知道，我就不说了。否则我越说，你越不高兴。

I. (Answers may vary.)
1. 我们是一家跨国绿色饮料公司，现在需要一位销售经理。申请者必须善于销售，中英文都好。有在海外工作、有销售经验、懂技术的，更好。这份工作男女都可以申请。我们公司男女平等、同工同酬。
2. 我今天的面试进行得很顺利。经理让我讲讲他们产品的优点与缺点。好在我准备得很好，我越解释，经理就越满意。我进他办公室之前,大家都告诉我经理很严肃,甚至可怕。可是只要你好好回答他的问题,他没有那么吓人。面试结束的时候,他竟跟我握手,让我回家等好消息。

J. (Answers may vary.)

K. (Answers may vary.)
1. 坐在书桌旁边的这个人看起来是一位总经理。他很严肃。一位年轻人走进总经理的办公室。我们把他叫做小田吧。小田刚刚研究生毕业,正在找工作。他今天来总经理这儿面试。他跟总经理握手,看起来很轻松,一点儿也不紧张。
2. 总经理坐在办公桌后边,小田坐在他的对面。总经理问小田一个跟公司管理有关的问题。小田不知道怎么回答,就用手机打电话给他的教授,请教授帮忙。
3. 总经理现在显得有点儿不高兴了。他接着问小田一个和产品销售有关的问题。小田又不知道怎么回答,就又用手机打电话,请他的教授帮忙。
4. 总经理很生气,他觉得不用再接着问问题了。面试可以结束了。他对小田说:"现在我请你去吃晚饭吧。你喜欢中国菜还是法国菜?"小田听了,用手机对他的教授说:"教授,这个问题不用您帮忙,我自己可以回答。"看得出来,总经理是不会录用小田的。

LESSON 20

外国人在中国

I. Listening Comprehension

A. (Answers may vary.)

1. Tianming, Lisa, Li Zhe, Li Wen, and Mark are attending the party. The party is a celebration of Xuemei's new job. Meanwhile, it is a farewell party because Tianming and Lisa are returning to the United States, and it is also a welcome party because Li Zhe has just arrived in Beijing.
2. It will be a trip to Europe promoting solar water heaters.
3. He has arrived in Beijing for an internship. Xuemei is excited because Li Zhe will intern in her company.
4. He is happy, even though his work is not stable.
5. No, because she has enjoyed living with Li Wen and her parents.
6. Because she thinks that Chinese people and foreigners are now in more frequent and closer contact with each other.

B. ［女：你是李哲先生吧？总经理知道你要来，可是他两点要开会，所以让我在这儿欢迎你。

男：谢谢。我非常高兴有机会到这儿来实习。

女：总经理已经把你的实习工作安排好了。你在这里的三个月都在销售部工作，销售部的经理是林雪梅小姐，她会帮你适应那里的工作的。

男：好极了，林小姐是我在美国的校友。

女：真的？那太好了，校友成了同事了。］

1. (F)
2. (F)
3. (F)
4. (T)
5. (F)

C. (Answers may vary.)

1. ［女：小王，我是张红。学期结束了，李新马上要回中国了，她已经在上海的一家公司找到了工作。另外，新的中国留学生也开始来了，昨天来了两位北京的同学。还会有上海的、天津的。明天晚上我这儿有个聚会，算是给李新饯行，也算是给从北京来的两位新朋友接风。希望你一定来。］

   Questions:

   a. Zhang Hong is a student from China. She wants to tell Little Wang about tomorrow's party.
   b. Li Xin is leaving soon for a new job in Shanghai.
   c. To send off Li Xin and welcome two new students from Beijing.

2. ［男：大家好。我叫田江，刚从北京来。我和我的同学钱明很高兴参加这个聚会。我们也要祝贺李新成为一只新的"海龟"。我们来了才两天，就已经看到听到不少新鲜事儿，不但认识了不少中国同学，而且交了几个美国朋友。我们想早点儿适应这里的生活，融入新的环境。请大家多关照！］

   a. He is a student who has just arrived from Beijing. He is speaking to all the guests at the party.
   b. He calls Li Xin a new "sea turtle."
   c. He has met many Chinese students and made a few American friends.

D. ［男：王经理，很高兴能跟您一起工作，请多关照。

女：

a. 你太客气了，欢迎你来我们单位工作。
b. 你虽然是经理，但是不可怕！
c. 你放心，我也很高兴在这儿工作。
d. 可不是吗？公司有很多同事照顾我。］

II. Speaking Exercises

A. (Answers may vary.)

B. (Answers may vary.)

III. Reading Comprehension

A. (English translations may vary.)

New Word	*Pinyin*	English
聚餐	jù cān	to dine together/to have a dinner party
庆功	qìnggōng	to celebrate a success
器材	qìcái	equipment
剧本	jùběn	script
听众	tīngzhòng	audience/listeners

B. (English translations may vary.)
1. a. reader
   b. author/writer
   c. elderly person/senior/senior citizen
   d. educator
   e. scholar
2. a. waiter/waitress/wait staff
   b. salesperson/salesclerk
   c. athlete
   d. team member/teammate
   e. actor/actress
3. a. philosopher
   b. scientist
   c. econmist
   d. inventor
   e. educator
   f. thinker

C. 1. 1. (F)
      2. (F)
      3. (F)
      4. (T)
      5. (c)
      6. (a)
   2. 1. (F)
      2. (F)
      3. (F)
      4. (c)

D. tutor(s)

E. (Answers may vary.)
这是社区超市的广告。他们卖很多东西。/小区超市的广告。他们卖很多东西。
(2 of the following:) They sell cigarettes, alcohol, recreational and sports items, daily necessities, metals or hardware, cosmetics, etc.

IV. Writing and Grammar Exercises

A. (Answers may vary.)
1. 是<u>欧</u>洲的<u>欧</u>。
2. 是<u>搞</u>点儿翻译的<u>搞</u>。
3. 是<u>校友/学校</u>的<u>校</u>。
4. 是<u>不值一提/值得</u>的<u>值</u>。
5. 是<u>友谊</u>的<u>谊</u>。

B. (Answers may vary.)
1. 把钱存在银行（里）。/把钱存进银行（里）。
2. 把钱投资到股票市场。/把钱投资到股市里。/把钱拿来炒股。
3. 把钱给父母。
4. 把钱借给同学。
5. 把钱放在枕头下面。/把钱放在枕头下边。
6. 把钱放在床下（边）。
7. 把钱（都）花了。

C. (Answers may vary.)

D. (Answers may vary.)
1. 别紧张，<u>(我)只请了五个人</u>而已。
2. 不累，<u>(我只有)三份工作</u>而已。
3. 不长，<u>(我只待了)半年</u>而已。

E. (Answers may vary.)
1. （在同事的帮助下，他很快地适应了新工作。）
2. （在老师的教育下，他顺利地拿到硕士学位。）
3. （在父母的说服下，他决定不投资股市。）

F. (Answers may vary.)
1. （A: 谢谢你的帮助。要不是你跟电视公司联系，他们不可能让我演那个电视剧。
   B: 我只是打个电话而已，不值一提。）
2. （A: 上个月热水器的销售情况怎么样？
   B: 您说呢？在您的领导下，我们成为全世界三大热水器公司之一。我们越推销，卖得越火。
   A: 太好了。我们今天晚上应该聚会，庆祝一下。
   B: 我举双手赞成。）

G. (Answers may vary.)
1. （同学们，谢谢大家为我饯行。四年的大学生活，没想到这么快就过去了。明天我就要坐飞机回墨西哥了。我来中国的时候一句中文都不会，由于大家经常帮助我、照顾我，这四年我在中国过得非常快乐。我每天都能看到、听到新鲜事儿，这些我永远也忘不了。我也要谢谢白老师教了我很多东西。来，我祝大家身体健康、事业成功。）
2. （裴佩和我做了四年的同屋，所以我得说几句。学校让我帮裴佩学习中文，但是我觉得我从裴佩那儿也学到了很多东西。裴佩是个足球迷。我现在身体那么好，就是因为裴佩不管学习多忙，每个周末都让我和他一起去足球场踢足球。他使我认识到身体健康和学习一样重要。我永远不会忘记你，裴佩。现在请白老师说几句话。）
3. （裴佩，我先要恭喜你找到了好工作。裴佩告诉没告诉大家他在墨西哥的一家中国公司找到了一份工作？听说裴佩面试的时候一点都不紧张，表现得非常好，面试他的经理觉得裴佩很有能力，优点很多，我非常高兴。裴佩，祝你明天一路平安！也祝你事业成功！）
4. （今天是我上班的第一天。下个月我要去欧洲出差为公司推销太阳能热水器。我们公司的产品价廉物美，加上环保，所以卖得很火。公司里有三个人是我的校友，他们说会关照我。这个周末我要给我妈打电话，告诉她我工作会很顺利，让她放心。）
5. （我的校友王子明大学毕业后来公司工作已经三年了。他说虽然工作很有意思，但是压力也很大，有的时候得熬夜。他很不简单，这么年轻就当上国际销售部的经理了。他不但懂销售，而且是个优秀的管理人材，只是我觉得他应该多注意休息。我希望他偶尔能出去旅游一下，轻松轻松。）

H. (Answers may vary.)

I. (Answers may vary.)

J. (Answers may vary.)
（1. 这位妇女叫米雪儿，她是英国人，可是住在中国已经好几年了。米雪儿没有稳定的工作。今天是星期一，有一个从英国来的旅游团。米雪儿在给那个旅游团当导游。他们正在游览一个公园，公园里的风景很美，米雪儿和游客都很高兴。
2. 今天是星期三，米雪儿现在在当家庭教师。她的学生看起来是个中国女孩子。米雪儿在教这个孩子英文。女孩子的父母都不在家，这样让他们上课的时候更安静一些。
3. 今天是星期五，米雪儿今天的工作是拍电影。一开始她有点紧张，可是很快就适应了。她演得不错，大家都很满意，她自己也很高兴。
4. 今天是星期天，米雪儿工作了一个星期，终于可以休息了。这个星期她很忙，做了好几种工作。现在她在想，我到底是导游，是家庭教师，还是电影演员呢？她又想，不管是当导游、当家庭教师，还是当演员都没关系，我永远是快乐的米雪儿。）

Let's Review (Lessons 16–20)

I. How Good Is Your Pronunciation?

(Answers may vary: space between pinyin syllables, some neutral tones, English translations.)

1. Xīnxiān, bú shòu wūrǎn de kōngqì yǒuyì yú shēntǐ jiànkāng.
   Fresh, unpolluted air is conducive to physical health.
2. Fēngnéng shì dà zìrán qǔ zhī bú jìn de néngyuán zhī yī.
   Wind energy is one of nature's inexhaustible energy sources.
3. Zhèngfǔ guīdìng, xiàtiān gōnggòng chǎngsuǒ de kōngtiáo wēndù bù kě dī yú Shèshì èrshí liù dù.
   The government has stipulated that temperatures for air conditioning in public venues in summer should not be lower than 26 degrees Celsius.
4. Hěn duō tuìxiū lǎorén bǎ zìjǐ shěng chī jiǎn yòng zǎn xià lai de qián, ná qù tóuzī fēngxiǎn jiào dà de gǔshì.
   Many retired elderly people save by living frugally and then invest their money in the risky stock market.
5. Zuìjìn shìjiè de jīngjì wēijī, yǐnqǐ hěn duō rén duì zìjǐ de lǐcái fāngshì jìnxíng sīkǎo.
   The recent world economic crisis has led many people to reconsider their methods of financial management.
6. Tā zhōngyú shuōfú qīzi bǎ cúnkuǎn cóng yínháng ná chū lai, xiǎoliǎngkǒu juédìng yào hǎo hǎo xiāofèi, hǎo hǎo xiǎngshòu shēnghuó.
   Finally, he managed to persuade his wife to withdraw their savings from the bank. The young couple decided to spend a lot and enjoy their lives.
7. "Yǒu péng zì yuǎnfāng lái, bù yì lè hū", zhè jù huà yǒu liǎng qiān duō nián de lìshǐ.
   The line, "Isn't it a pleasure to have a friend visiting from afar?" has a history of over two millenia.
8. Qínshǐhuáng duì Zhōngguó wénzì de tǒngyī yǒu gòngxiàn, dàn tā xiū fénmù, xiū gōngdiàn, shā dúshū rén, shāo gǔshū, yě yǐnqǐ lǎobǎixìng duì tā de bùmǎn.
   Qin Shihuangdi/the First Emperor of the Qin Dynasty made contributions to the unification of Chinese script, but by building his mausoleum and palaces, killing scholars, and burning ancient books, he also incurred resentment from the common people.
9. Zhōngguó lìshǐ fēicháng cháng, céngjīng shì kējì fādá, jìshù xiānjìn de wénmíng gǔguó.
   Chinese history is very long; China was once a cultured ancient nation with scientific developments and technological advances.
10. Tā xué yǒu suǒ chéng, cóng hǎiwài guīlái, jīntiān qù mǒu jiā kuàguó gōngsī miànshì. Tā duì zìjǐ de biǎoxiàn hěn bù mǎnyì, juéde shífēn yùmèn.
    He returned from overseas an academic success. Today he went for an interview at a transnational company. He was not satisfied with his own performance, and felt rather distressed.
11. Nàwèi zǒng jīnglǐ suīrán yǒu xiē yánsù, dàn díquè shì guǎnlǐ fāngmiàn de yōuxiù réncái.
    Although that general manager is somewhat solemn, he is truly talented in business management.
12. Shōu dào lùyòng tōngzhī shí, tā de liǎn shang mǎshàng duō yún zhuǎn qíng, xiào le qǐ lai.
    When he received the employment offer, his face changed from cloudy to sunny as he smiled.
13. Měi zhōu gōngzuò jùhuì shí, tā dōu xīwàng jīnglǐ, tóngshì gàosu tā zìjǐ de yōu quēdiǎn.
    At each weekly workplace gathering, he hoped that the managers and colleagues would inform him of his strengths and weaknesses.

14. Zhè wèi yǎnyuán bùjǐn niánqīng, piàoliang, érqiě shànyú tuīxiāo xīn chǎnpǐn, hěn duō gōngsī dōu zhǎo tā pāi guǎnggào, zuìjìn tèbié huǒ.

    This actress is not only young and pretty but also good at marketing new products. Since many companies want her to do commercials for them, she has become extremely popular recently.

15. Tā yào yímín qù Ōuzhōu, péngyou men gěi tā jiànxíng, dàjiā wèi yǒuyì gān bēi, bìng hù zhù shēntǐ jiànkāng, shēnghuó xìngfú, shìyè chénggōng.

    He is emigrating to Europe, so his friends threw him a farewell party. Everybody toasted to friendship and wished each other good health, happy lives, and successful careers.

II. Put Your Chinese to Good Use!

(Answers may vary.)

III. Getting to Know Yourself!

(Answers may vary.)

IV. Express Yourself!

(Answers may vary.)

LESSON 11

学生版

Name: _____ Section: _____

Character Quiz

A. Write down the *Chinese characters* for the following along with *pinyin* and *tone marks*. (40%)

1. to end; to finish _____

2. feeling; emotion; affection _____

3. happy; happiness _____

4. meal _____

5. to drink a toast; cheers! _____

B. Write down the *Chinese characters* for the following *pinyin*. In the parentheses, write down the *meaning in English*. (40%)

1. niányèfàn _____ (_____)

2. chuántǒng _____ (_____)

3. nónglì _____ (_____)

4. zhēngyuè _____ (_____)

5. gōngxǐ _____ (_____)

C. Translate the following sentences into English. (20%)

1. 他们住的小区环境很好，房子是一套三房两厅两卫的公寓，家具都很新、很漂亮，每个房间都很干净，住起来很舒服。

   _____

2. 为你们在新的一年里找工作顺利、学习进步。干杯！

   _____

LESSON 11

教师版

Character Quiz
Suggested duration of quiz: 10 minutes

A. Write down the *Chinese characters* for the following along with *pinyin* and *tone marks*. (40%)

1.	to end; to finish	结束	jiéshù
2.	feeling; emotion; affection	感情	gǎnqíng
3.	happy; happiness	幸福	xìngfú
4.	meal	餐	cān
5.	to drink a toast; cheers!	干杯	gān bēi

B. Write down the *Chinese characters* for the following *pinyin*. In the parentheses, write down the *meaning in English*. (40%)

1.	niányèfàn	年夜饭	(Chinese New Year's Eve dinner)
2.	chuántǒng	传统	(tradition; traditional)
3.	nónglì	农历	(traditional Chinese lunar calendar)
4.	zhēngyuè	正月	(first month of the lunar year)
5.	gōngxǐ	恭喜	(to congratulate)

C. Translate the following sentences into English. (20%)

1. 他们住的小区环境很好，房子是一套三房两厅两卫的公寓，家具都很新、很漂亮，每个房间都很干净，住起来很舒服。

   The environment of their residential subdivision is very nice. Their apartment has three bedrooms, a living room, a dining room, and two bathrooms. The furniture is all new and very beautiful. Every room is very clean and very comfortable to live in.

2. 为你们在新的一年里找工作顺利、学习进步。干杯！

   I hope that in the New Year your search for work goes off without a hitch, and that you make [a lot of] progress academically. Cheers!

LESSON 12

学生版

Name: _____ Section: _____

Character Quiz

A. Write down the *Chinese characters* for the following along with *pinyin* and *tone marks*. (40%)

1. change; to change _____

2. always _____

3. unfamiliar; strange _____

4. to merge into; to meld into _____

5. common folk; (ordinary) people _____

B. Write down the *Chinese characters* for the following *pinyin*. In the parentheses, write down the *meaning in English*. (40%)

1. díquè _____(_____)

2. yóukè _____(_____)

3. jiànzhù _____(_____)

4. fúzhuāng _____(_____)

5. nánguò _____(_____)

C. Translate the following sentences into English. (20%)

1. 民以食为天。

    _____

2. 看来，南京人真的是想尽可能保留老南京的特色，老南京的传统啊。

    _____

Lesson 12

教师版

Character Quiz
Suggested duration of quiz: 10 minutes

A. Write down the *Chinese characters* for the following along with *pinyin* and *tone marks*. (40%)

1. change; to change — 变化 — biànhuà
2. always — 总 — zǒng
3. unfamiliar; strange — 陌生 — mòshēng
4. to merge into; to meld into — 融入 — róngrù
5. common folk; (ordinary) people — 老百姓 — lǎobǎixìng

B. Write down the *Chinese characters* for the following *pinyin*. In the parentheses, write down the *meaning in English*. (40%)

1. díquè — 的确 — (indeed)
2. yóukè — 游客 — (tourist)
3. jiànzhù — 建筑 — (architecture; to build)
4. fúzhuāng — 服装 — (clothing; apparel)
5. nánguò — 难过 — (sad; hard to bear)

C. Translate the following sentences into English. (20%)

1. 民以食为天。

   People think of food as important as heaven.

2. 看来，南京人真的是想尽可能保留老南京的特色，老南京的传统啊。

   It seems that people in Nanjing really want to preserve Old Nanjing's character and tradition as much as possible.

LESSON 13

Name: _____ Section: _____

学生版

Character Quiz

A. Write down the *Chinese characters* for the following along with *pinyin* and *tone marks*. (40%)

1. to share _____

2. admission ticket _____

3. sleeping berth or bunk on a train _____

4. box lunch _____

5. ancient; old _____

B. Write down the *Chinese characters* for the following *pinyin*. In the parentheses, write down the *meaning in English*. (40%)

1. fēnbié _____ (_____)

2. měilì _____ (_____)

3. dǎ hūlu _____ (_____)

4. yóulǎn _____ (_____)

5. yōumò _____ (_____)

C. Translate the following sentences into English. (20%)

1. 来云南旅游，可以亲眼看看不同民族的建筑服装饮食，了解各个民族的风俗习惯。

   _____

2. 最特别的是有一条非常干净的小河从城中间流过。

   _____

LESSON 13

教师版

Character Quiz

Suggested duration of quiz: 10 minutes

A. Write down the *Chinese characters* for the following along with *pinyin* and *tone marks*. (40%)

1. to share   分享   fēnxiǎng

2. admission ticket   门票   ménpiào

3. sleeping berth or bunk on a train   卧铺   wòpù

4. box lunch   盒饭   héfàn

5. ancient; old   古老   gǔlǎo

B. Write down the *Chinese characters* for the following *pinyin*. In the parentheses, write down the *meaning in English*. (40%)

1. fēnbié   分别   (separately; to part from each other)

2. měilì   美丽   (beautiful)

3. dǎ hūlu   打呼噜   (to snore)

4. yóulǎn   游览   (to go sightseeing; excursion)

5. yōumò   幽默   (humorous)

C. Translate the following sentences into English. (20%)

1. 来云南旅游，可以亲眼看看不同民族的建筑服装饮食，了解各个民族的风俗习惯。

   If you take a trip to Yunnan, you can see firsthand the architecture, costumes, food and drink of different ethnic groups, as well as understand each group's customs.

2. 最特别的是有一条非常干净的小河从城中间流过。

   The most unusual thing is the very clean and small river running through the city.

LESSON 14

学生版

Name: _____ Section: _____

Character Quiz

A. Write down the *Chinese characters* for the following along with *pinyin* and *tone marks*. (40%)

1. museum _____

2. tai chi _____

3. to perform; performance _____

4. fitness center; gym _____

5. to stay up late or all night _____

B. Write down the *Chinese characters* for the following *pinyin*. In the parentheses, write down the *meaning in English*. (40%)

1. sàn bù _____ (_____)

2. ǒu'ěr _____ (_____)

3. děngyú _____ (_____)

4. yíngyǎng _____ (_____)

5. kějiàn _____ (_____)

C. Translate the following sentences into English. (20%)

1. 退休老人们有的站成一个圈，高高兴兴地跳舞，有的排成队，慢慢地打太极拳。

   _____

2. 如果常常开夜车，就必须尽可能找时间补充睡眠，否则两只眼睛就会变成熊猫眼。

   _____

LESSON 14

教师版

Character Quiz
Suggested duration of quiz: 10 minutes

A. Write down the *Chinese characters* for the following along with *pinyin* and *tone marks*. (40%)

1. museum — 博物馆 — bówùguǎn
2. tai chi — 太极拳 — tàijíquán
3. to perform; performance — 表演 — biǎoyǎn
4. fitness center; gym — 健身房 — jiànshēnfáng
5. to stay up late or all night — 熬夜 — áo yè

B. Write down the *Chinese characters* for the following *pinyin*. In the parentheses, write down the *meaning in English*. (40%)

1. sàn bù — 散步 (to take a walk)
2. ǒu'ěr — 偶尔 (occasionally)
3. děngyú — 等于 (to equal; to amount to)
4. yíngyǎng — 营养 (nutrition; nourishment)
5. kějiàn — 可见 (it is obvious that; it can be seen that)

C. Translate the following sentences into English. (20%)

1. 退休老人们有的站成一个圈，高高兴兴地跳舞，有的排成队，慢慢地打太极拳。
   Some of the retirees stand in a circle and have a good time dancing, while some of them form rows and slowly practice tai chi.

2. 如果常常开夜车，就必须尽可能找时间补充睡眠，否则两只眼睛就会变成熊猫眼。
   If you often have to burn the midnight oil, you must find time to make up for your sleep deficit as much as possible, otherwise your two eyes will turn into panda eyes.

LESSON 15

Name: _____ Section: _____

学生版

Character Quiz

A. Write down the *Chinese characters* for the following along with *pinyin* and *tone marks*. (40%)

1. after all _____

2. to appear, to rise, to emerge _____

3. wife _____

4. to lose, to be defeated _____

5. opportunity _____

B. Write down the *Chinese characters* for the following *pinyin*. In the parentheses, write down the *meaning in English*. (40%)

1. chéngjì _____ (_____)

2. tǎoyàn _____ (_____)

3. mófàn zhàngfu _____ (_____)

4. qìguǎnyán _____ (_____)

5. chāoguò _____ (_____)

C. Translate the following sentences into English. (20%)

1. 要想有一个公平健康的工作环境，同工同酬、男女平等是非常重要的。

   _____

2. 2000年以来，职业运动员的薪水和社会地位都提高得很快。这是由他们的表现和市场决定的。

   _____

教师版

Character Quiz
Suggested duration of quiz: 10 minutes

A. Write down the *Chinese characters* for the following along with *pinyin* and *tone marks*. (40%)

1. after all — 毕竟 — bìjìng
2. to appear, to rise, to emerge — 出现 — chūxiàn
3. wife — 妻子 — qīzi
4. to lose, to be defeated — 输 — shū
5. opportunity — 机会 — jīhuì

B. Write down the *Chinese characters* for the following *pinyin*. In the parentheses, write down the *meaning in English*. (40%)

1. chéngjì — 成绩 (achievement)
2. tǎoyàn — 讨厌 (disgusting)
3. mófàn zhàngfu — 模范丈夫 (model husband)
4. qìguǎnyán — 气管炎 (tracheitis)
5. chāoguò — 超过 (surpass)

C. Translate the following sentences into English. (20%)

1. 要想有一个公平健康的工作环境，同工同酬、男女平等是非常重要的。

   Equal pay for equal work and gender equality are very important for a fair and healthy work environment.

2. 2000年以来，职业运动员的薪水和社会地位都提高得很快。这是由他们的表现和市场决定的。

   Since 2000, professional athletes' salaries and social status have rapidly increased. This is due to their performance, as well as to market considerations.

LESSON 16

学生版

Name: _____ Section: _____

Character Quiz

A. Write down the *Chinese characters* for the following along with *pinyin* and *tone marks*. (40%)

1. (of resources) inexhaustible _____

2. country; nation _____

3. bottled water _____

4. to protect _____

5. crisis _____

B. Write down the *Chinese characters* for the following *pinyin*. In the parentheses, write down the *meaning in English*. (40%)

1. gōnggòng chǎngsuǒ _____ (_____)

2. zànchéng _____ (_____)

3. tàiyángnéng _____ (_____)

4. guīdìng _____ (_____)

5. sùliào dài _____ (_____)

C. Translate the following sentences into English. (20%)

1. 如果不保护环境，不节约能源，后果会不堪设想。

_____

2. 现在很多人都不用一次性筷子了。

_____

LESSON 16

教师版

Character Quiz
Suggested duration of quiz: 10 minutes

A. Write down the *Chinese characters* for the following along with *pinyin* and *tone marks*. (40%)

1. (of resources) inexhaustible   取之不尽   qǔ zhī bú jìn

2. country; nation   国家   guójiā

3. bottled water   瓶装水   píngzhuāng shuǐ

4. to protect   保护   bǎohù

5. crisis   危机   wēijī

B. Write down the *Chinese characters* for the following *pinyin*. In the parentheses, write down the *meaning in English*. (40%)

1. gōnggòng chǎngsuǒ   公共场所   (public place)

2. zànchéng   赞成   (to approve)

3. tàiyángnéng   太阳能   (solar energy)

4. guīdìng   规定   (to regulate; rules and regulations)

5. sùliào dài   塑料袋   (plastic bag)

C. Translate the following sentences into English. (20%)

1. 如果不保护环境，不节约能源，后果会不堪设想。

   If we do not protect the environment, if we do not conserve energy, the consequences will be unimaginable.

2. 现在很多人都不用一次性筷子了。

   Nowadays, a lot of people do not use disposable chopsticks.

LESSON 17

学生版

Name: _____ Section: _____

Character Quiz

A. Write down the *Chinese characters* for the following along with *pinyin* and *tone marks*. (40%)

1. bank savings _____

2. to persuade _____

3. stock market _____

4. to be left over _____

5. contract _____

B. Write down the *Chinese characters* for the following *pinyin*. In the parentheses, write down the *meaning in English*. (40%)

1. shěng chī jiǎn yòng _____ (_____)

2. xīnkǔ _____ (_____)

3. xiāofèi _____ (_____)

4. tūrán _____ (_____)

5. yùmèn _____ (_____)

C. Translate the following sentences into English. (20%)

1. 我觉得买房子是一种很好的投资。

   _____

2. 炒股有风险,你有可能会赔很多钱。

   _____

LESSON 17

教师版

Character Quiz

Suggested duration of quiz: 10 minutes

A. Write down the *Chinese characters* for the following along with *pinyin* and *tone marks*. (40%)

1. bank savings — 存款 — cúnkuǎn
2. to persuade — 说服 — shuōfú
3. stock market — 股市 — gǔshì
4. to be left over — 剩余 — shèngyú
5. contract — 合同 — hétong

B. Write down the *Chinese characters* for the following *pinyin*. In the parentheses, write down the *meaning in English*. (40%)

1. shěng chī jiǎn yòng — 省吃俭用 — (to be frugal)
2. xīnkǔ — 辛苦 — (hard; strenuous)
3. xiāofèi — 消费 — (to consume)
4. tūrán — 突然 — (sudden)
5. yùmèn — 郁闷 — (gloomy; depressed)

C. Translate the following sentences into English. (20%)

1. 我觉得买房子是一种很好的投资。

   I believe that purchasing a house is a good investment.

2. 炒股有风险，你有可能会赔很多钱。

   Speculating on stocks is risky; you might lose a lot of money.

LESSON 18

学生版

Name: _____ Section: _____

Character Quiz

A. Write down the *Chinese characters* for the following along with *pinyin* and *tone marks*. (40%)

1. to develop _____

2. compass _____

3. to contribute _____

4. civilization; civilized _____

5. palace _____

B. Write down the *Chinese characters* for the following *pinyin*. In the parentheses, write down the *meaning in English*. (40%)

1. bīngmǎyǒng _____ (_____)

2. màoyì _____ (_____)

3. wěidà _____ (_____)

4. jìshù _____ (_____)

5. gémìng _____ (_____)

C. Translate the following sentences into English. (20%)

1. 中国唐朝的经济和文化都非常发达。

   _____

2. 秦始皇统一了中国，还统一了文字。

   _____

LESSON 18

教师版

Character Quiz

Suggested duration of quiz: 10 minutes

A. Write down the **Chinese characters** for the following along with **pinyin** and **tone marks**. (40%)

1. to develop   发展   fāzhǎn

2. compass   指南针   zhǐnánzhēn

3. to contribute   贡献   gòngxiàn

4. civilization; civilized   文明   wénmíng

5. palace   宫殿   gōngdiàn

B. Write down the **Chinese characters** for the following **pinyin**. In the parentheses, write down the **meaning in English**. (40%)

1. bīngmǎyǒng   兵马俑   (terracotta warriors and horses)

2. màoyì   贸易   (trade)

3. wěidà   伟大   (great; outstanding)

4. jìshù   技术   (technology)

5. gémìng   革命   (revolution)

C. Translate the following sentences into English. (20%)

1. 中国唐朝的经济和文化都非常发达。

   The economy and culture of China's Tang Dynasty were both very developed.

2. 秦始皇统一了中国,还统一了文字。

   The First Emperor unified China and its script.

LESSON 19

学生版

Name: _____ Section: _____

Character Quiz

A. Write down the *Chinese characters* for the following along with *pinyin* and *tone marks*. (40%)

1. shortcoming _____

2. capacity _____

3. overseas; abroad _____

4. manager _____

5. to explain _____

B. Write down the *Chinese characters* for the following *pinyin*. In the parentheses, write down the *meaning in English*. (40%)

1. mǎnyì _____ (_____)

2. yánsù _____ (_____)

3. huídá _____ (_____)

4. chǎnpǐn _____ (_____)

5. xué yǒu suǒ chéng _____ (_____)

C. Translate the following sentences into English. (20%)

1. 实习的时候，我常常熬夜加班。

_____

2. 第一次面试的时候我很紧张。

_____

LESSON 19

教师版

Character Quiz

Suggested duration of quiz: 10 minutes

A. Write down the **Chinese characters** for the following along with **pinyin** and **tone marks**. (40%)

1. shortcoming   缺点   quēdiǎn

2. capacity   能力   nénglì

3. overseas; abroad   海外   hǎiwài

4. manager   经理   jīnglǐ

5. to explain   解释   jiěshì

B. Write down the **Chinese characters** for the following **pinyin**. In the parentheses, write down the **meaning in English**. (40%)

1. mǎnyì   满意   (to be satisfied)

2. yánsù   严肃   (serious)

3. huídá   回答   (to reply)

4. chǎnpǐn   产品   (product)

5. xué yǒu suǒ chéng   学有所成   (to have achieved academic success)

C. Translate the following sentences into English. (20%)

1. 实习的时候，我常常熬夜加班。

   When I have an internship, I always stay up late and work overtime.

2. 第一次面试的时候我很紧张。

   I was very nervous during my first job interview.

LESSON 20

学生版

Name: _____ Section: _____

Character Quiz

A. Write down the *Chinese characters* for the following along with *pinyin* and *tone marks*. (40%)

1. TV series _____

2. to celebrate _____

3. alumni _____

4. colleague _____

5. Europe _____

B. Write down the *Chinese characters* for the following *pinyin*. In the parentheses, write down the *meaning in English*. (40%)

1. jiēfēng _____ (_____)

2. miànshú _____ (_____)

3. zhòngrén _____ (_____)

4. guānzhào _____ (_____)

5. jùhuì _____ (_____)

C. Translate the following sentences into English. (20%)

1. 昨天我们在四川饭店吃又香又辣的火锅，为我们的外国演员朋友饯行。

_____

2. 那个年轻人一直想把二流的热水器推销给我们。

_____

Character Quiz

Suggested duration of quiz: 10 minutes

教师版

A. Write down the **Chinese characters** for the following along with *pinyin* and *tone marks*. (40%)

1. TV series   电视剧   diànshìjù

2. to celebrate   庆祝   qìngzhù

3. alumni   校友   xiàoyǒu

4. colleague   同事   tóngshì

5. Europe   欧洲   Ōuzhōu

B. Write down the **Chinese characters** for the following *pinyin*. In the parentheses, write down the *meaning in English*. (40%)

1. jiēfēng   接风   (to give a welcome dinner for a visitor from afar)

2. miànshú   面熟   (familiar-looking)

3. zhòngrén   众人   (everybody; the crowd)

4. guānzhào   关照   (to take care of; to look after)

5. jùhuì   聚会   (to get together; social gathering)

C. Translate the following sentences into English. (20%)

1. 昨天我们在四川饭店吃又香又辣的火锅，为我们的外国演员朋友饯行。

   Yesterday, we had delicious spicy hotpot at a Sichuan restaurant. It was a farewell dinner for our foreign actor friend.

2. 那个年轻人一直想把二流的热水器推销给我们。

   That young man keeps trying to sell that mediocre water heater to us.

LESSON 11

Name: _____ Section: _____

Test

Section I Listening Comprehension (30%)
Listen, then answer the following questions in English.

A: For each question in this part, you will hear a short conversation between two speakers.

1. What is the first speaker looking for?
   _____

2. What does the second speaker suggest?
   _____

3. What is Ke Lin probably doing now?
   _____

4. What is the second speaker's suggestion to the first speaker's problem?
   _____

B: For questions 5–6, you will hear a short narration.

5. Which dish will definitely be included in the Chinese New Year's Eve Dinner?
   _____

6. Why don't people finish the fish included in the Chinese New Year's Eve Dinner?
   _____

学生版

Section II Translation (30%)

Translate the following dialogues into Chinese characters or English as appropriate.

A:	新年到了，我以茶代酒，祝大家新年快乐，身体健康！	
B:		Yes, let's drink to everyone's health!

A:		Happy New Year! Come get some red envelopes.
B:	谢谢舅舅、舅妈，恭喜发财！	

A:	天明一个人在美国，不能回家过年，一定很难过吧。	
B:		Don't forget to send a text message to Tianming to wish him a Happy New Year.

Section III Reading Comprehension (20%)

Read the passage below and decide whether the statements that follow it are true or false.

每年的农历正月初一，是中国新年。中国人过春节的时候，家家都会打扫房间，在门上贴春联和倒了的"福"字。春节的前一天晚上叫"除夕"，全家人都会在一起，热热闹闹地吃年夜饭。这些年来，越来越多的家庭还会一边吃年夜饭，一边在电视上看春节晚会。不过，各个地方的年夜饭不一样。北方人喜欢吃饺子，南方人常常吃年糕。可是不管吃饺子还是年糕，大家希望的都是能够生活美满，一年比一年好。

1. (　) The first day of the first month on the solar calendar is Chinese New Year.
2. (　) Chinese people have dinner as a family on New Year's Day.
3. (　) Southern Chinese people have dumplings while northern Chinese people like "niangao" for Chinese New Year's Eve Dinner.
4. (　) More and more families like watching the "Spring Festival Evening Show" on TV while having Chinese New Year's Eve Dinner.

Section IV Writing (20%)

You will host a Chinese New Year's Eve celebration at your place. Write a letter to your friends and describe how they can help decorate and cook for the holiday, what they should wear, what they should bring, what they should expect to do at the celebration, etc.

Test Listening Script

Suggested duration of test: 30 minutes

Section I Listening Comprehension (30%)
Listen, then answer the following questions in English.
Suggested duration: 6 minutes

A. For each question in this part, you will hear a short conversation between two speakers.

1. Speaker 1: 您好，我想租一套两房一厅一卫的公寓。

   Speaker 2: 请问要不要带家具？

2. Speaker 1: 今年春节又不能回家了，我真难过。

   Speaker 2: 别难过了，打电话回家给爸爸妈妈拜个年吧。

3. Speaker 1: 您好，请问柯林在家吗？

   Speaker 2: 他刚刚急着去见朋友，没吃晚饭就出去了。

4. Speaker 1: 我最不愿意跟病人打交道，可是妈妈非让我上医学院不可。

   Speaker 2: 你跟妈妈说清楚嘛，要是上了医学院想再换专业，就难了。

B. For questions 5–6, you will hear a short narration.

春节的时候，如果你去中国人家里吃年夜饭，你一定会吃到鱼。可是吃鱼的时候，你一定不要把鱼吃完。为什么？你听说过"年年有鱼，年年有余"吗？"鱼"跟"余"的发音一样，"余"有"剩下"的意思。这样，人们希望每年都有剩下的钱。

Section II Translation (30%)
Translate the following dialogues into Chinese characters or English as appropriate.
Suggested duration: 6 minutes

Section III Reading Comprehension (20%)
Read the passage below and decide whether the statements that follow it are true or false.
Suggested duration: 6 minutes

Section IV Writing (20%)
You will host a Chinese New Year's Eve celebration at your place. Write a letter to your friends and describe how they can help decorate and cook for the holiday, what they should wear, what they should bring, what they should expect to do at the celebration, etc.
Suggested duration: 12 minutes

LESSON 12

Name: _____ Section: _____

Test

Section I Listening Comprehension (30%)
Listen, then answer the following questions in English.

A: For each question in this part, you will hear a short conversation between two speakers.

1. What happened to the father's high school in Nanjing?
   _____

2. What allows the speakers to identify that they are still in Nanjing, instead of an American city?
   _____

3. Why did Zhang Tianming's mother look sad?
   _____

4. Why can't the second speaker count on the first speaker to help make 元宵?
   _____

B: For questions 5–6, you will hear a short narration.

5. Why is Beijing the speaker's favorite city in China?
   _____

6. When has he been to Beijing, and for what reason?
   _____

Section II Translation (30%)

Translate the following dialogues into Chinese characters or English as appropriate.

A:	他真的给你道歉了？	
B:		She did apologize to me, and was sincere about it.

A:		Should we walk to the movie theater?
B:	那么远，走路可走不到。咱们还是打车吧！	

A:	南京人在尽可能地保护孔子庙，在发展旅游的同时保护古老的建筑。	
B:		It seems that people are really trying to preserve old Nanjing's character and tradition, as much as possible.

Section III Reading Comprehension (20%)

Read the passage below and decide whether the statements that follow it are true or false.

　　张天明的爸爸熟悉的那个南京已经没有了，今天的南京对他来说其实是一个完全陌生的地方。第一，他以前的中学搬家了，那儿变成了购物中心。第二，南京新盖了很多高楼大厦，有外国商店、银行什么的。第三，南京过去很安静，现在街上人多，车多，还有很多外国游客，很热闹。

1. (　) Zhang Tianming's father's high school has moved to a place where there used to be a shopping mall.
2. (　) There aren't many foreign stores in Nanjing.
3. (　) There are many foreign tourists in Nanjing nowadays.
4. (　) Zhang Tianming's father finds it difficult to recognize Nanjing now.

Section IV Writing (20%)

What is the most memorable city or town that you have ever visited? What was it like? Recap what you heard (or didn't hear) and what you saw (or didn't see) during your visit there.

_____
_____
_____
_____
_____
_____
_____
_____

教师版

Test Listening Script
Suggested duration of test: 30 minutes

Section I Listening Comprehension (30%)
Listen, then answer the following questions in English.
Suggested duration: 6 minutes

A. For each question in this part, you will hear a short conversation between two speakers.

1. Speaker 1: 你找到爸爸几十年前在南京的中学了吗？

   Speaker 2: 那儿已经变成了一个购物中心，完全不是以前的样子了。

2. Speaker 1: 美国快餐店、日本银行、法国服装店，还有到处都能看到的外国游客，现在的南京就像美国的城市一样。

   Speaker 2: 是啊，要不是街上的这些中国字，我还以为是在美国呢。

3. Speaker 1: 今天是张天明的母亲的生日，没想到他竟然忘记了！

   Speaker 2: 哎呀，难怪他妈妈看起来非常难过！

4. Speaker 1: 虽然我在中国出生、长大，可是我在家能不进厨房就尽可能不进厨房。

   Speaker 2: 看来这次做元宵可得完全靠我了。

B. For questions 5–6, you will hear a short narration.

我最喜欢的中国城市是北京。北京可真漂亮！在那里你可以看到很多有中国特色的建筑，也有一座座新盖的高楼大厦，还可以吃到各种各样的传统小吃。两年前我曾经去北京上过暑期学校，在那儿学习了两个月的中文。我好想再去北京！

Section II Translation (30%)
Translate the following dialogues into Chinese characters or English as appropriate.
Suggested duration: 6 minutes

Section III Reading Comprehension (20%)
Read the passage below and decide whether the statements that follow it are true or false.
Suggested duration: 6 minutes

Section IV Writing (20%)
What is the most memorable city or town that you have ever visited? What was it like? Recap what you heard (or didn't hear) and what you saw (or didn't see) during your visit there.
Suggested duration: 12 minutes

LESSON 13

Name: _____ Section: _____

Test

Section I Listening Comprehension (30%)

Listen, then answer the following questions in English.

A: For each question in this part, you will hear a short conversation between two speakers.

1. Why was the first speaker unable to recognize Little Zhang?
   _____

2. What about Yunnan left the second speaker with a deep impression?
   _____

3. What amenities does the tour group fee include?
   _____

4. How did the second speaker enjoy the weekend? Why?
   _____

B: For questions 5–6, you will hear a short narration.

5. Where did the speaker get the money to buy a plane ticket to China?
   _____

6. What specific aspects of China made a deep impression on the speaker?
   _____

学生版

Section II Translation (30%)
Translate the following dialogues into Chinese characters or English as appropriate.

A:	这盘清蒸鱼真新鲜！	
B:		The fish comes from the river behind the hotel!

A:		What are you going to do when you travel to this new place?
B:	我一定会尝特色小吃，买纪念品，还要了解当地老百姓的风俗习惯。	

A:	你们买了什么火车票去云南？	
B:		The soft sleeper tickets were too expensive, so we got two hard sleeper tickets.

Section III Reading Comprehension (20%)
Read the passage below and decide whether the statements that follow it are true or false.

去年夏天我去了中国的很多地方旅游。为了省钱，我在中国都坐火车或者大巴。坐火车的时候，我总是买最便宜的硬座票。硬座车厢里又挤又不舒服，晚上也很吵，使我睡不着觉。可是坐硬座可以跟很多中国人聊天儿，练习中文。去云南的时候，我在火车上认识了一个中国大学生，叫张朋。张朋是南京人，现在在北京上大学二年级。我们除了一起去各个景点以外，还一起合租家庭旅馆，省了不少住宿费。

1. (　) I always get a hard sleeper train ticket when I travel to save money.
2. (　) When I travel by train, I like sitting in the hard seat railway compartments, because it provides me with a good opportunity to practice my Chinese, and because the compartments bustle with noise and excitement.
3. (　) I know Zhang Peng from when we studied together in Beijing.
4. (　) Zhang Peng and I shared a room at the bed-and-breakfast to save money.

Section IV Writing (20%)

Propose a three-day itinerary for tourists visiting your hometown or your favorite place. Make sure to include information about transportation, lodging, attractions, tour guides, typical expenses, etc. Don't forget to give your itinerary the following title: 《[Name of place] 三日游》.

_____

_____

_____

_____

_____

_____

_____

Test Listening Script
Suggested duration of test: 30 minutes

Section I Listening Comprehension (30%)
Listen, then answer the following questions in English.
Suggested duration: 6 minutes

A. For each question in this part, you will hear a short conversation between two speakers.

1. Speaker 1: 我跟小张分别已经十年了，一直没有见面。

   Speaker 2: 原来这么多年没见了，难怪你都不认识小张了。

2. Speaker 1: 听说你去过云南，你对那里的印象怎么样？

   Speaker 2: 中国的火车、导游和云南美丽的风景给我留下了很深的印象。

3. Speaker 1: 旅行团的团费包括哪些？

   Speaker 2: 团费一共是两千八百元，包括交通、旅馆和三餐，不包括部分景点门票。

4. Speaker 1: 周末去海边玩得怎么样？

   Speaker 2: 我们本来打算去海边，可是没想到竟然下起大雨来，只好待在家里看电视。

B. For questions 5–6, you will hear a short narration.

我学中文学了两年了，一直都很想去中国旅行。去年暑假，我用平时打工挣的钱买飞机票去了中国。我没有报名参加旅游团，而是选择了自助游。我一个人游览了北京和上海等大城市，也游览了很多的小城镇。中国各地多样的风景，不同的风俗习惯，还有少数民族的饮食和服装，给我留下了深刻的印象。我的父母担心我的安全，朋友们想了解中国，所以我天天都写博客，在博客上和他们分享我的快乐。

Section II Translation (30%)
Translate the following dialogues into Chinese characters or English as appropriate.
Suggested duration: 6 minutes

Section III Reading Comprehension (20%)
Read the passage below and decide whether the statements that follow it are true or false.
Suggested duration: 6 minutes

Section IV Writing (20%)
Propose a three-day itinerary for tourists visiting your hometown or your favorite location. Make sure to include information about transportation, lodging, attractions, tour guides, typical expenses, etc. Don't forget to give your itinerary the following title: 《[Name of the place] 三日游》.
Suggested duration: 12 minutes

LESSON 14

Name: _____   Section: _____

Test

Section I Listening Comprehension (30%)
Listen, then answer the following questions in English.

A: For each question in this part, you will hear a short conversation between two speakers.

1. Why is Ke Lin always so busy?

   _____

2. What kind of exercising are these people doing in the park?

   _____

3. Why is the second speaker so nervous?

   _____

4. Why does the second speaker look sick/unenergetic?

   _____

B: For questions 5–6, you will hear a short narration.

5. What are the healthy diet habits recommended in this paragraph?

   _____

6. According to this paragraph, what should we do to live a healthy lifestyle besides eating well?

   _____

Section II Translation (30%)

Translate the following dialogues into Chinese characters or English as appropriate.

A:	你想吃什么菜？	
B:		Whatever you like.

A:		I got three letters from the companies I applied to. They all offered me jobs!
B:	你申请哪个公司，哪个公司就要你，可见你很棒！	

A:	这次考试我又没考好。	
B:		It's okay. As long as you study diligently, your Chinese will definitely improve.

Section III Reading Comprehension (20%)

Read the passage below and decide whether the statements that follow it are true or false.

我有一条狗叫肥肥，它胖死了。它每天都吃很多东西，而且不喜欢喝水。它的饮食习惯非常差，而且又懒又不运动，所以它有很多健康问题。我的姐姐说这是因为我的生活习惯也不好。她说我根本没有活力，我应该多锻炼，还要注意饮食。她让我每天带肥肥去慢跑。有的人说狗会长得像主人，可是我的姐姐说我得注意，否则我会越来越像肥肥。

1. (　) My dog is fat because it does not like drinking water.
2. (　) I am not energetic because I resemble my dog.
3. (　) My sister suggested that I go to the gym with my dog, so that we could both exercise there.
4. (　) My sister said that I have to pay attention; otherwise, I will resemble my dog more and more.

Section IV Writing (20%)

As a fitness expert, give some advice to people about how to build a healthy diet, exercise regime, general lifestyle, etc.

Test Listening Script
Suggested duration of test: 30 minutes

Section I Listening Comprehension (30%)
Listen, then answer the following questions in English.
Suggested duration: 6 minutes

A. For each question in this part, you will hear a short conversation between two speakers.

1. Speaker 1: 为什么柯林总是那么忙呢？

   Speaker 2: 为了减轻家里的经济压力，他自己打工交学费。

2. Speaker 1: 公园里，有的人在散步，有的人排成队打太极，有的人站成圈跳舞。

   Speaker 2: 这些锻炼的人真是美丽的风景。

3. Speaker 1: 指导教授叫你去一下他的办公室。

   Speaker 2: 教授叫我去有什么事儿呢？我真紧张。

4. Speaker 1: 你是不是生病了？

   Speaker 2: 没有。我昨天又熬夜了，所以今天显得很没有精神。

B. For questions 5–6, you will hear a short narration.

一个人要想身体好，就应该重视锻炼身体，除了锻炼身体以外，还要注意饮食，要多喝水，多吃青菜水果。早餐吃得好，午餐吃得饱，晚餐吃得少。另外，还要有良好的生活习惯，不吸烟，不喝酒，早睡早起，最好不熬夜。

Section II Translation (30%)
Translate the following dialogues into Chinese characters or English as appropriate.
Suggested duration: 6 minutes

Section III Reading Comprehension (20%)
Read the passage below and decide whether the statements that follow it are true or false.
Suggested duration: 6 minutes

Section IV Writing (20%)
As a fitness expert, give some advice to people about how to build a healthy diet, exercise regime, general lifestyle, etc.
Suggested duration: 12 minutes

Midterm Exam

Name: _____ Section: _____

Section I Listening Comprehension (30%)
You will hear two narratives. Listen, then answer the following questions in English.

Narrative A

1. What do you know from the passage about the speaker's lifestyle?

2. What did the speaker and his roommate do for summer vacation, and where did they go?

3. What method of transport did they use, and why this particular one?

4. What did their parents think of their plans? Why?

5. Did their parents' concern come true? What really happened to them on the trip?

6. Because of his experience during this vacation, what does the speaker plan to do? Why?

Narrative B

7. What issues mentioned in the passage do Chinese people face after the Reform and Opening-Up of China?

8. What's the work situation for women?

9. What's the situation at home for women?
   _____

10. What does "男主外，女主内" mean in the passage?
    _____

Section II Reading Comprehension (30%)
Read each passage and answer the questions that follow it.

Part A: Read the paragraph below and decide whether the statements that follow it are true or false.

在北京的一条小街里有一家家常菜饭馆。这附近并没有什么旅游景点也不是热闹的商业区，可是这家饭馆的生意特别火。他们不接受预约，每天吃饭的时间外面等座的人就排起了队。这家餐馆看起来没什么特别，可是老板以诚信为本经营生意又为客人着想，饭菜的质量好、分量足，环境干净、整齐，有很多回头客。

1. (　) This particular restaurant serves exotic cuisine.
2. (　) The restaurant's business is good because it's close to tourist spots and commercial areas.
3. (　) If you want to eat in the restaurant, you have to make a reservation in advance.
4. (　) The restaurant owner runs his business based on honesty and consideration for his customers.
5. (　) Most people who eat in the restaurant are tourists.

Part B: Read the paragraph below and answer the questions that follow it, paying attention to the specific instructions for each question.

除了中国大陆、台湾和一些亚洲国家以外，在西方很多城市的唐人街的华人和一些当地的居民也很重视庆祝中国的传统节日。他们吃节日特有的食品，还对每一个传统节日背后的故事了如指掌。

比如端午节的来历，屈原的故事感动了很多人。屈原是战国时代楚国的臣子，有智慧、有胆识、口才好、又很会写文章、作诗。最重要的，他有满腔的爱国热忱，时时刻刻为国操心。楚国的臣子，看见才华洋溢的屈原，心中十分嫉妒，在楚王面前说尽屈原的坏话，楚王不能明辨是非，大怒之下，便把屈原赶出国去了。屈原看自己既不能报效国家，又找不到志同道合的人，活在这个世界上，还有什么意义呢？就悲痛的抱起大石头，往汨罗江一跳。附近居民听说屈原投江，赶忙划船来救，可惜太迟了。他们只有敲锣打鼓吓走鱼群。又用竹筒装米放入江中喂饱鱼虾，这样鱼虾就不会去吃屈原的身体了。

　　人们都非常敬重屈原爱国的精神，以后每年到了农历五月初五，都要去河边纪念他。当年划船敲锣打鼓的紧张情形，逐渐演变成今天端午节的划龙船比赛，竹筒装米也变成箬叶包粽子的习俗了。

1. Besides Chinese mainlanders and Taiwanese people, who else celebrates traditional Chinese holidays? (Answer in **English**.)

2. What does the phrase "了如指掌" (written in the first paragraph) mean? (Answer in **English**.)

3. Why do people eat "粽子" every year on the 5th day of the 5th month of the lunar calendar? (Answer in **English**.)

4. Who is Qu Yuan? What happened to him? (Answer in **English**.)

5. What is your favorite traditional Chinese festival? How do people typically celebrate it? (Answer in **Chinese**.)

Section III Writing (40%)

Translate the following two passages into Chinese.

Passage A

Some people like to travel alone, but others like to travel with friends or family. I prefer to have an outgoing friend to share the journey with, so I always try my best to find such a travel buddy. However, since everyone is already busy this summer, I have no choice but to visit China by myself.

Passage B

A healthy lifestyle is important for one's quality of life. Many people don't smoke or drink alcohol. They don't stay up late at night. Besides doing those things, people also pay attention to their diet. They eat less meat, and more fruits and vegetables. Some people even become vegetarians. Exercising regularly is also important. According to most doctors, people should exercise at least three times a week to stay in shape.

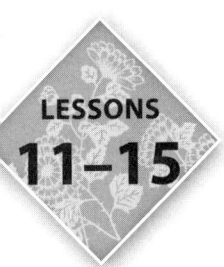

Midterm Exam Listening Script

Suggested duration of test: 50 minutes

Section I Listening Comprehension (30%)
You will hear two narratives. Listen, then answer the following questions in English.
Suggested duration: 15 minutes

Narrative A

  我和我的室友都很喜欢运动和旅行，虽然我们俩经常抽烟，喝酒和熬夜，但是我们觉得自己很健康。今年放暑假以后，我们一起开车从北京去西藏旅行，在路上我们游览了中国中部和西部的8个省。我们决定开车去西藏，一方面是要看看中国不同地方的不同的风景，另一方面是因为可以省钱。但是我们的父母反对我们的计划，他们要我们坐火车或者坐飞机去。他们担心开车旅行在路上会不安全。我们没有听他们的。我们一共游览了一个半月，在路上没有遇到什么安全问题。不过我们的身体有点受不了这样的旅行，我们在路上感冒了，有时候还闹肚子。回来以后我们决定要养成健康的生活习惯，不再抽烟，喝酒和熬夜了。

Narrative B

  改革开放以后，中国老百姓的工资增加了，但是要面对一些新的问题，比如看病，养老，买房子，上学，找工作等等。对妇女来说，困难可能更多一些，在很多公司和工厂有同工不同酬的现象。不过在很多家庭里男人帮太太做家务带孩子。甚至有一些家庭是妻子在外面工作赚钱，丈夫不工作在家里照顾家庭，和传统的"男主外，女主内"正好反过来了。

Section II Reading Comprehension (30%)
Read each passage and answer the questions that follow it.
Suggested duration: 15 minutes

Section III Writing (40%)
Translate the following two passages into Chinese.
Suggested duration: 20 minutes

Name: _____ Section: _____

Test

Section I Listening Comprehension (30%)
Listen, then answer the following questions in English.

A: For each question in this part, you will hear a short conversation between two speakers.

1. What did the second speaker suggest?
   _____

2. What did the second speaker say about what the first speaker asked about?
   _____

3. Why did the second speaker bring a shopping bag?
   _____

4. Why is it so cold inside?
   _____

B: For questions 5–6, you will hear a short narration.

5. What does Little Wang do to preserve the environment?
   _____

6. What does Little Wang say to the neighbors?
   _____

Section II Translation (30%)

Translate the following dialogues into Chinese characters or English as appropriate.

A:	我们明天怎么去长城比较好?	
B:		Taking a cab would be too expensive, but the bus would be too crowded.

A:	下个月的今天就是爷爷的八十岁生日了。	
B:		Yes, we should throw a big celebration, and have a good time!

A:		Energy conservation is a big problem.
B:	是啊，现在很多国家都在闹能源危机啊。	

Section III Reading Comprehension (20%)

Read the passage below and decide whether the statements that follow it are true or false.

现在在中国的很多大学，教学楼里都装有可以灌热水或是凉水的公共饮水机。学生们不用买瓶装水，也不带家里装好的水去上课，而是只要带着自己的空杯子，就可以在教学楼里接到免费的水，喝完了就再去饮水机接。越来越多的同学都自己买杯子接水，不再用去商店买瓶装水。喜欢喝茶的同学还常常会在杯子里装上茶叶，再到教学楼里泡茶。这样真是既方便了同学，又保护了环境。

1. (　) More and more students bring their cups to school these days to get free water from the drinking fountains.
2. (　) The drinking fountains provide both hot and cold water.
3. (　) The fountain water at school is not cheaper than bottled water.
4. (　) Water fountains are now set up in most schools in China.

Section IV Writing (20%)

Discuss how pollution affects our environment. What have you seen people doing or what have you been doing to protect the environment?

_____

_____

_____

_____

_____

_____

Test Listening Script

Suggested duration of test: 30 minutes

Section I Listening Comprehension (30%)
Listen, then answer the following questions in English.
Suggested duration: 6 minutes

A. For each question in this part, you will hear a short conversation between two speakers.

1. Speaker 1: 这个周末我们出去轻松轻松吧。

   Speaker 2: 我周六有事儿，要不周日去爬山？

2. Speaker 1: 那边房顶上有些亮亮的东西，是什么？

   Speaker 2: 是利用太阳能发电吧。太阳能和风能都是环保的新能源。

3. Speaker 1: 不用带自己的购物袋，超市有塑料袋儿啊！

   Speaker 2: 你不知道吗，现在为了环保，超市都没有免费的塑料袋儿了。

4. Speaker 1: 外边华氏100度，里面华氏60度！

   Speaker 2: 是啊，教室里的空调总是开得这么低。

B. For questions 5–6, you will hear a short narration.

小王平时非常保护环境、节约能源。他每次去超市买东西都带自己的购物袋，去饭馆儿吃饭也从来不用一次性的餐具，去不远的地方也不开车而是走路。除了这些以外，小王还参加了小区的环保队，向邻居们介绍环保知识。

Section II Translation (30%)
Translate the following dialogues into Chinese characters or English as appropriate.
Suggested duration: 6 minutes

Section III Reading Comprehension (20%)
Read the passage below and decide whether the statements that follow it are true or false.
Suggested duration: 6 minutes

Section IV Writing (20%)
Discuss how pollution affects our environment. What have you seen people doing or what have you been doing to protect the environment?
Suggested duration: 12 minutes

LESSON 17

Name: _____ Section: _____

Test

Section I Listening Comprehension (30%)
Listen, then answer the following questions in English.

A: For each question in this part, you will hear a short conversation between two speakers.

1. What warning did the second speaker give the first speaker?
   _____

2. Why do some people invest so much money in their children's education?
   _____

3. How does the second speaker manage his money?
   _____

4. Why does the first speaker want to speculate on stocks?
   _____

B: For questions 5–6, you will hear a short narration.

5. What did the speaker's aunt initially save money for?
   _____

6. Why does the speaker's aunt change her mind about purchasing the house?
   _____

Section II Translation (30%)

Translate the following dialogues into Chinese characters or English as appropriate.

A:	我父母终于买了一套房子。	
B:		They have worked hard for years. It's time for them to enjoy some comfort.

A:	我开始炒股了，希望可以赚到很多钱。	
B:		Do you know how risky that is?

A:		Saving your money in the bank is a very safe thing to do.
B:	是啊，但是利息太少，钱增加得太慢。	

Section III Reading Comprehension (20%)

Read the passage below and decide whether the statements that follow it are true or false.

现在很多中国人都开始投资理财。以前，人们习惯把钱存在银行，但是现在有的人用钱炒股票，有的人买房子，还有的人把钱投资到子女的教育上。任何一种投资方式都是有风险的，所以投资真不是一件简单的事。

1. (   ) Nowadays, most Chinese people deposit their money in the bank.
2. (   ) People in China have started speculating on stocks to make money.
3. (   ) Purchasing real estate is the best way to manage money.
4. (   ) Since making investments is risky, depositing money in the bank is the safest option.

Section IV Writing (20%)
Discuss your opinion about managing money and investments. Among the different ways to invest, which method do you prefer?

_____

_____

_____

_____

_____

_____

_____

Test Listening Script
Suggested duration of test: 30 minutes

Section I **Listening Comprehension** (30%)
Listen, then answer the following questions in English.
Suggested duration: 6 minutes

A. For each question in this part, you will hear a short conversation between two speakers.

1. Speaker 1: 我觉得买房子是一种不错的投资。

   Speaker 2: 但是在房价太高的时候买房子有风险。

2. Speaker 1: 听说有些人愿意把钱花在子女教育上。

   Speaker 2: 是啊，他们觉得让子女受到最好的教育才是最好的投资。

3. Speaker 1: 你怎么理财？

   Speaker 2: 我觉得钱只有花了才是自己的，有钱就应该消费享受。

4. Speaker 1: 我有一个朋友这两年炒股赚了不少钱，我也想炒股。

   Speaker 2: 炒股不一定赚钱，我父母的一个朋友就赔了很多钱。

B. For questions 5–6, you will hear a short narration.

　　我的姑妈省吃俭用存了一笔钱，本来要留给孙子上大学用，后来又想买一个房子。但是签购房合同前她的想法突然变了。她打算投资股市，因为她听说炒股能赚不少钱。

Section II **Translation** (30%)
Translate the following dialogues into Chinese characters or English as appropriate.
Suggested duration: 6 minutes

Section III **Reading Comprehension** (20%)
Read the passage below and decide whether the statements that follow it are true or false.
Suggested duration: 6 minutes

Section IV **Writing** (20%)
Discuss your opinion about managing money and investments. Among the different ways to invest, which method do you prefer?
Suggested duration: 12 minutes

LESSON 18

Name: _____ Section: _____

Test

Section I Listening Comprehension (30%)

Listen, then answer the following questions in English.

A: For each question in this part, you will hear a short conversation between two speakers.

1. Who is Confucius?
   _____

2. What contribution did the First Emperor make?
   _____

3. Please list three of the Four Great Inventions.
   _____

4. What is the second speaker's comment on the Tang Dynasty?
   _____

B: For questions 5–6, you will hear a short narration.

5. When did trade with the West start?
   _____

6. Why was the Qing Dynasty the last dynasty in China?
   _____

学生版

Section II Translation (30%)

Translate the following dialogues into Chinese characters or English as appropriate.

A:	我对中国的诗很感兴趣。	
B:		I suggest that you read Li Bai's poetry, then.

A:	汉朝在秦朝的基础上有很大发展。	
B:		The term "Han" for the Han ethnicity originated with the Han Dynasty.

A:	中国哪个朝代给你印象最深？	
B:		The Qin Dynasty, because it was the first one.

Section III Reading Comprehension (20%)

Read the passage below and decide whether the statements that follow it are true or false.

秦始皇是中国历史上第一个皇帝，他对中国有很多贡献，比如他统一了中国，也统一了文字。他还修建了长城。很多人觉得他是一个很好的皇帝，但是他也做了一些不对的事情。他杀了几百个读书人，烧了很多古书，而且他还让千千万万的人给他修宫殿和坟墓。

1. (　　) The First Emperor was a uniformly good emperor in Chinese history.
2. (　　) The First Emperor killed a lot of people.
3. (　　) The Qin Dynasty was the last dynasty in Chinese history.
4. (　　) The First Emperor forced a lot of people to build palaces for him.

Section IV Writing (20%)

Among the Chinese dynasties discussed in this lesson, which one impresses you the most? Why?

Test Listening Script

Suggested duration of test: 30 minutes

Section I **Listening Comprehension** (30%)
Listen, then answer the following questions in English.
Suggested duration: 8 minutes

A. For each question in this part, you will hear a short conversation between two speakers.

1. Speaker 1: 你听说过孔子吗？

   Speaker 2: 听说过，他是中国历史上最伟大的教育家和思想家。

2. Speaker 1: 秦始皇对中国有很多贡献。

   Speaker 2: 是啊，他统一了中国，还统一了文字。

3. Speaker 1: 中国的四大发明是什么？

   Speaker 2: 是造纸、火药、指南针、活字印刷。

4. Speaker 1: 唐朝的经济发达吗？

   Speaker 2: 发达，唐朝的文化也很发达，那个时候有很多外国留学生到中国留学。

B. For questions 5–6, you will hear a short narration.

中国历史上有很多朝代。秦始皇是中国的第一个皇帝，秦朝的时间不长。秦朝以后是汉朝，汉朝开始跟西方进行贸易。唐朝的经济和文化都很发达，唐诗也很有名。清朝是中国最后的一个朝代，因为孙中山领导革命，建立了中华民国。

Section II **Translation** (30%)
Translate the following dialogues into Chinese characters or English as appropriate.
Suggested duration: 6 minutes

Section III **Reading Comprehension** (20%)
Read the passage below and decide whether the statements that follow it are true or false.
Suggested duration: 6 minutes

Section IV **Writing** (20%)
Among the Chinese dynasties discussed in this lesson, which one impresses you the most? Why?
Suggested duration: 10 minutes

LESSON 19

Name: _____ Section: _____

Test

Section I Listening Comprehension (30%)
Listen, then answer the following questions in English.

A: For each question in this part, you will hear a short conversation between two speakers.

1. Why is the second speaker nervous?
   _____

2. Why did the second speaker come back to China?
   _____

3. Does the second speaker often stay up late to work overtime now?
   _____

4. According to the second speaker, why are a lot of Chinese students who study abroad going back to China to find a job?
   _____

B: For questions 5–6, you will hear a short narration.

5. What is Little Lin's plan after graduation?
   _____

6. List the two reasons why Little Lin is choosing to work in China.
   _____

Section II Translation (30%)

Translate the following dialogues into Chinese characters or English as appropriate.

A:	你最大的缺点是什么？	
B:		I work too hard and don't know how to rest well.

A:	既然你喜欢美国，为什么不留在美国工作呢？	
B:		All my family and friends are in China.

A:	The busier I am the more difficult it is for me to fall asleep.	
B:		你应该注意休息，否则会生病的。

Section III Reading Comprehension (20%)

Read the passage below and decide whether the statements that follow it are true or false.

我昨天去面试。因为是第一次，所以非常紧张。给我面试的经理是个非常严肃的人，所以我就更紧张了。他让我说说自己的优点和缺点。我说我的优点是工作很努力，而且能科学地安排自己的时间。但是如果工作压力大，我就会熬夜加班，就不太会休息了。经理听了我的话，一直点头微笑。

1. (   ) The manager makes the interviewee nervous.
2. (   ) The interviewee's strength is his tendency to never stay up late.
3. (   ) The interviewee is able to manage his time with scientific precision.
4. (   ) The manager seems to like the interviewee's answers.

Section IV Writing (20%)
Please describe the kind of job you would like to do in the future and your reasons for choosing this profession.

_____

_____

_____

_____

_____

_____

Test Listening Script

Suggested duration of test: 30 minutes

Section I Listening Comprehension (30%)
Listen, then answer the following questions in English.
Suggested duration: 6 minutes

A. For each question in this part, you will hear a short conversation between two speakers.

1. Speaker 1: 你是不是很紧张？你出了好多汗。

   Speaker 2: 是啊，我很紧张，因为这是我第一次面试。

2. Speaker 1: 你是不是在美国找不到工作才回中国来的？

   Speaker 2: 不是，因为我男朋友在中国留学，所以我打算在中国找工作。

3. Speaker 1: 你常常熬夜加班吗？

   Speaker 2: 我以前实习的时候常常加班，现在不了。

4. Speaker 1: 为什么有很多留学生毕业以后都回到中国找工作？

   Speaker 2: 因为中国的经济高速发展，在中国有很多工作机会。

B. For questions 5–6, you will hear a short narration.

小林从美国大学毕业以后就回到中国找工作。虽然有好几家美国公司都录取了他，但是他还是想回国发展。第一个原因是因为中国的经济越来越好，第二个原因是因为小林的爸爸妈妈在中国，他们的年纪都很大了，小林希望照顾他们。

Section II Translation (30%)
Translate the following dialogues into Chinese characters or English as appropriate.
Suggested duration: 6 minutes

Section III Reading Comprehension (20%)
Read the passage below and decide whether the statements that follow it are true or false.
Suggested duration: 6 minutes

Section IV Writing (20%)
Please describe the kind of job you would like to do in the future and your reasons for choosing this profession.
Suggested duration: 12 minutes

学生版

Name: _____ Section: _____

Final Exam

Section I Listening Comprehension (30%)
You will hear three narratives. Listen, then answer the following questions in English.

Narrative A

1. What specifically do you know about Xiao Gao's job situation after graduation? What is the overall job situation in society? Provide details.

2. What are Xiao Gao's job-finding advantages or disadvantages, as mentioned in the passage?

3. What is the outcome of Xiao Gao's job search? How does it affect his mood?

Narrative B

4. Who is the historic figure mentioned in the passage? What do historians think of him?

5. What were his contributions? Did common folks like him? Why or why not?

Narrative C

6. What does Lao Zhang's son Xiao Zhang do? What does he always persuade Lao Zhang to do?

7. What was the first suggestion Xiao Zhang made to Lao Zhang? Did Lao Zhang listen to him? If yes, what was the result? If not, why?

8. What was the second suggestion Xiao Zhang made to Lao Zhang? Did Lao Zhang listen to him? If yes, what was the result? If no, why?

   _____

9. What was the third suggestion Xiao Zhang made to Lao Zhang? Did Lao Zhang listen to him? If yes, what was the result? If no, why?

   _____

10. What did Lao Zhang say to Xiao Zhang at the end? What did he mean by that?

    _____

Section II Reading and Grammar (20%)

Fill in the blanks.

1. 小高在微博上和大家分享他在夏威夷度假的照片。他在那里_____体验了冲浪运动的美妙。
   A. 亲手　　B. 亲自　　C. 亲身　　D. 亲眼

2. 现在的大城市非常忙碌和现代化，传统节日的热闹_____已经很难找到了。
   A. 印象　　B. 气氛　　C. 味道　　D. 环境

3. 明天总公司的人事经理要来面试你，你可_____别迟到啊！
   A. 千万　　B. 重视　　C. 否则　　D. 只要

4. 就_____李林和他妻子_____，他们的薪水一样高，在家里一起分担家务、互相照顾，很平等。
   A. 有的…有的　　B. 吧…吧　　C. 拿…来说　　D. 在…下

5. 明天柯林要和他的同事们一起去_____那家很有名的生产绿色食品的工厂。
   A. 游览　　B. 看望　　C. 旅游　　D. 参观

6. 中国人_____喜欢为孩子的教育投资,他们给孩子请家教、送他们去最好的学校。
   A. 常常　　　B. 往往　　　C. 经常　　　D. 平常

7. 小黄和父母参加了一个去香港和澳门的购物旅行团,玩得很不开心,他决定以后出门游览_____参加旅行团了。
   A. 尽可能　　B. 从来　　　C. 只好　　　D. 再也不

8. 老张身体很棒,已经70岁了还在那家中餐馆作全职厨师;不过_____"年纪不饶人",他还是要考虑退休的事了。
   A. 毕竟　　　B. 逐渐　　　C. 难怪　　　D. 不仅

9. 这只是一份工作_____,不要给自己太大的压力,否则会影响健康的。
   A. 之一　　　B. 其中　　　C. 而已　　　D. 方面

10. 他在大学读了十年书,_____拿到博士学位了。
    A. 算是　　　B. 终于　　　C. 不得不　　D. 突然

Section III Reading Comprehension (20%)

Part A: Read the paragraph below and answer the questions that follow it, paying attention to the specific instructions for each question.

在小林住的城市空气污染比较严重,垃圾回收的工作也不太顺利,有很多环保方面的事需要做。小林和朋友决定在学校和公司里介绍平常节能和其他有益于环境的做法,比如,去外面吃饭时自己带筷子不用一次性的餐具,出门时随手关灯,夏天空调的温度不要调得太低,多骑自行车少开车等等。他们的活动取得了很好的效果,很多人的生活方式都更有利于环保了。

1. What is the environmental protection situation where Xiao Lin lives? Please provide supporting detail. (Answer in **English**.)

2. What did Xiao Lin and his friends decide to do? (Answer in **English**.)

3. What specific measures have they taken to promote environmental protection? (Answer in **English**.)

4. What effects have these measures had on their school and workplace? (Answer in **English**.)

5. What would you do to protect the environment in your daily life, besides the measures mentioned in the passage? (Answer in **Chinese**.)

Part B: Read the paragraph below and decide whether the statements that follow it are true or false.

　　足球运动是世界上最流行的体育运动之一，尤其是在欧洲、亚洲和南美洲。喜欢踢足球的人很多，有小孩子，有大学生，甚至还有中老年人，男女都有。他们常常自己组队参加各种社区的足球比赛。对他们中的大部分人来说，体验踢足球的乐趣要比胜负更重要。还有很多人是足球迷，他们自己不踢球，但是很喜欢看各种各样的足球比赛，从各国的国内联赛到世界杯、奥运会的足球赛，男足女足的比赛都不会错过，真是"有球必看"。很多人都知道现代足球是从英国开始的，算起来有一百多年的历史。有一些中国人认为最早的足球运动是中国人发明的。从古代中国的画中看，有一种运动跟现在的足球很像，它叫"蹴鞠"。和别的国家一样，中国人现在玩的足球运动，包括服装、场地和比赛规则等，都是从英国传来的。

1. (　) Many people like to watch soccer games, but only children, college students and other young people play it for fun.
2. (　) For those who like to play soccer games, winning the game is more important than anything else.
3. (　) Most Chinese people believe that they invented soccer.

Answer the following questions about the passage in English.

1. Explain the meaning of the phrase "有球必看" in the passage.
   _____

2. According to the passage, what is "蹴鞠"?
   _____

Section IV Writing (30%)
Use Chinese characters to complete the following tasks.

Task A
Write a job announcement for the editor position at your school newspaper. List all the requirements in detail.

_____
_____
_____
_____

Task B
Imagine one of your academic advisors is a typical middle-aged professor who is under stress, doesn't live a healthy lifestyle, and is facing potential health problems. Make a health improvement plan for or suggest healthier lifestyle options to the professor.

_____
_____
_____
_____

Task C

Imagine that you and your friends just graduated from college. You are trying to open a small business together and you need a startup loan. Write a compelling statement that persuades either the bank or your parents/friends to loan you money.

_____

_____

_____

_____

Final Exam Listening Script
Suggested duration of test: 90 minutes

Section I Listening Comprehension (30%)
You will hear three narratives. Listen, then answer the following questions in English.
Suggested duration: 20 minutes

Narrative A

　　小高从研究所毕业以后一直在找工作，他寄出了上百份的工作申请，只得到了十几个电话面试的机会。现在的经济形势不好，再加上有很多的优秀人才从大学毕业，一个职位就有五六十个人竞争。好在小高不仅成绩好、有实习经验，而且诚实又勤劳，公司老板和经理们往往喜欢雇佣象他这样的人。最近他终于收到了一家跨国公司的录用通知，他的脸上也多云转晴了。

Narrative B

　　在中国历史上秦始皇是一个很有争议的人物，历史学家们和学者们对他的贡献和过失争论不休。他统一了中国、中国的文字和货币，在他建立的秦朝的基础上，中国成为了一个封建帝国。但他修建巨大的坟墓和宫殿、杀死了千千万万的人、烧了很多古书，也引起了老百姓对他的不满。

Narrative C

　　过去中国的老人往往把一辈子赚的一点儿钱存在银行里。现在越来越多的老年人开始寻找新的理财方式。老张的儿子小张最近在一家投资咨询公司找到了一份工作，总是给老张出主意让他把在银行的存款拿出来投资。小张先是劝老张买股票，因为股市很热、炒股票赚钱快。很快，股票市场就不行了，股价下跌得很厉害，老张赔了不少钱。小张又劝老张投资国债，说是比股票安全稳定。因为经济危机，国债的利息越来越低，什么时候才能把在股市赔的钱赚回来呀？房价一直在涨，最近更是涨了好几倍。小张又劝老张炒房，比股票安全又比国债来钱快。可是投资房地产需要老张把所有的存款都拿出来还要贷款。老张有点儿犹豫。这时候房地产市场突然变冷了，大家都租房住，不买房了，房价降了很多。老张对小张说："幸亏没听你的炒房，要不然后果不堪设想！看来做投资，你还有很多东西要学！"

Section II Reading and Grammar (20%)
Suggested duration: 20 minutes

Section III Reading Comprehension (20%)
Suggested duration: 20 minutes

Section IV Writing (30%)
Suggested duration: 30 minutes